MOSCOW SPRING FEVER

With

HELGA
Works as a model and DJ

VALERIE
Coordinator of the main project,
Moscow Biennale of Contemporary Art

SIMON
Cultural attaché from Vienna, organizes exhibitions in his own apartment from time to time

SLAVA
Works as a model and writes little poems

ANASTASIA
Model, actress and singer

ANTON
Has founded his own fashion label and models for magazines

IRA
Student and model

NIKA
Designs leather wallets and bags for her own label

DARIA
Artist who works in different kinds of media, performance as well as painting and photography

KATJA
Works as an artist and is exploring new painting techniques

JOSEPH
Artistic director, Moscow Biennale of Contemporary Art

ANNA
Director of the exhibion program, Moscow Biennale of Contemporary Art

USTINA
Artist who paints, draws and works with mixed media

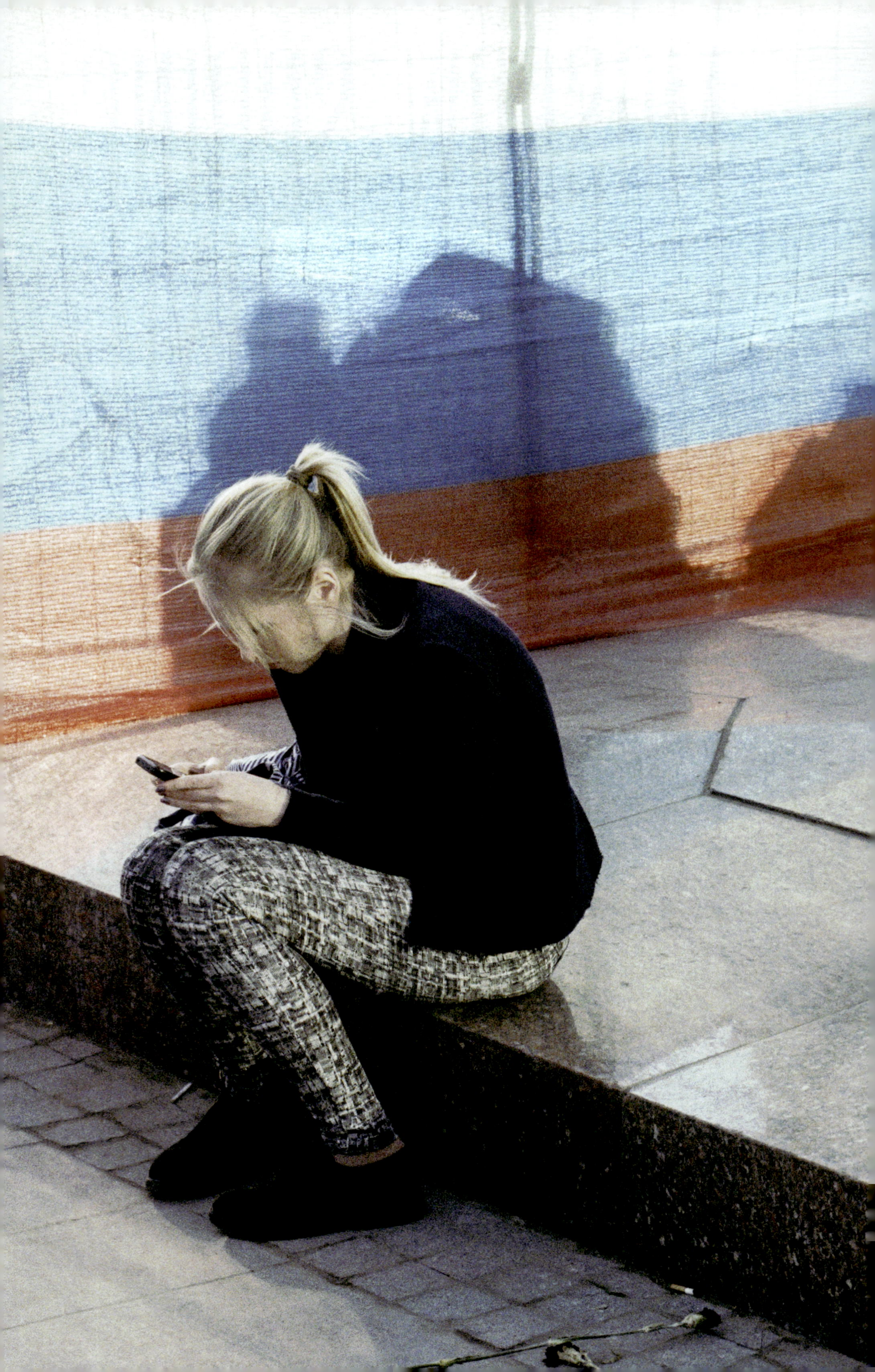

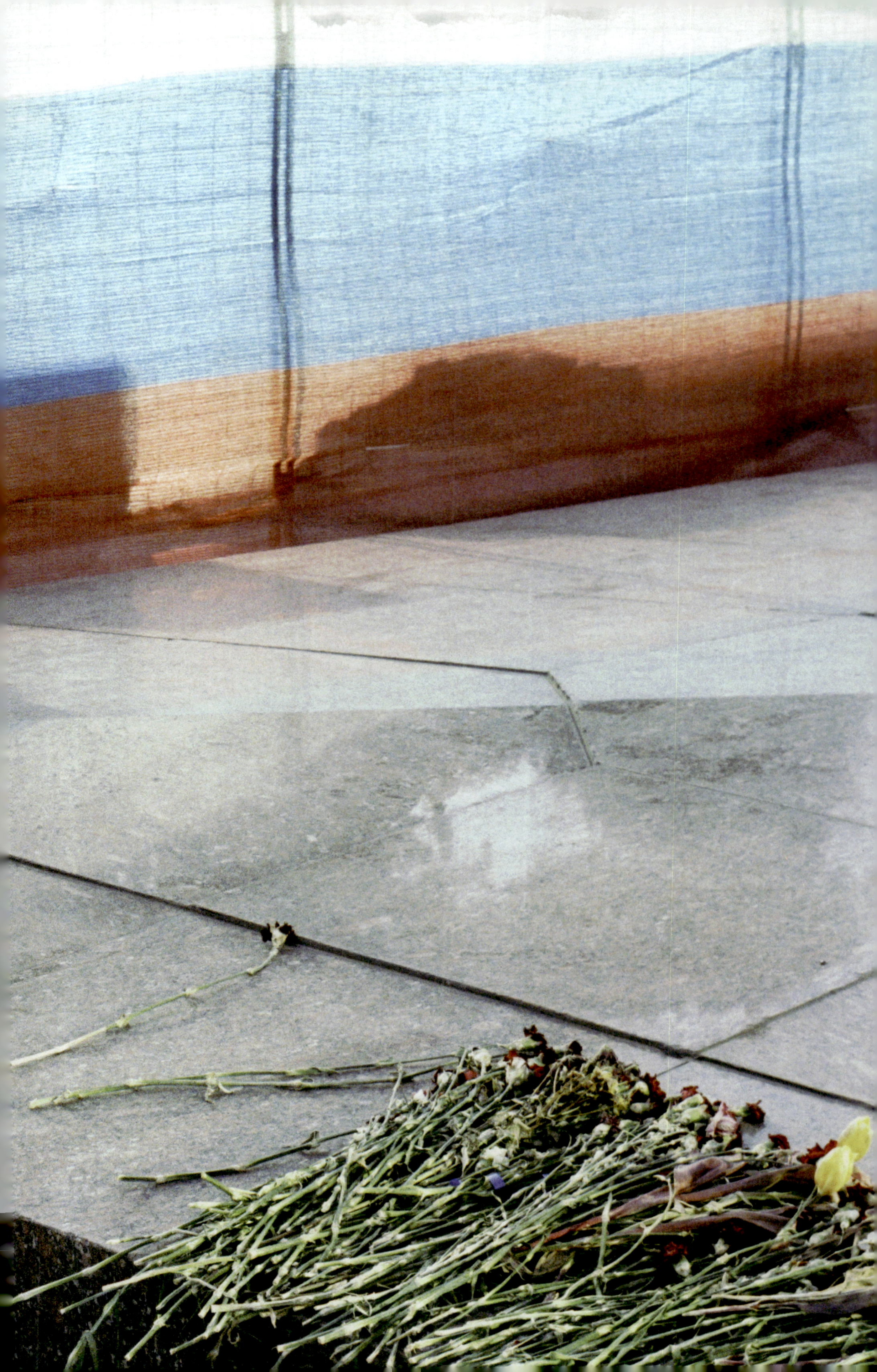

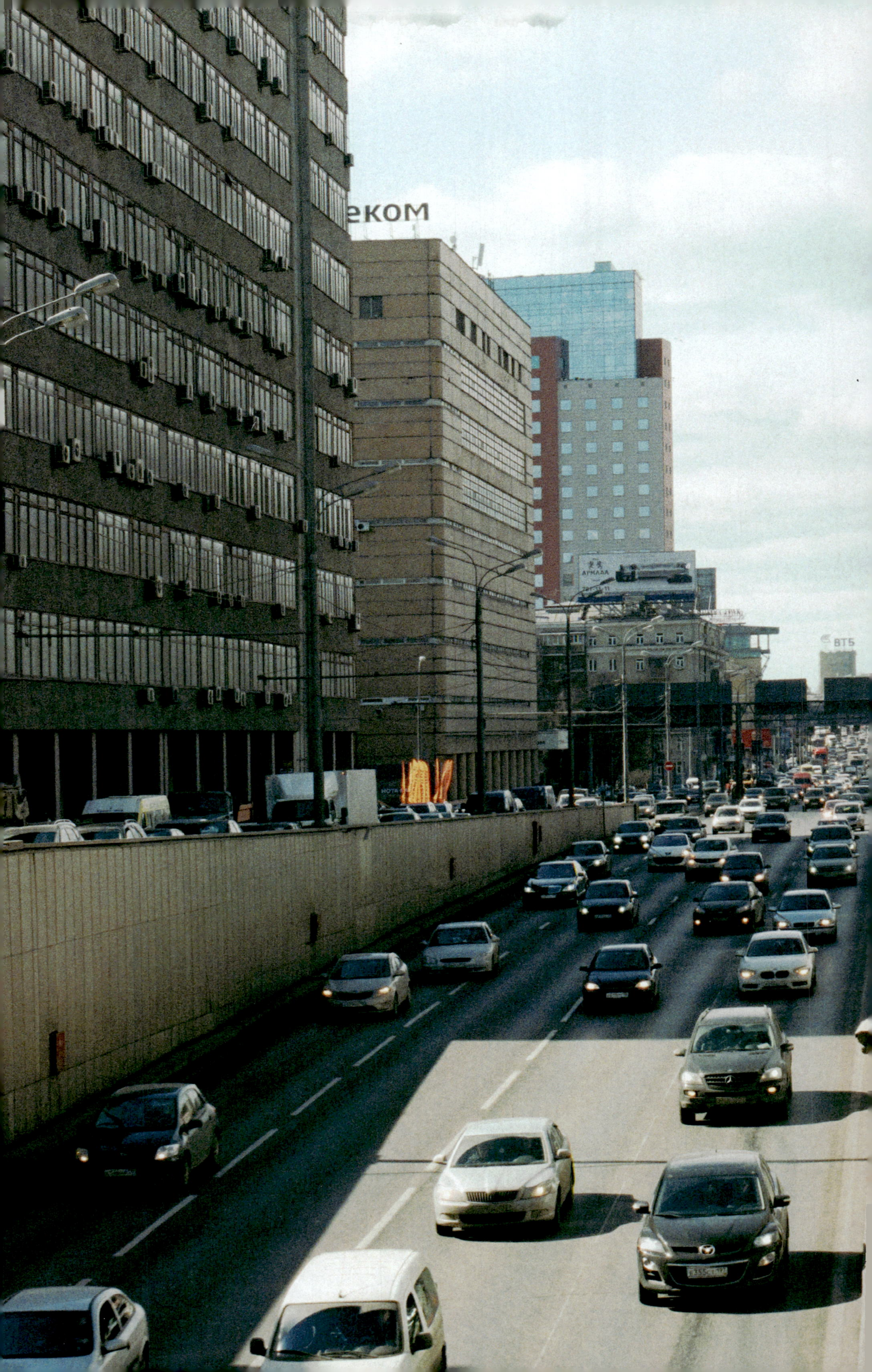
еком
ВТБ

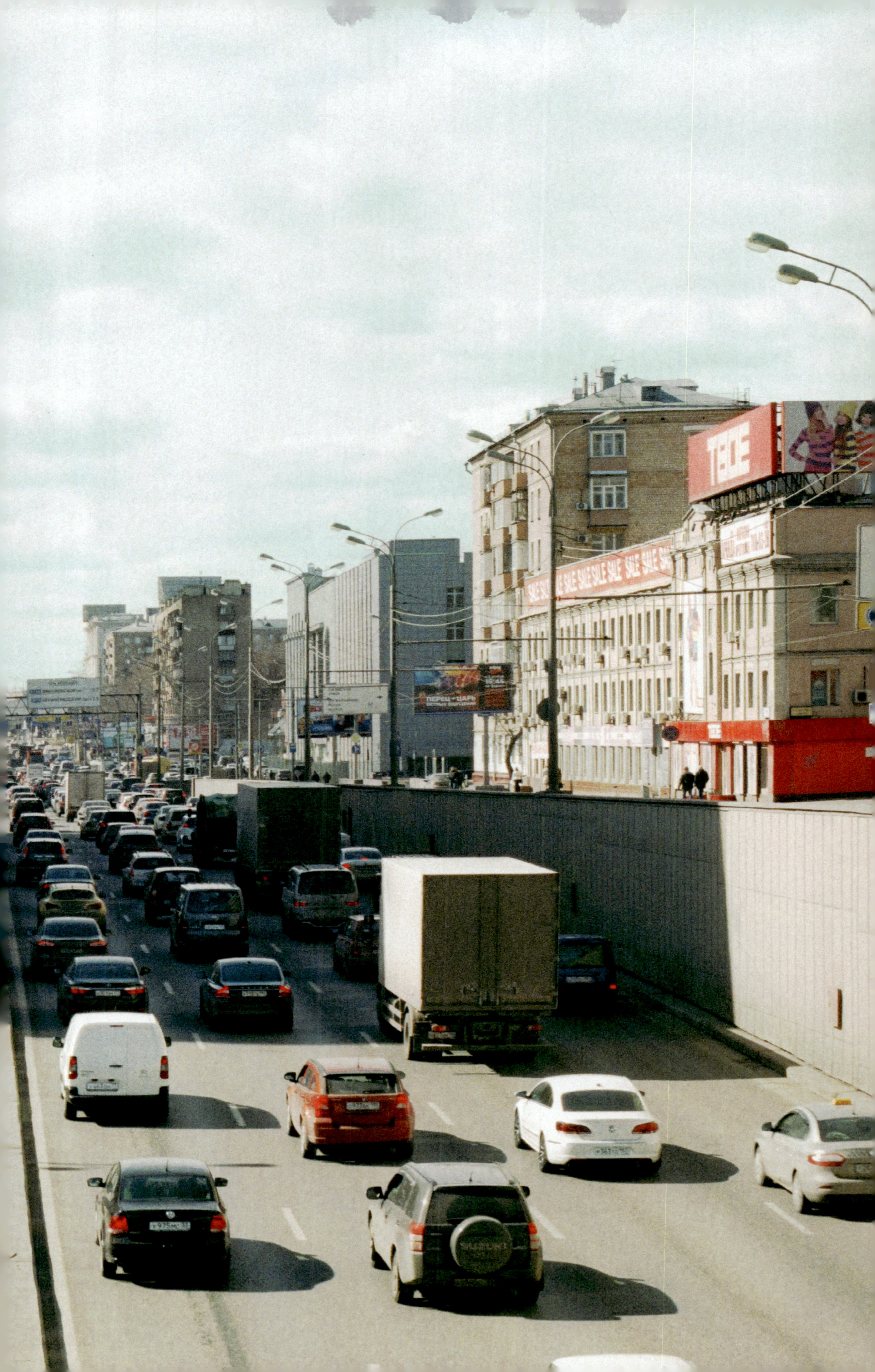
ТВОЕ

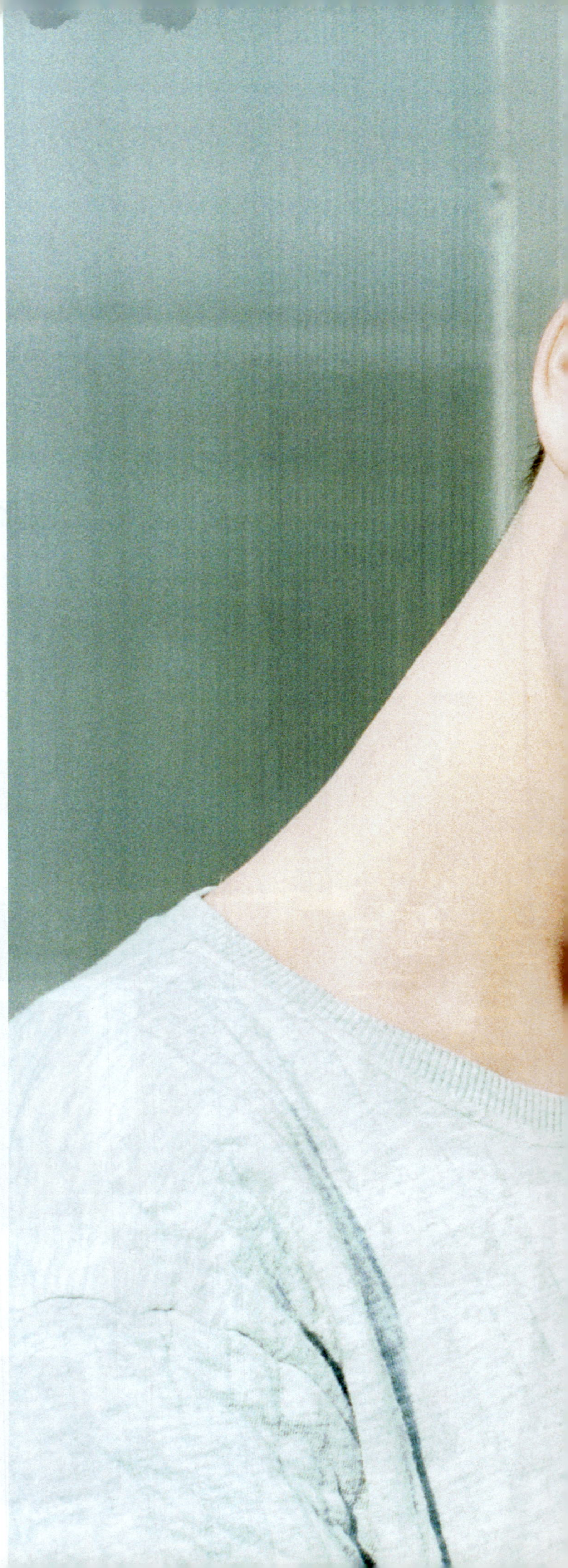

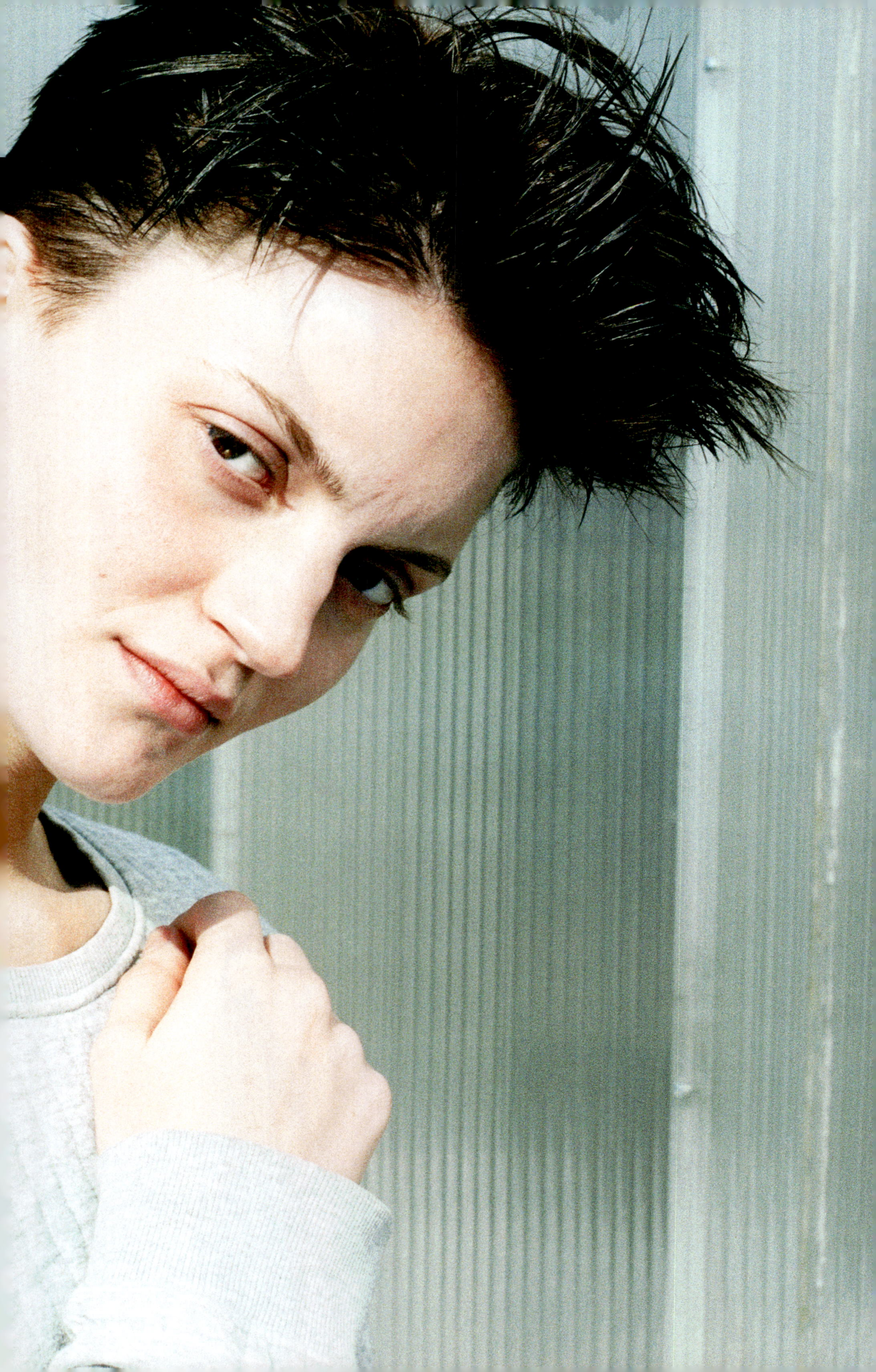

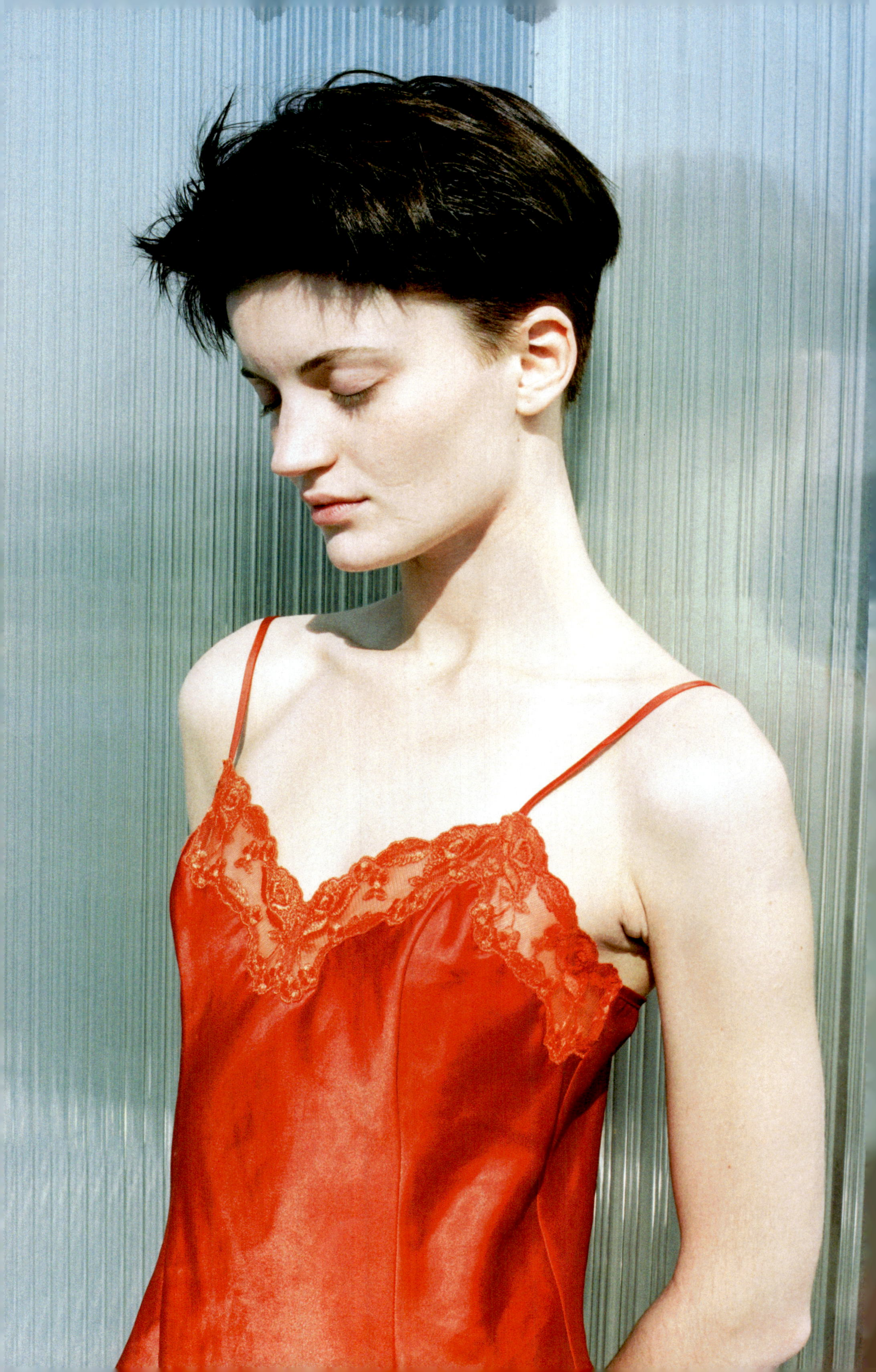

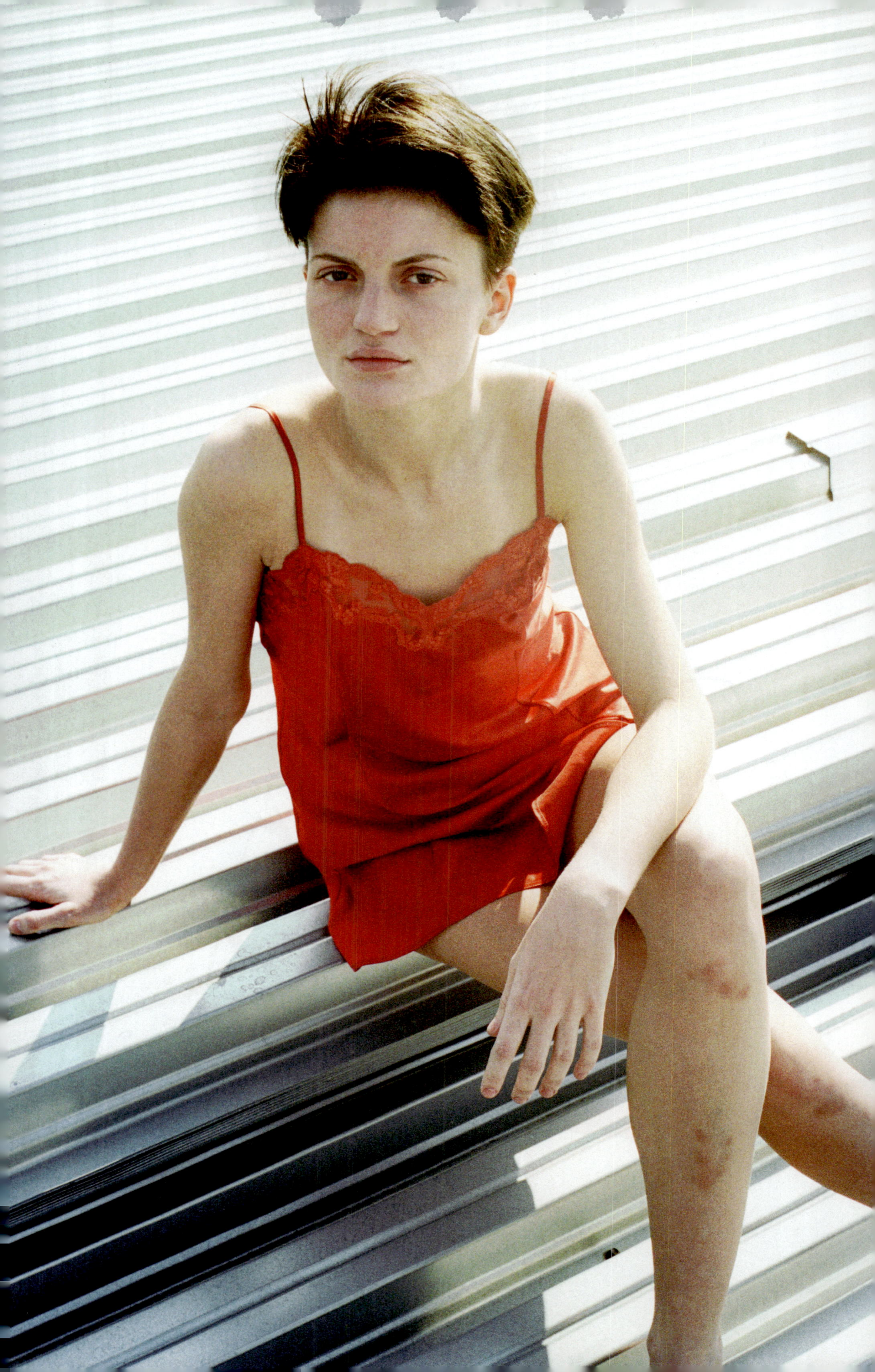

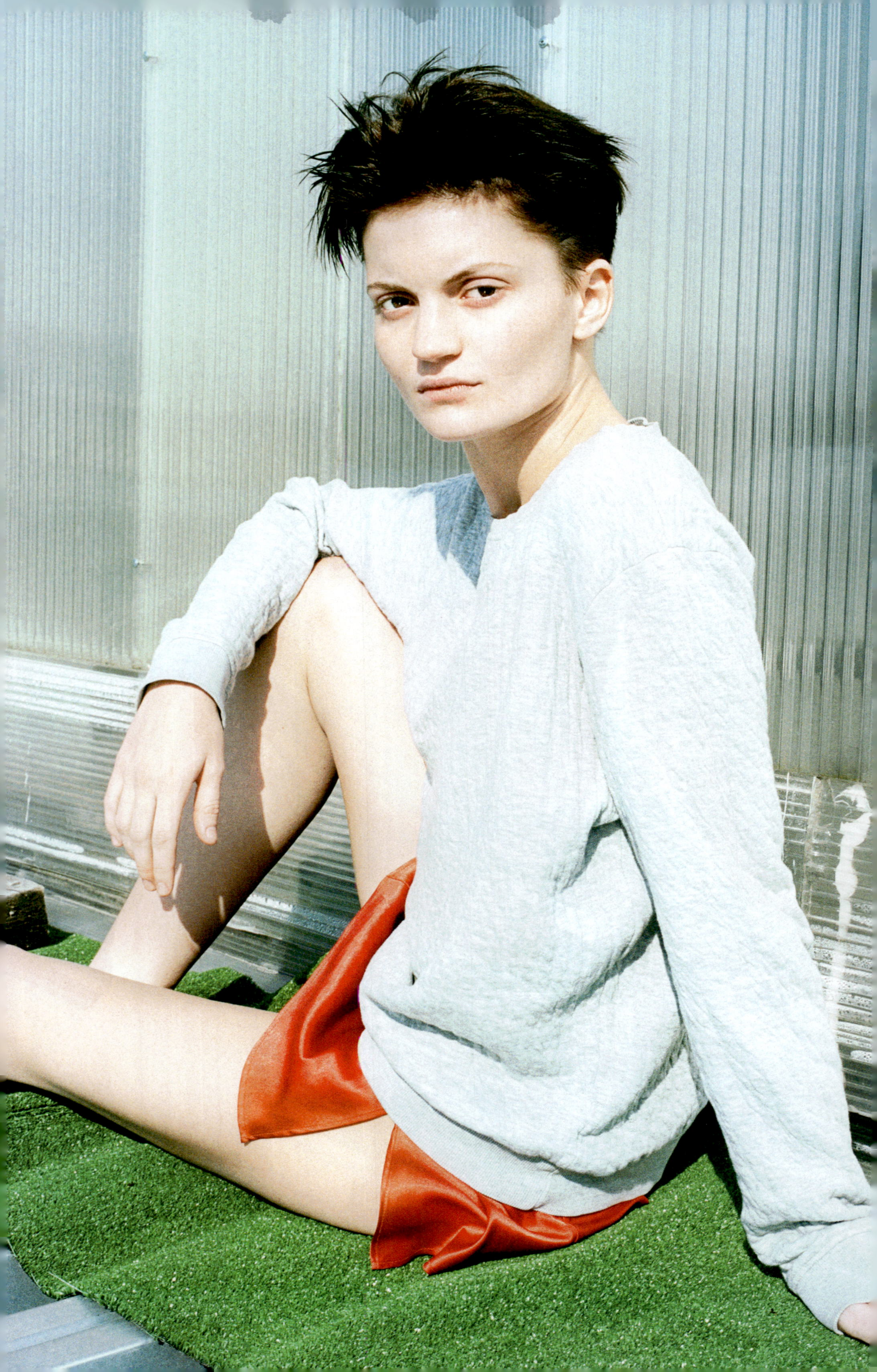

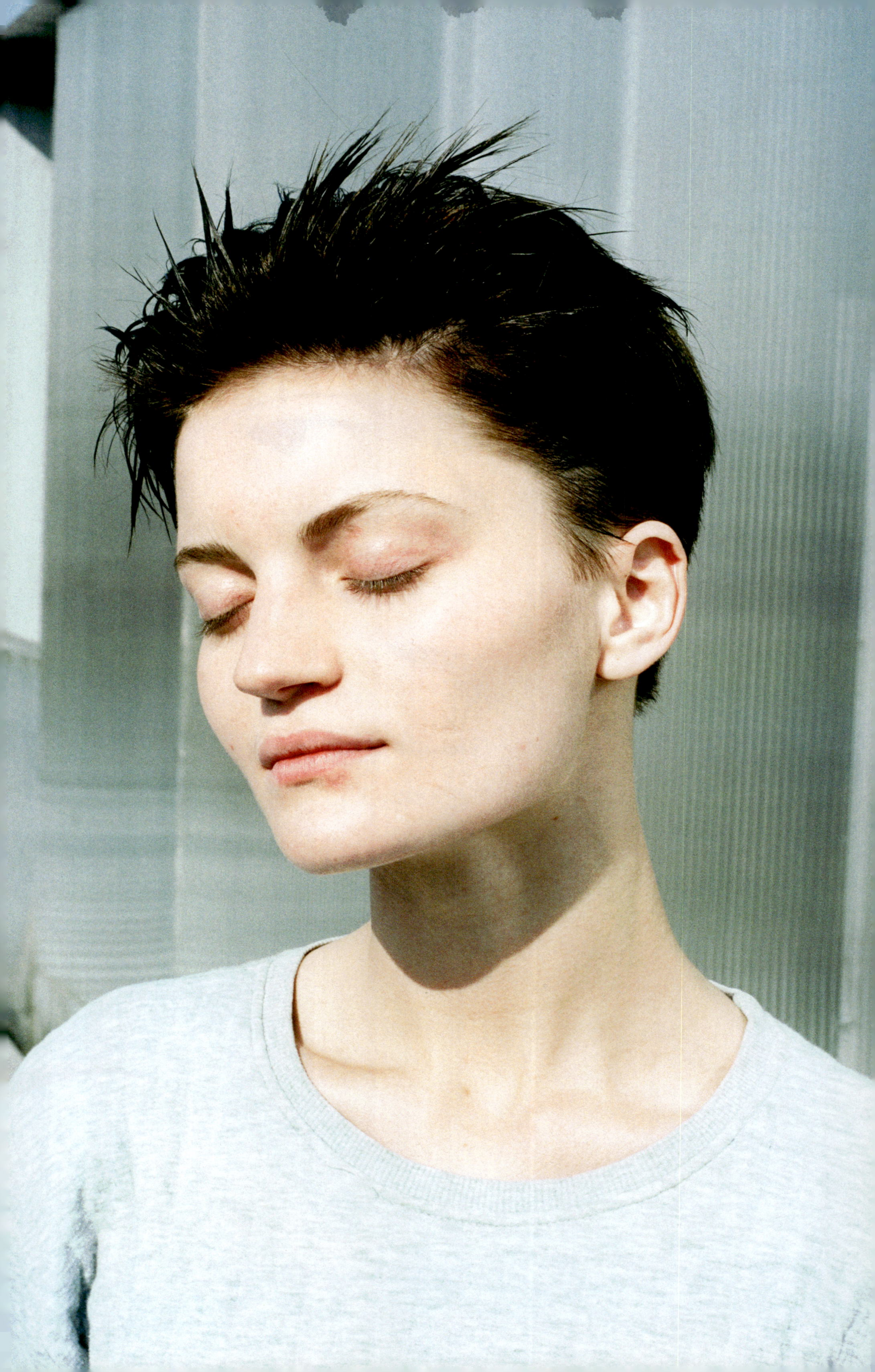

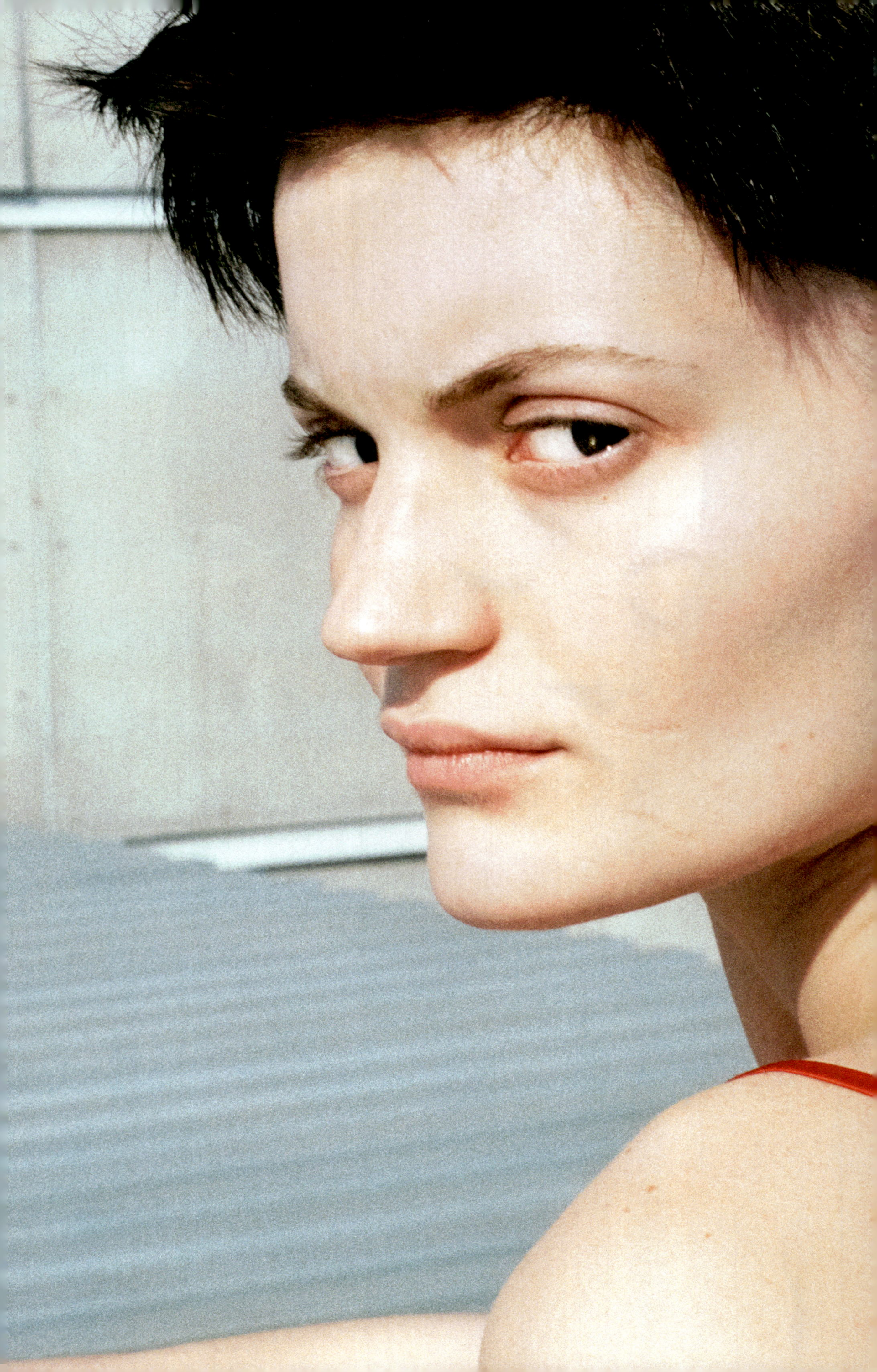

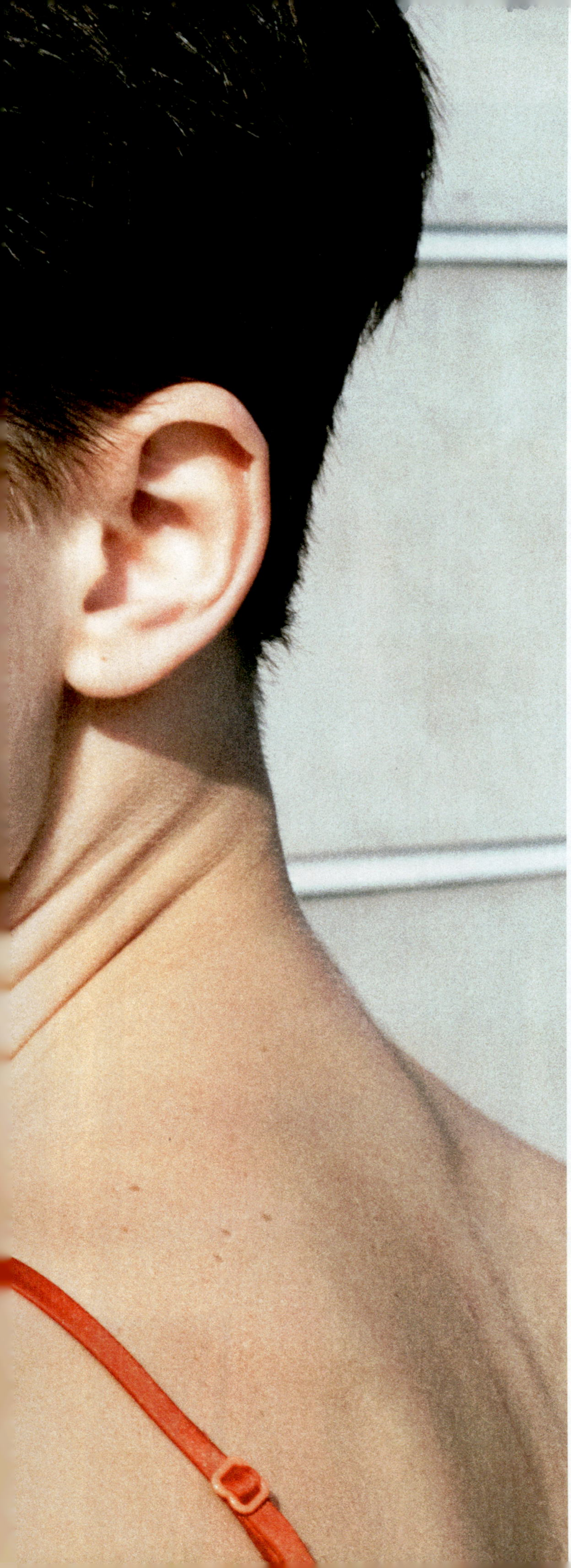

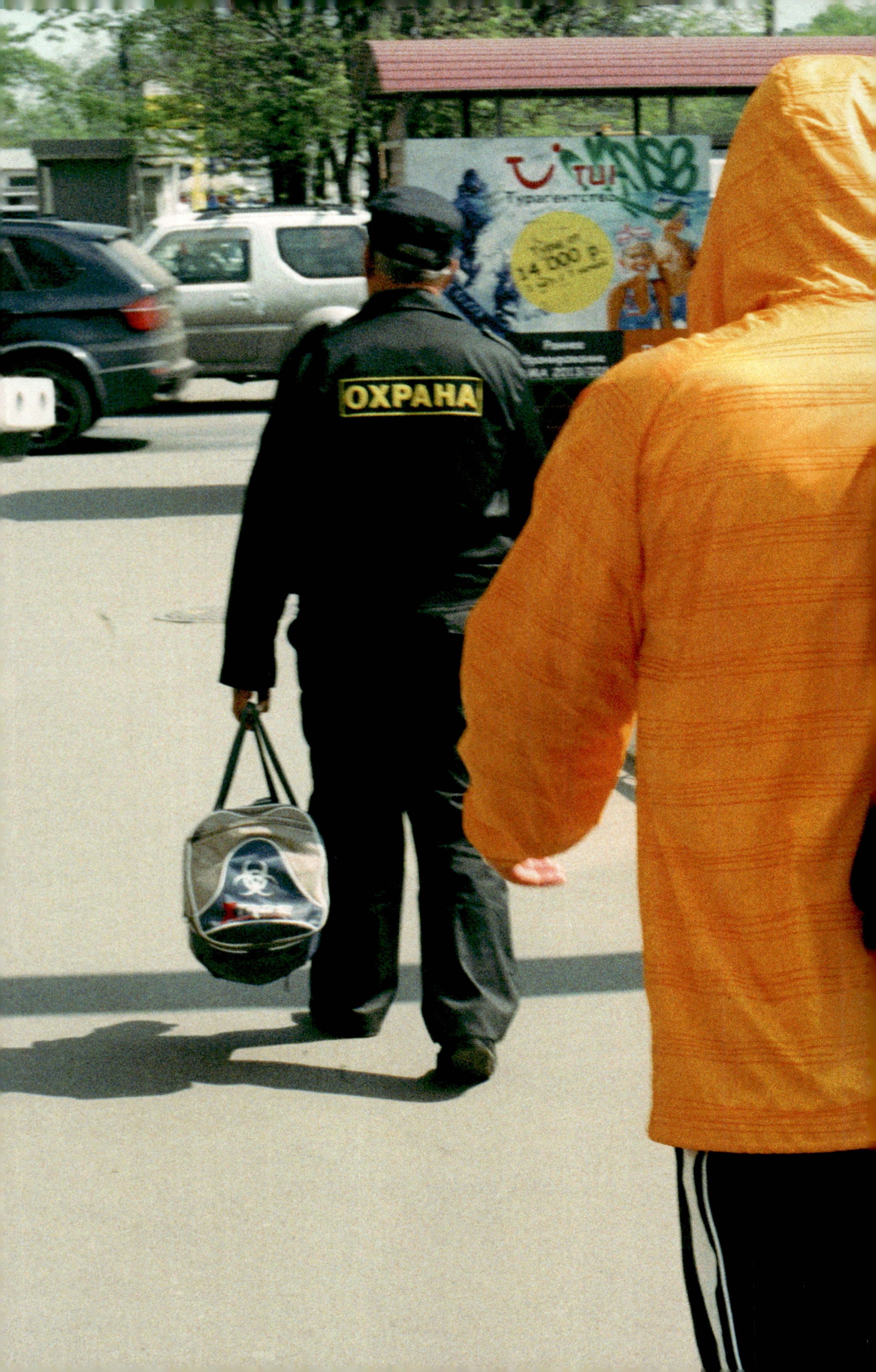
TUI
ОХРАНА

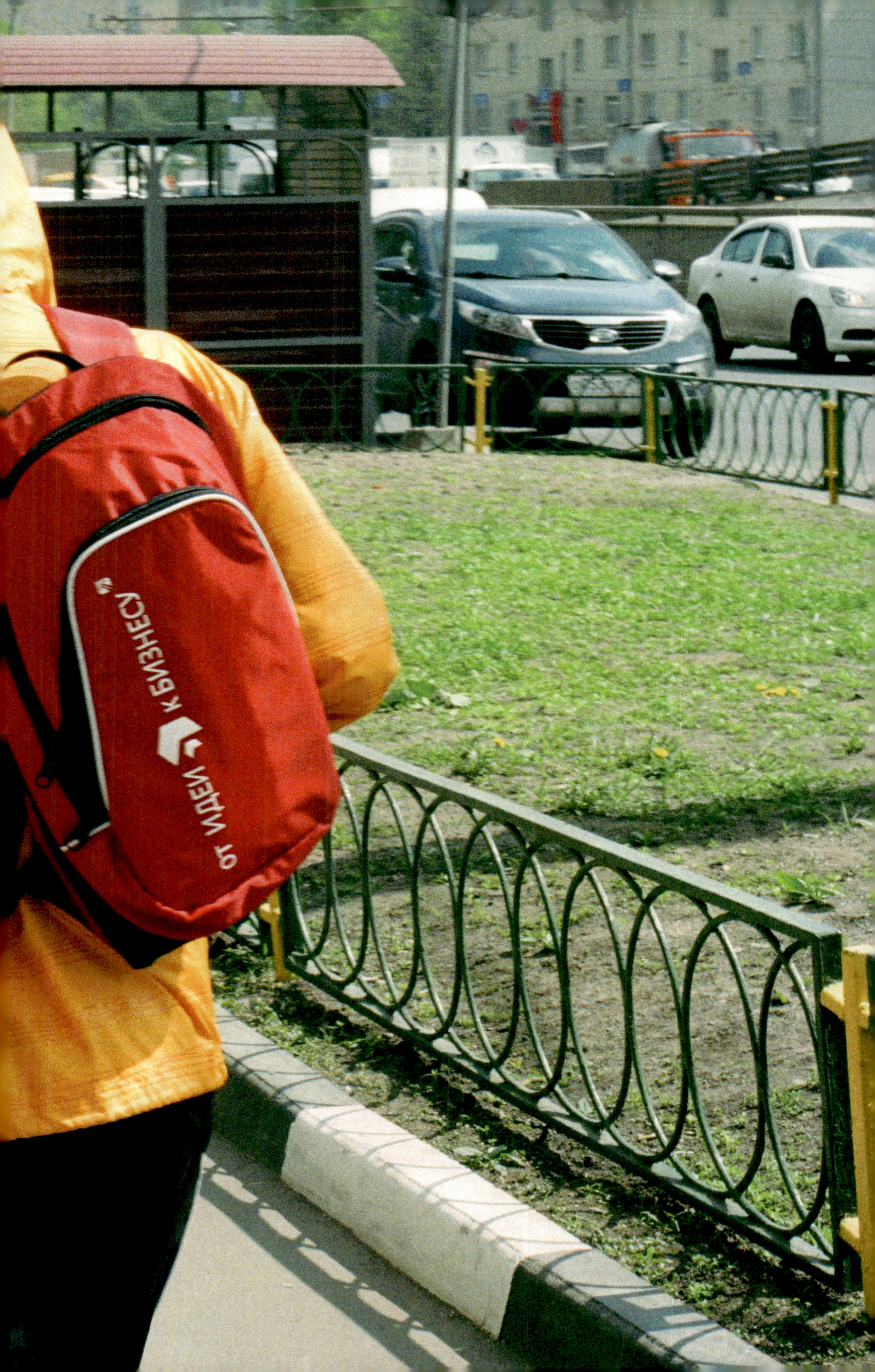
ОТ ИДЕИ К БИЗНЕСУ

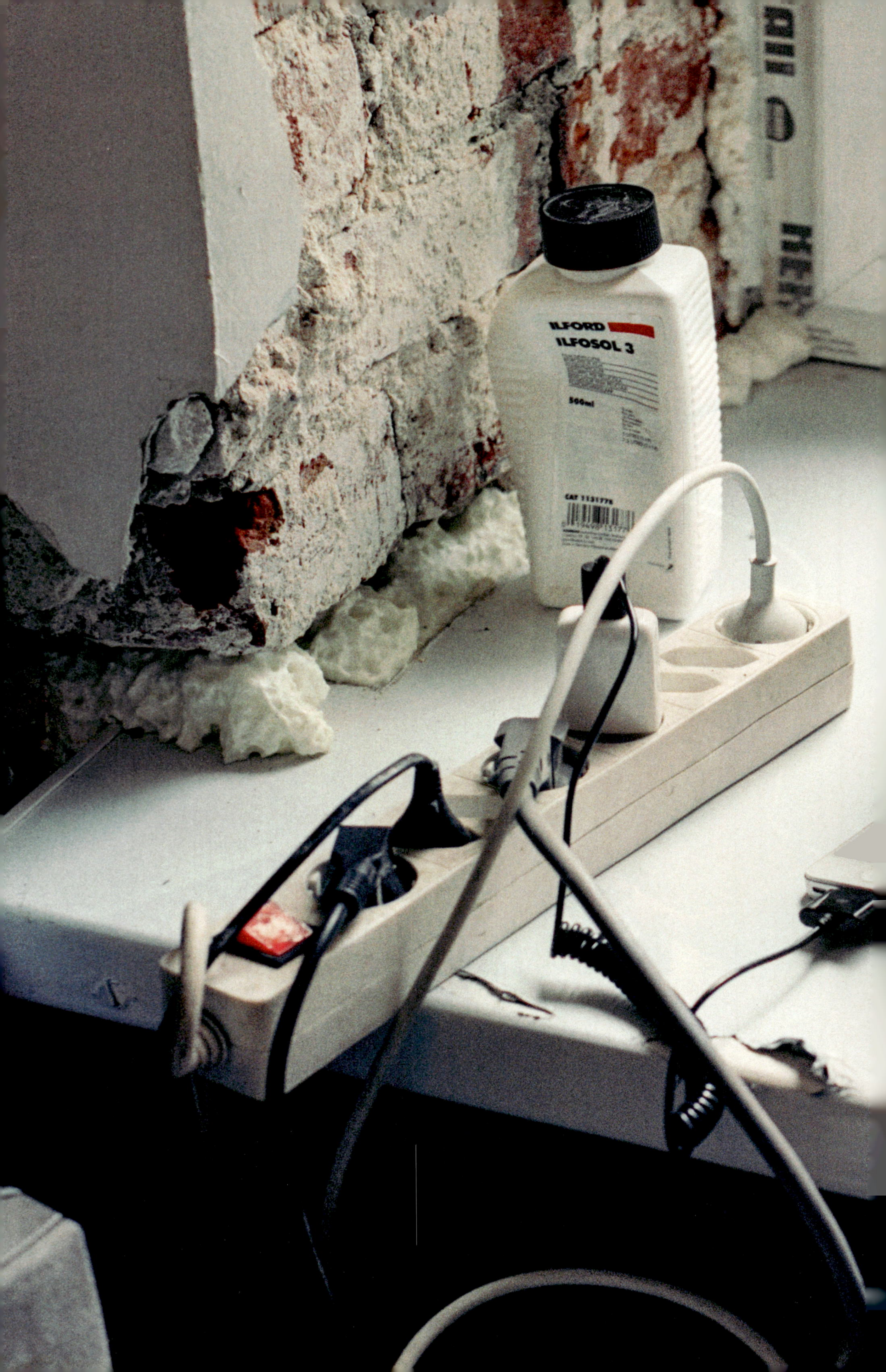
ILFORD
ILFOSOL 3
500ml
CAT 1131775

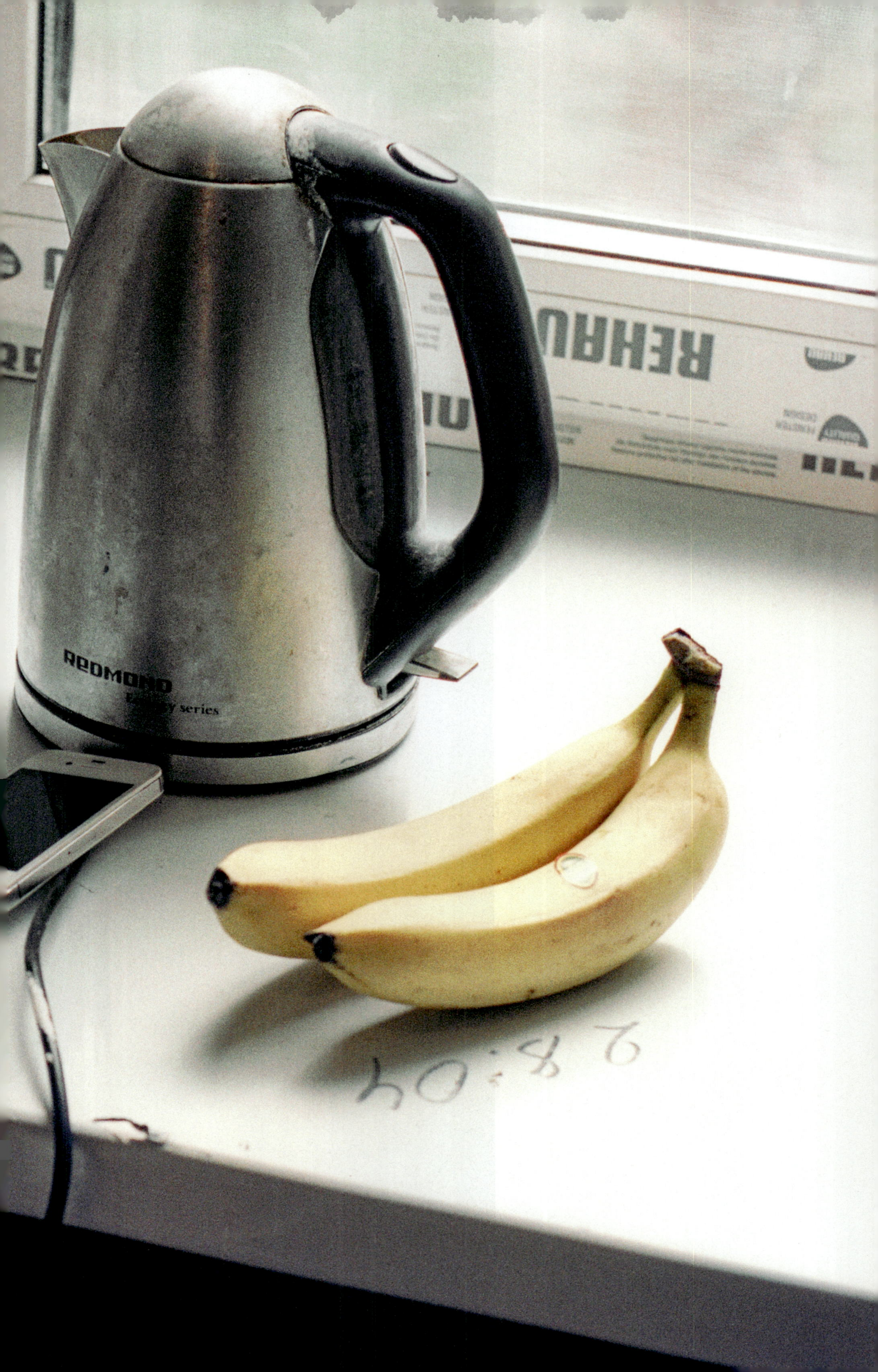
REDMOND
series

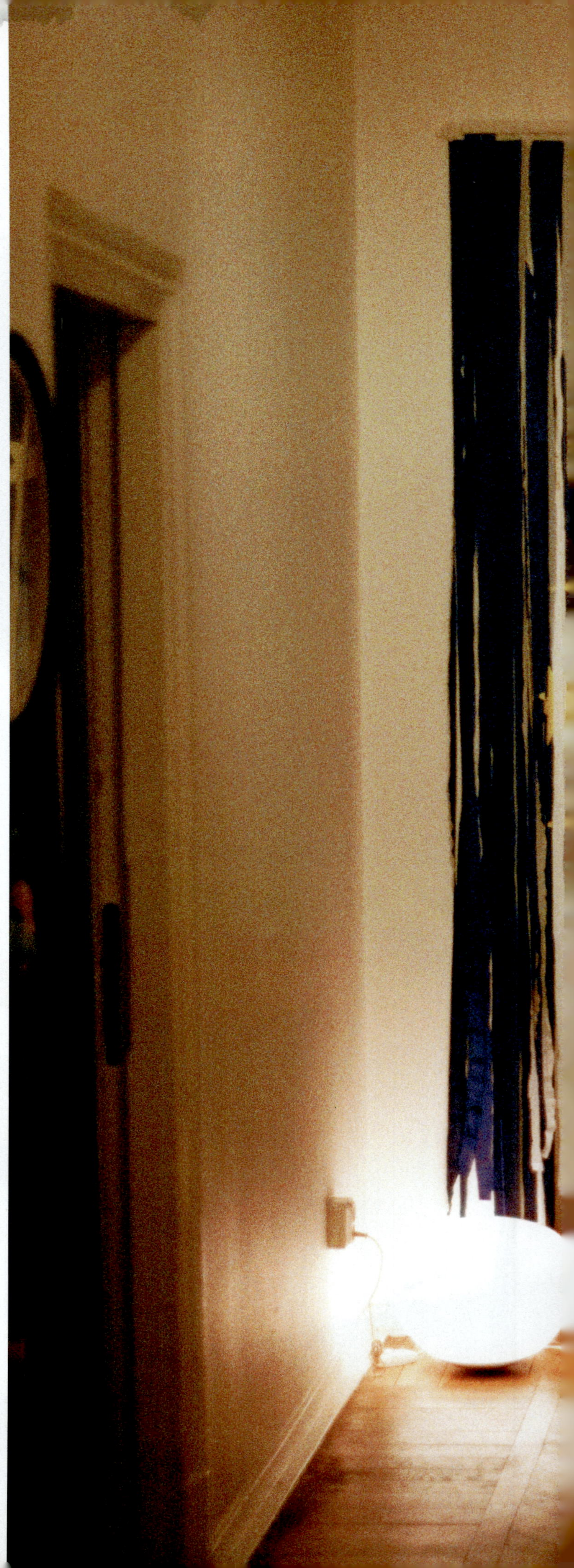

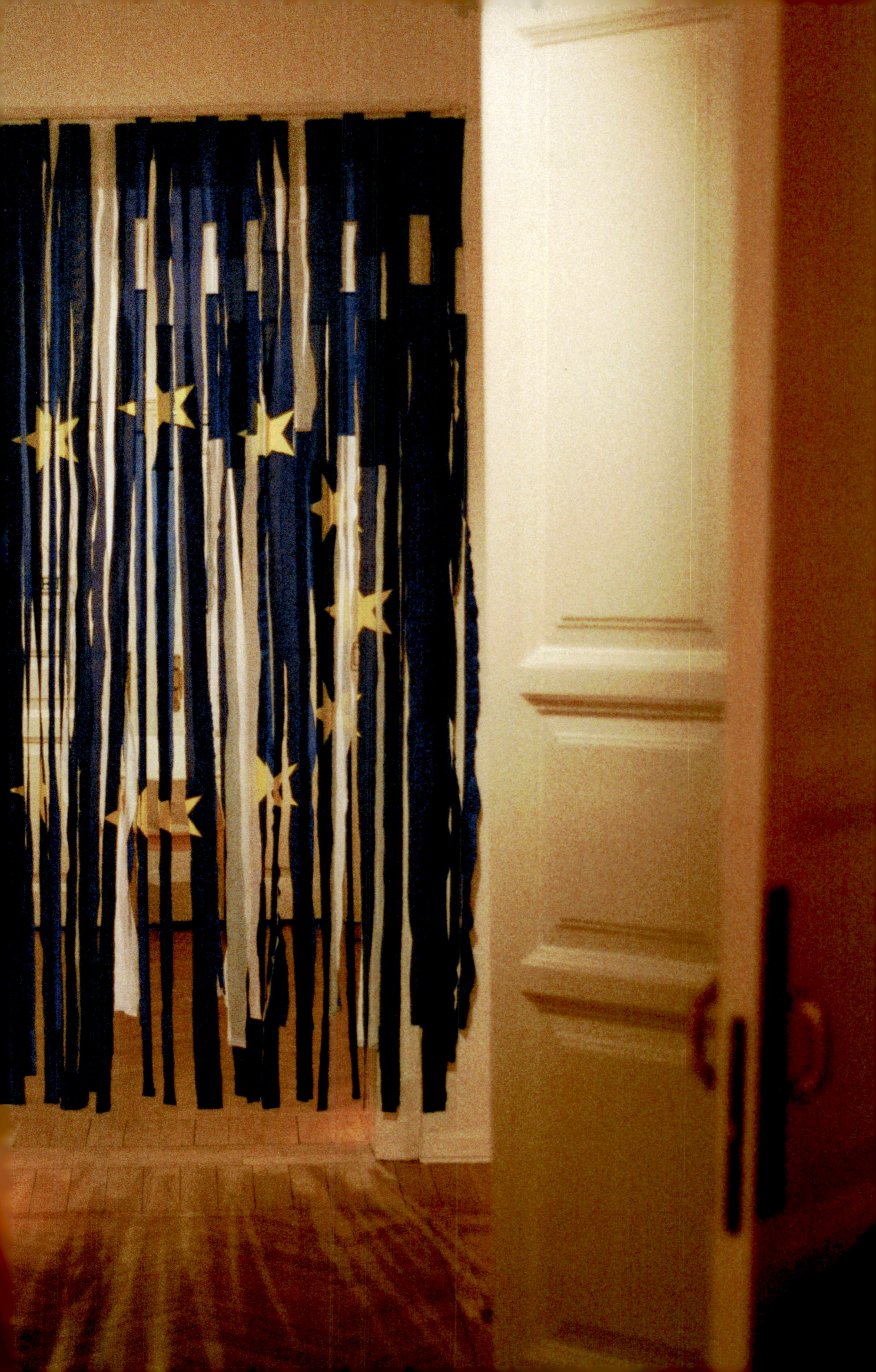

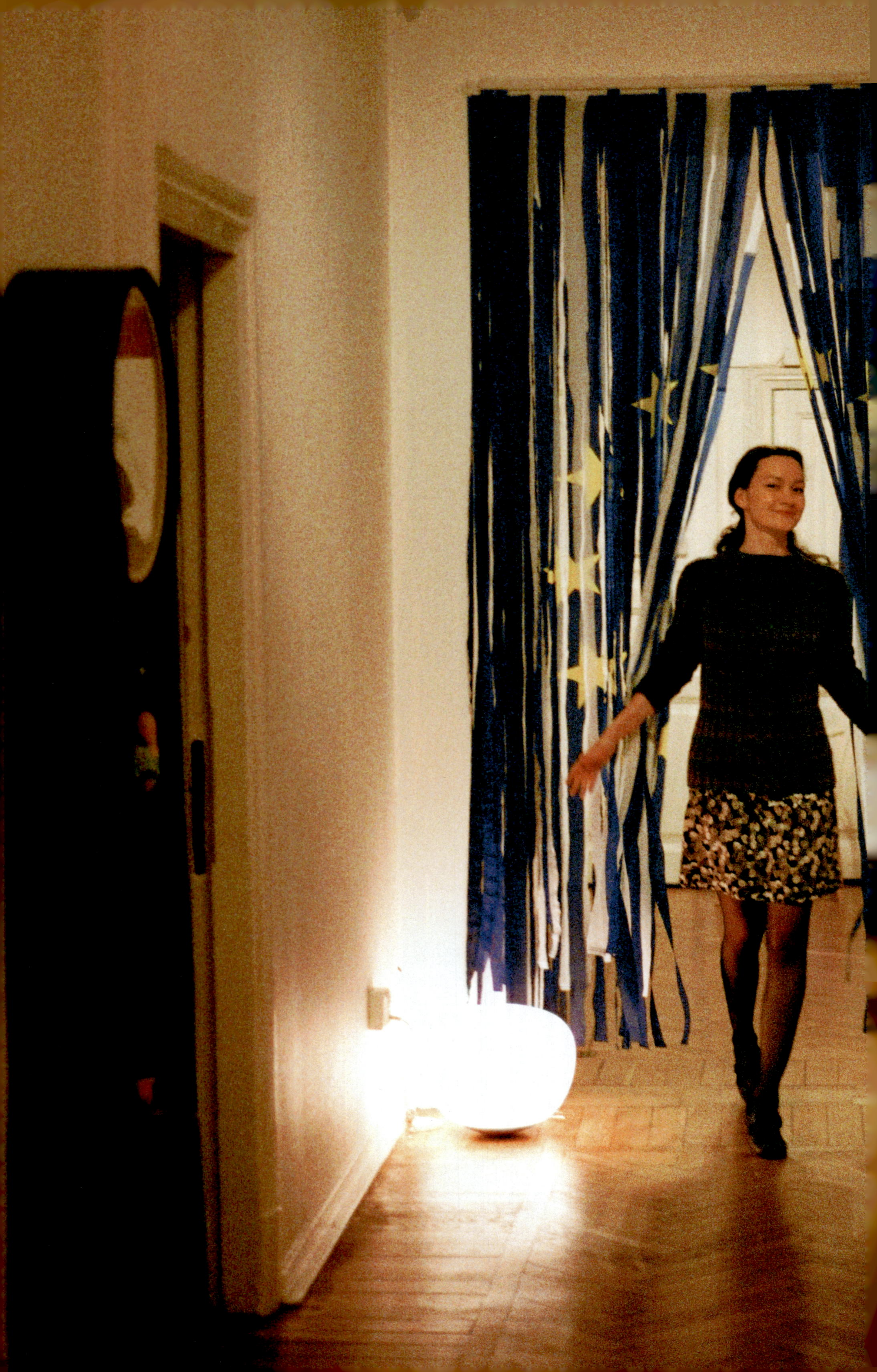

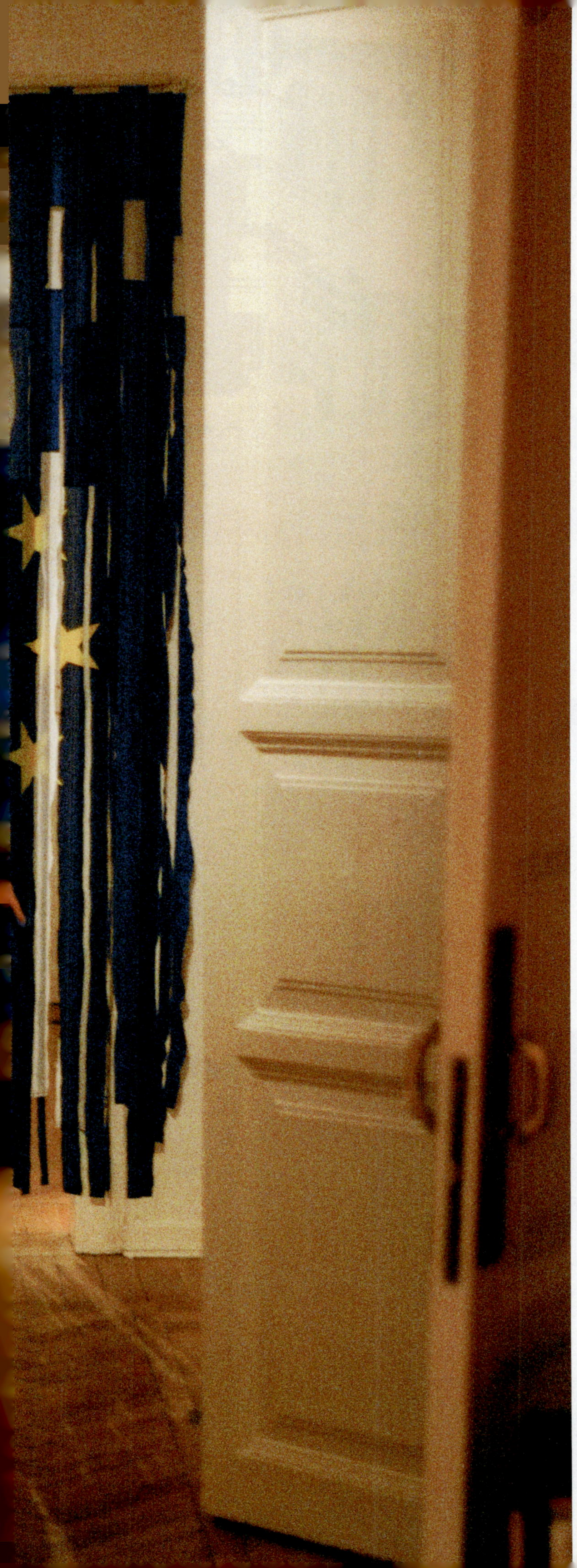

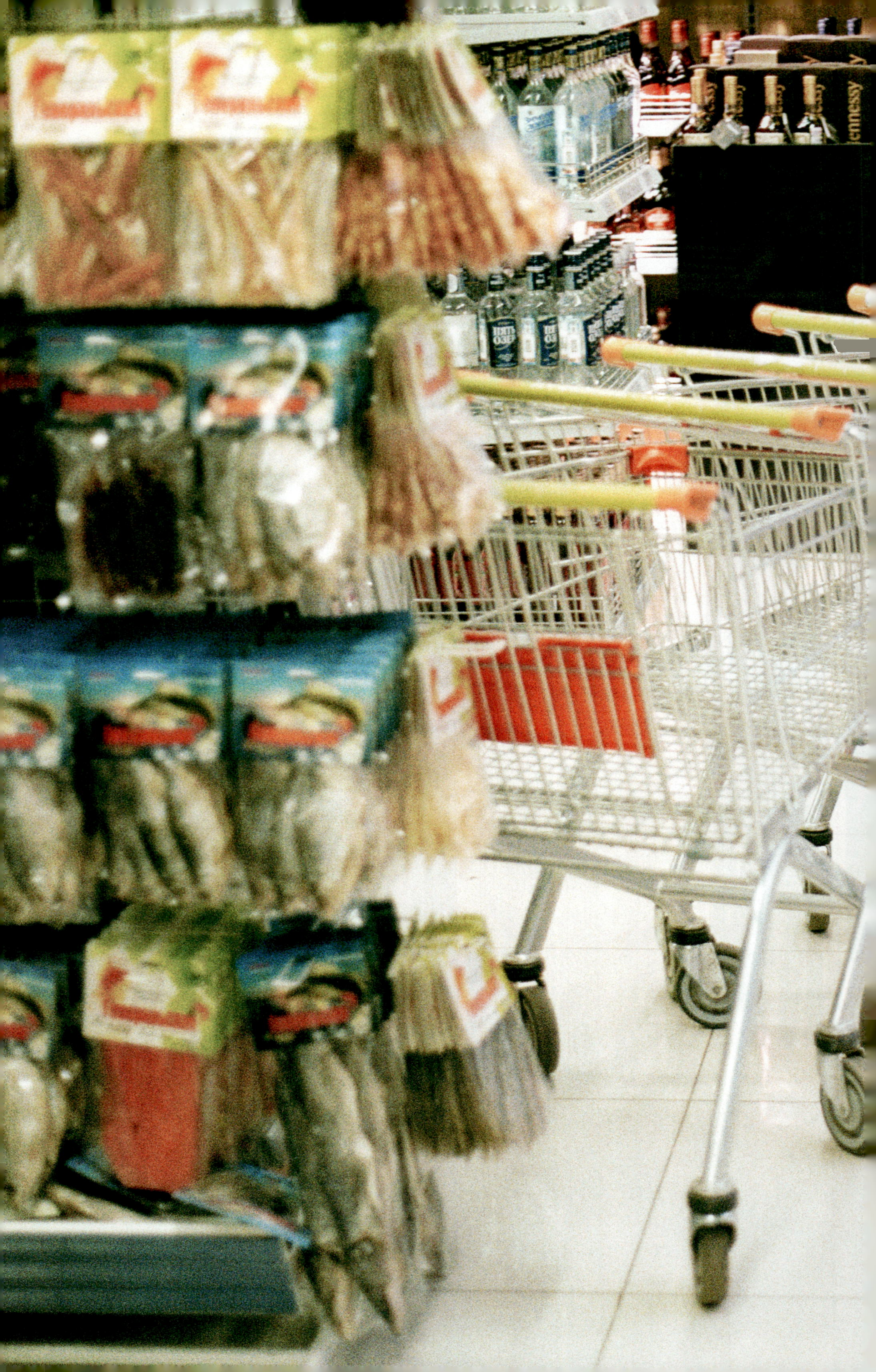

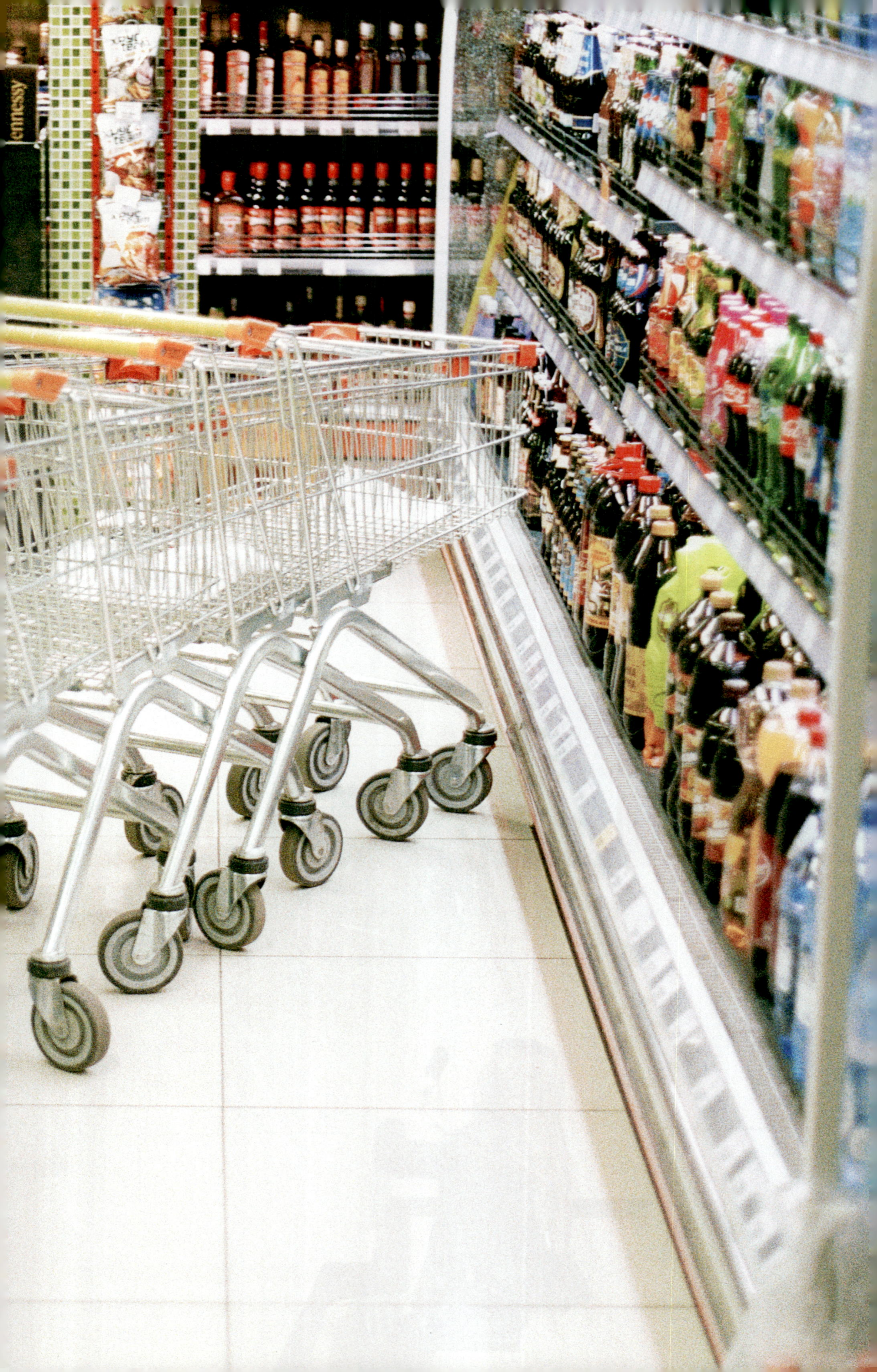

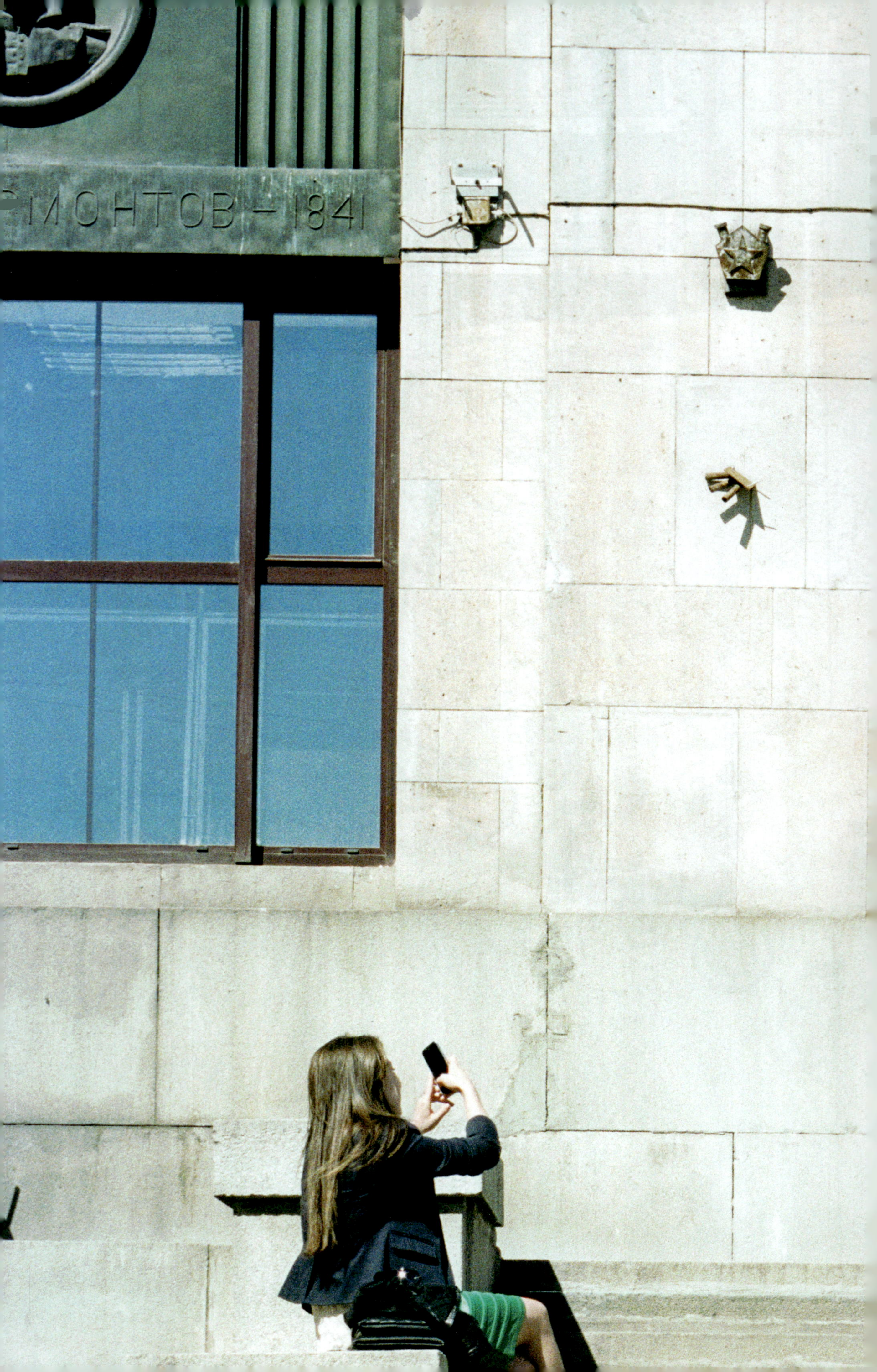
ИОНТОВ – 1841

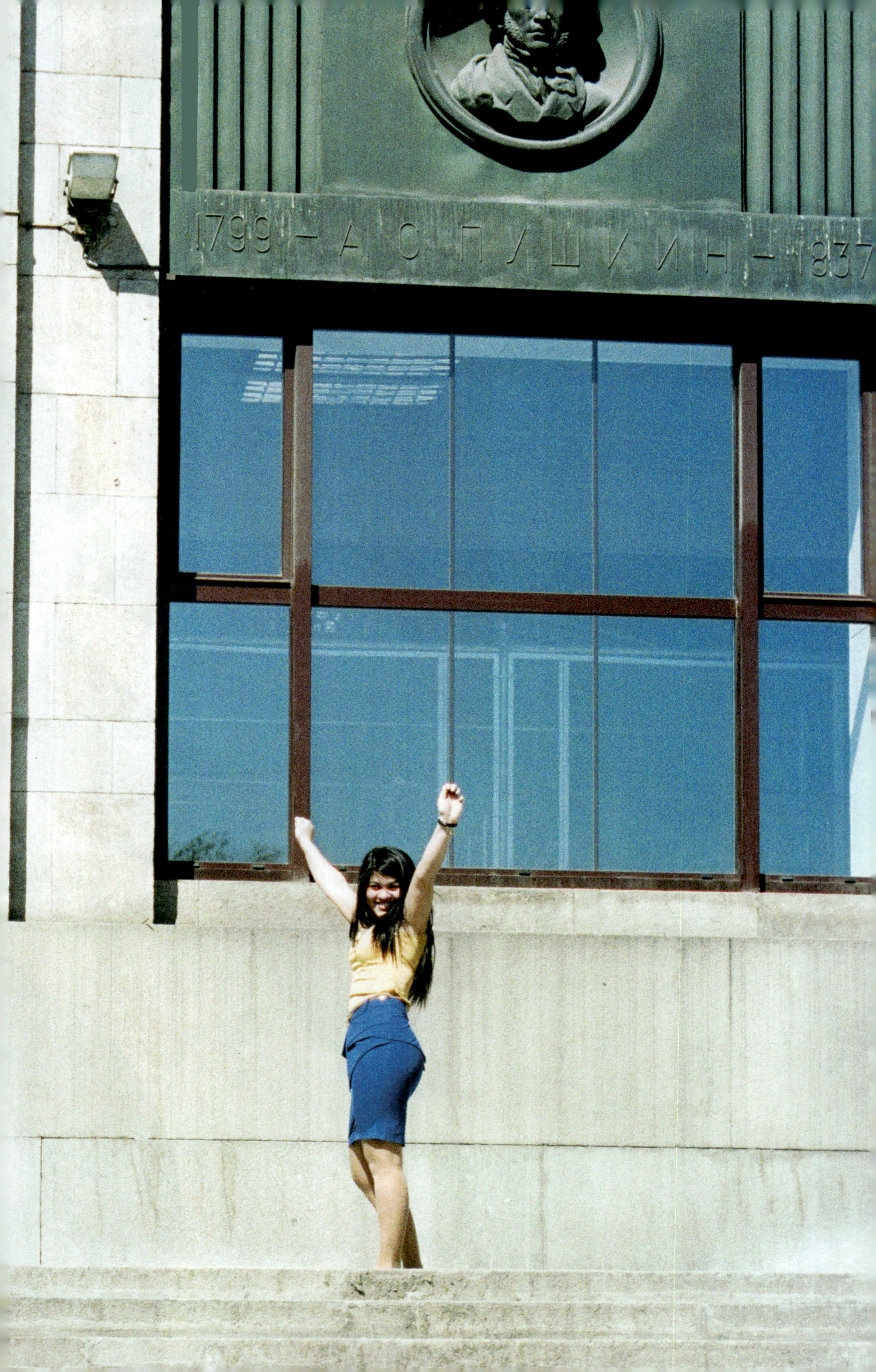
1799 — А С ПУШКИН — 1837

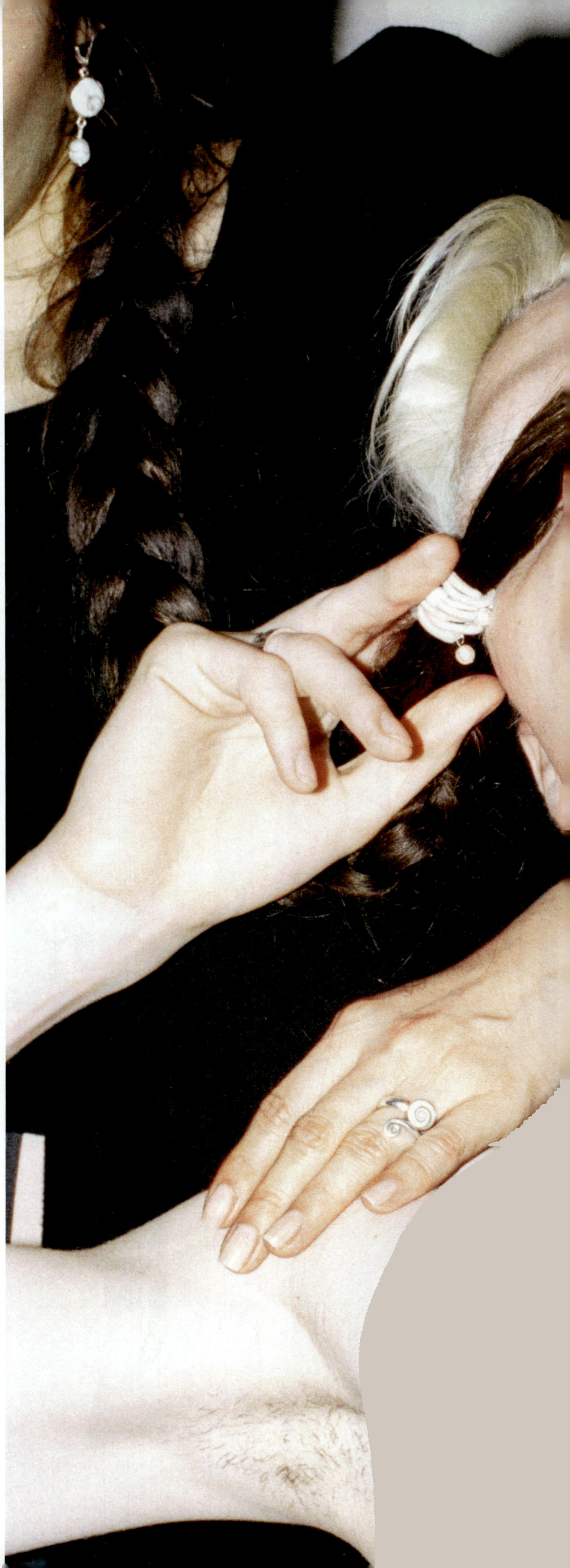

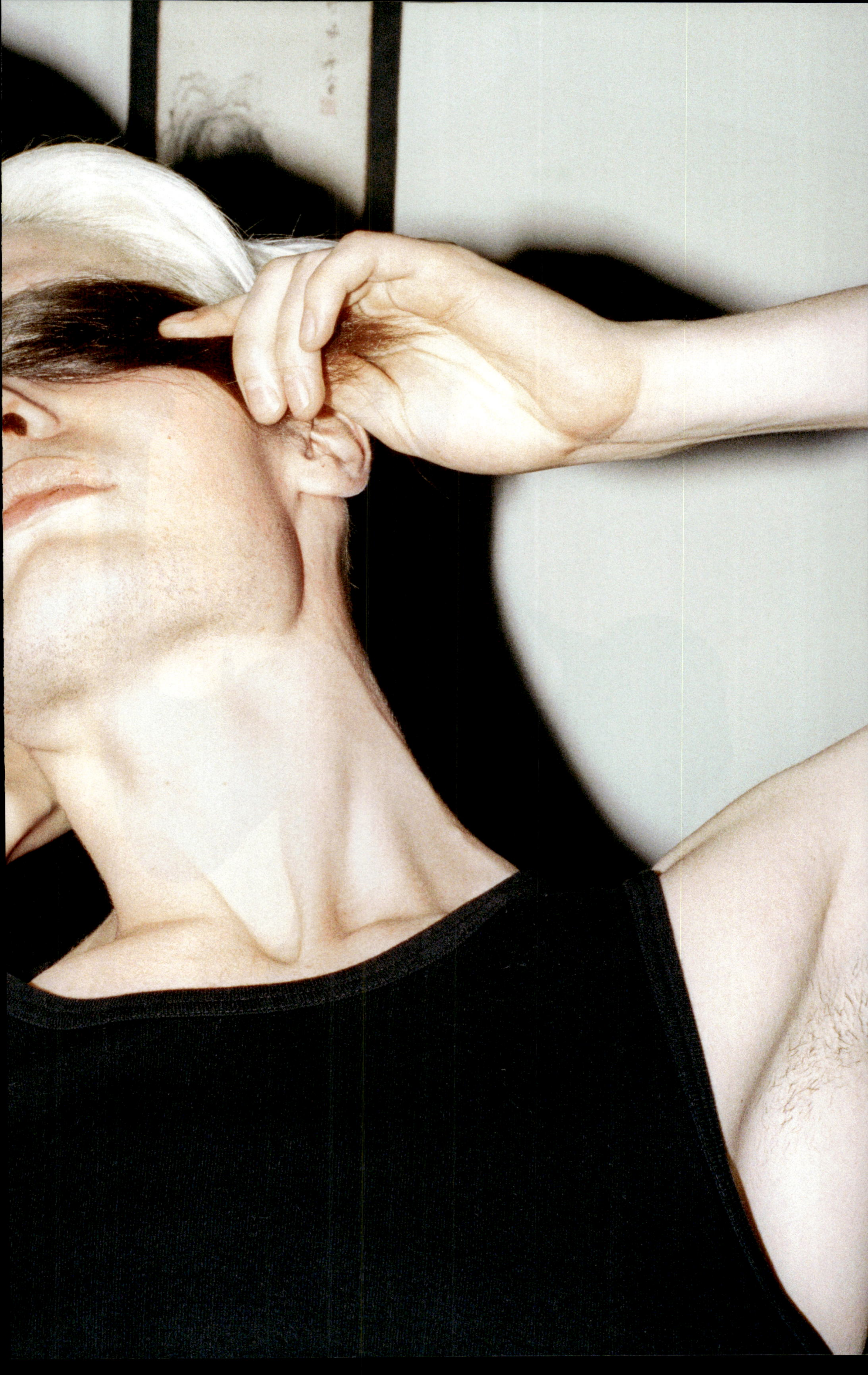

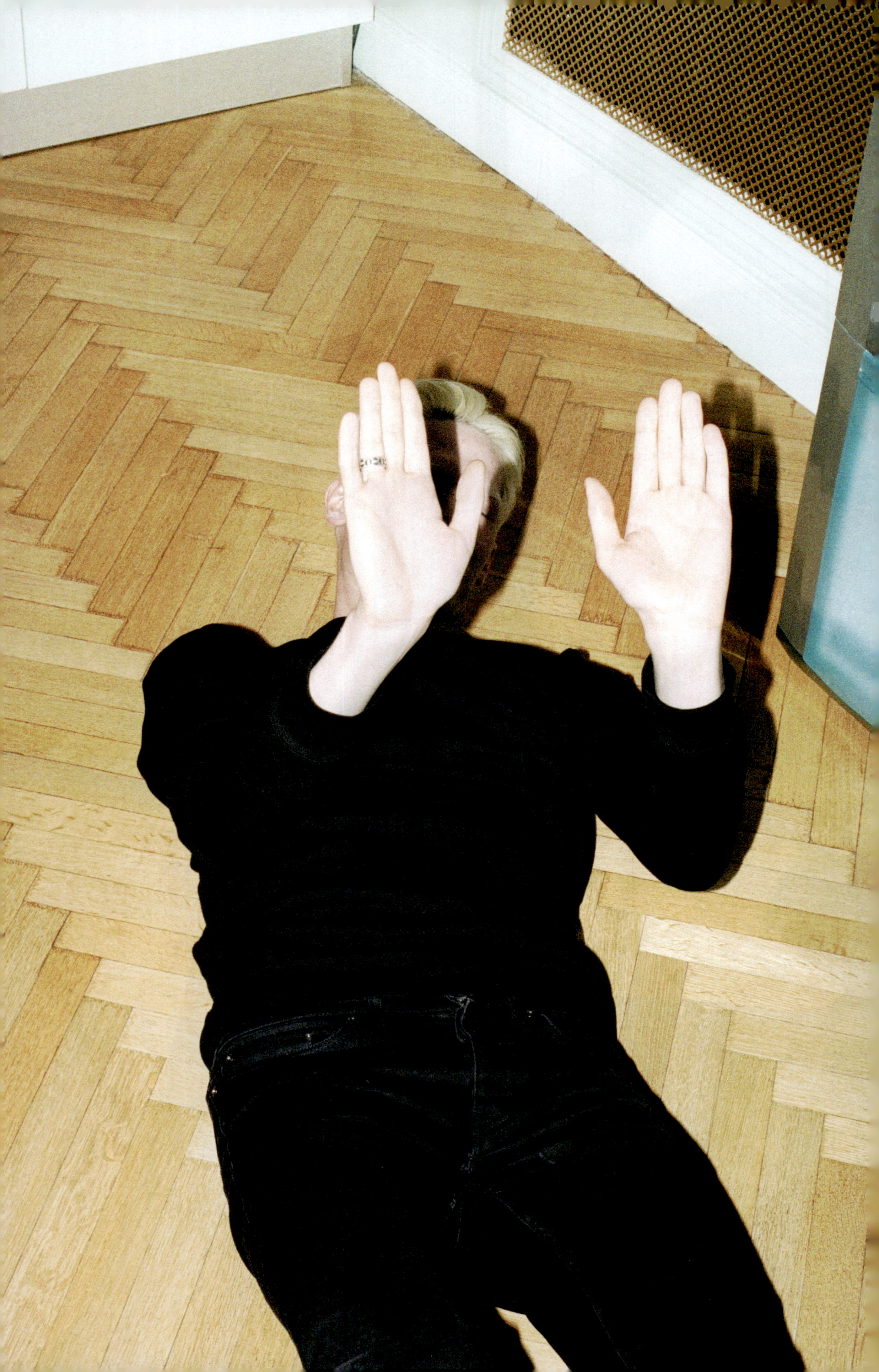

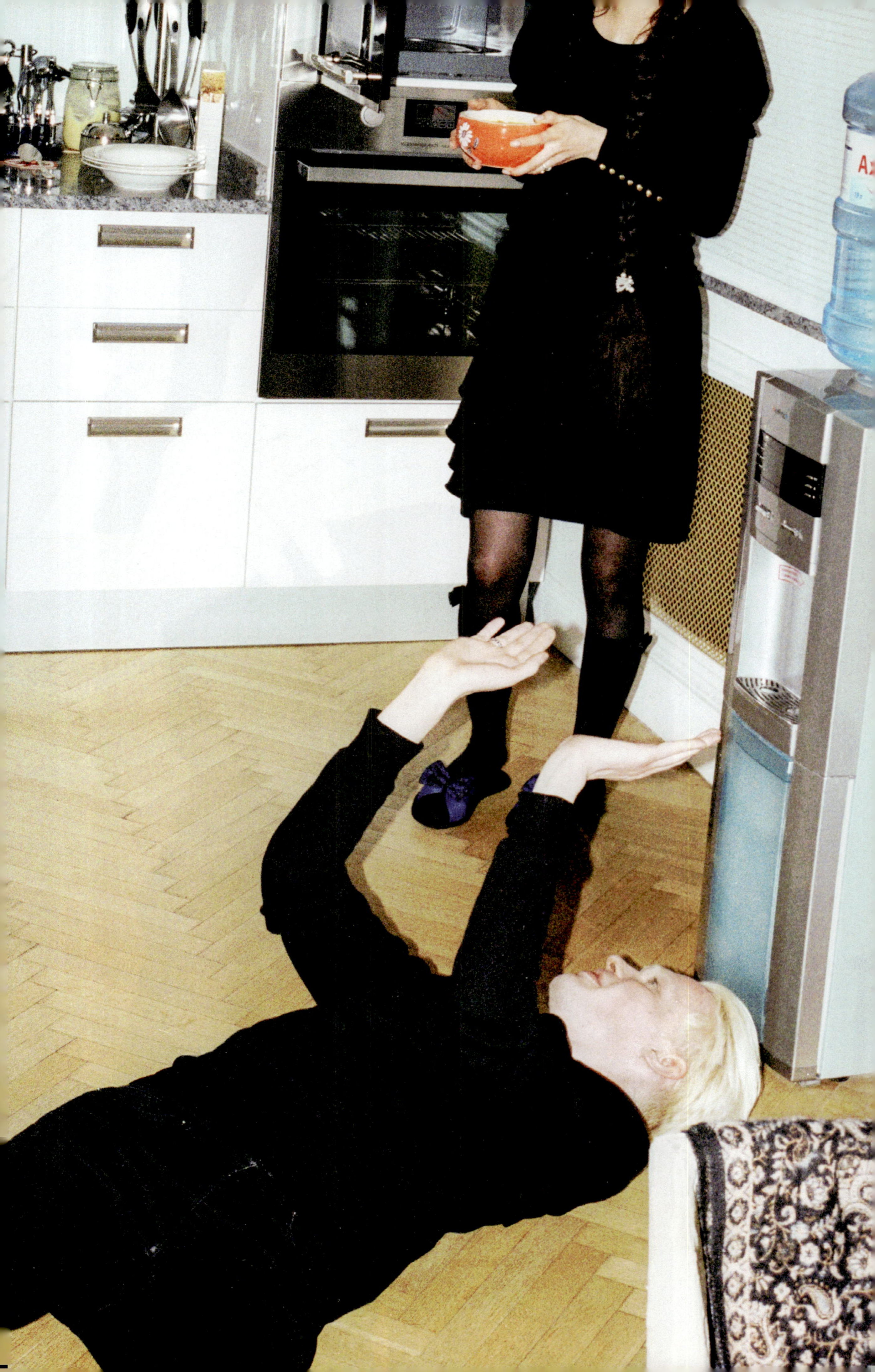

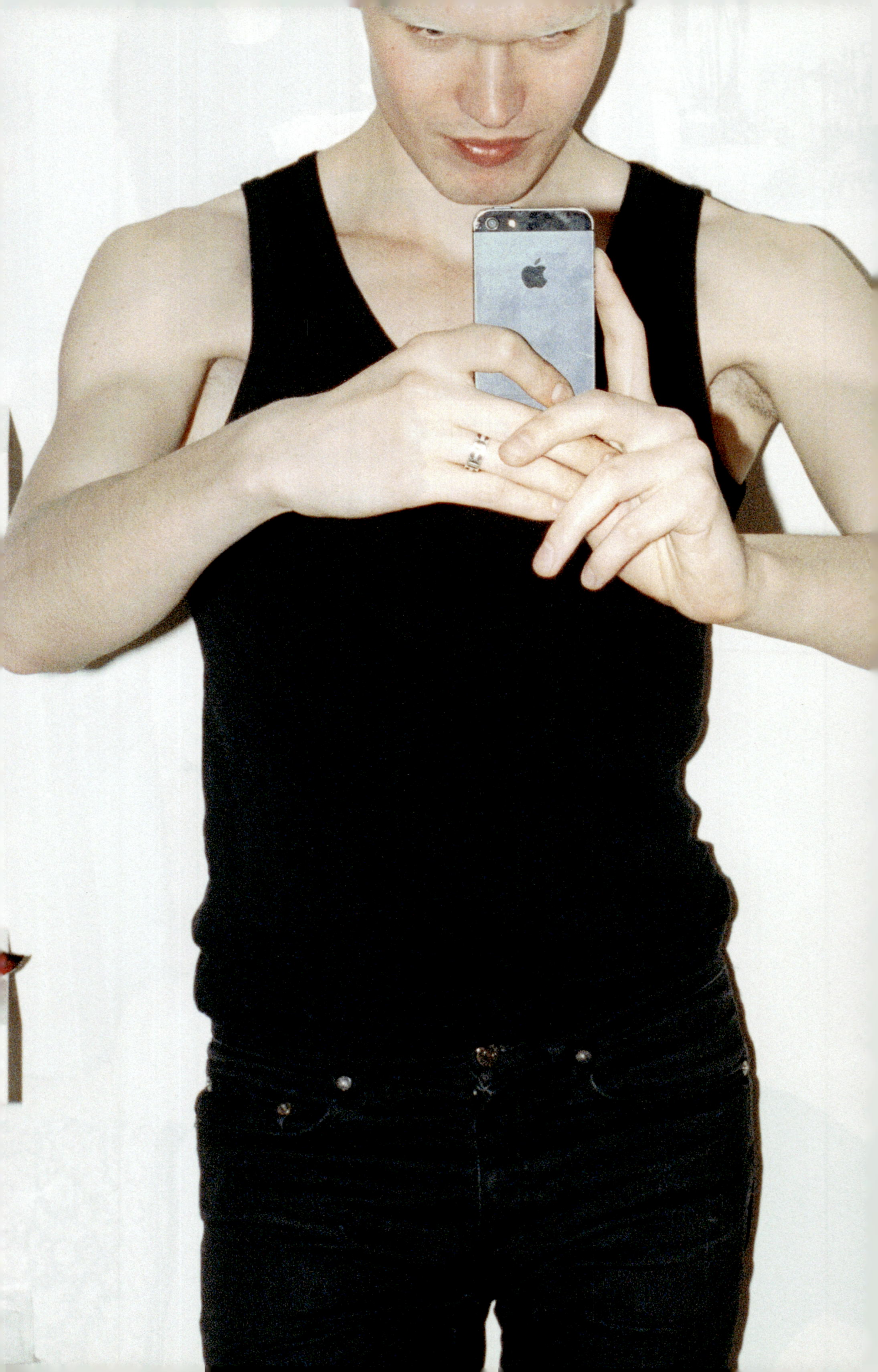

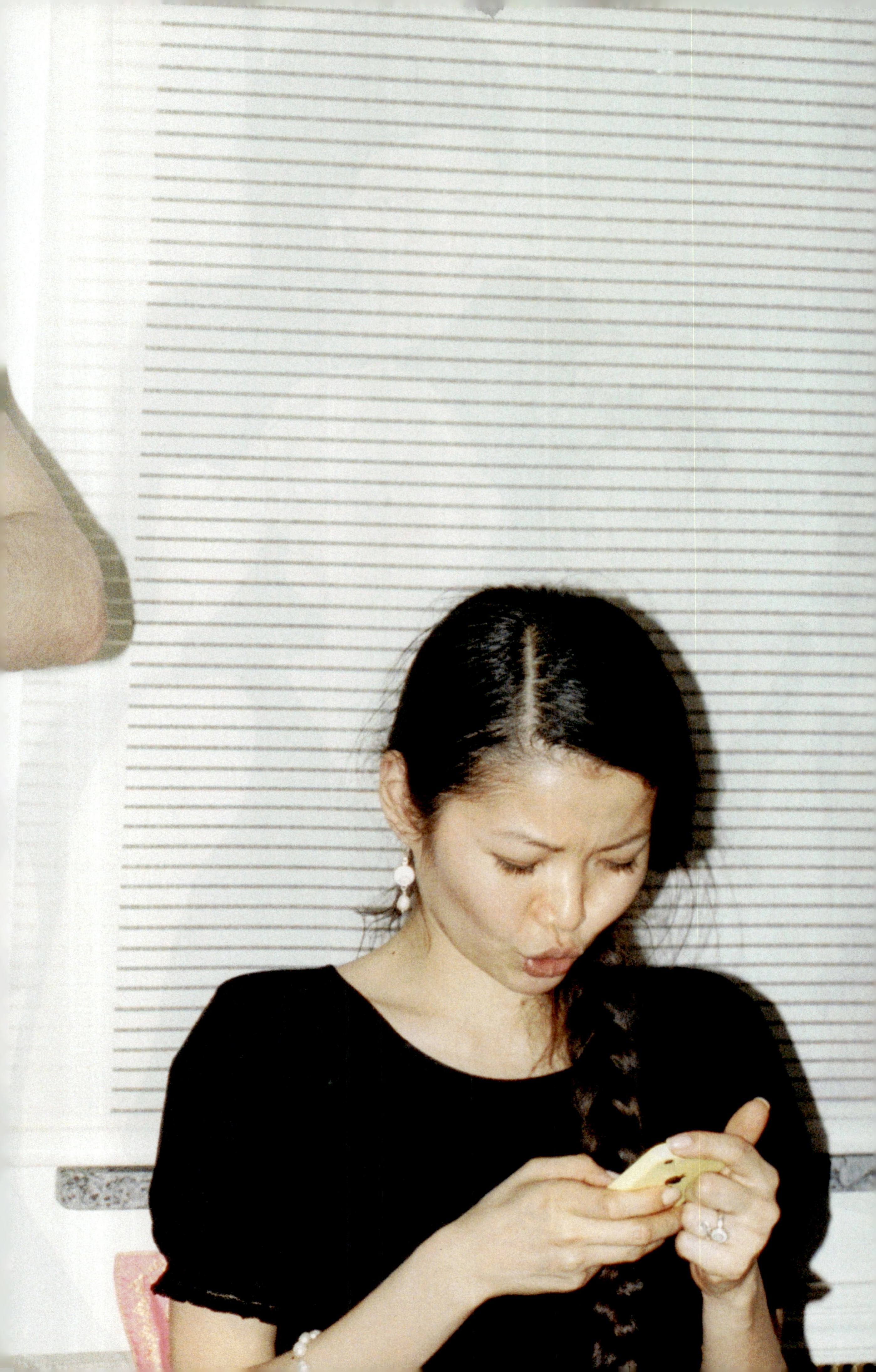

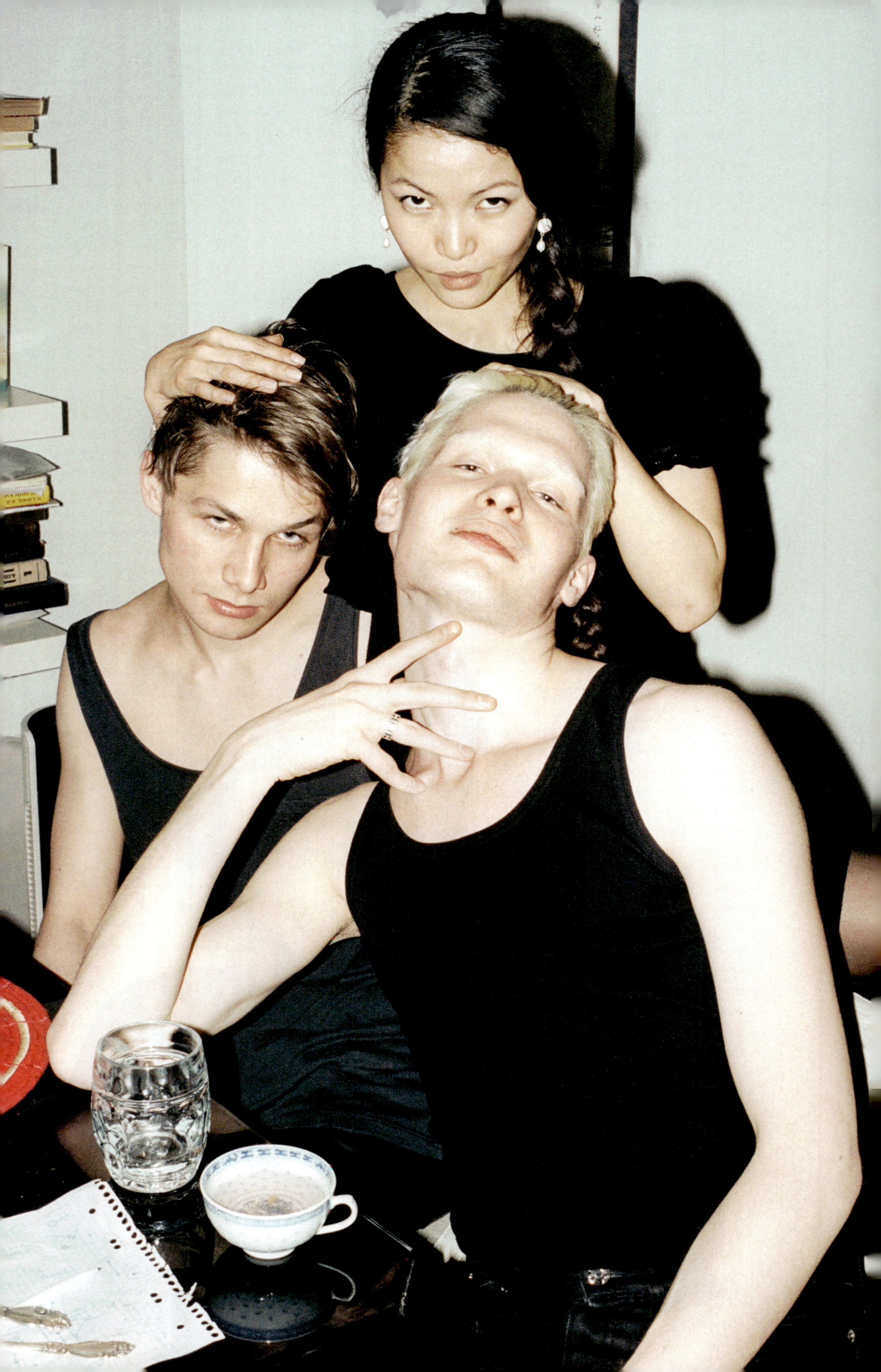

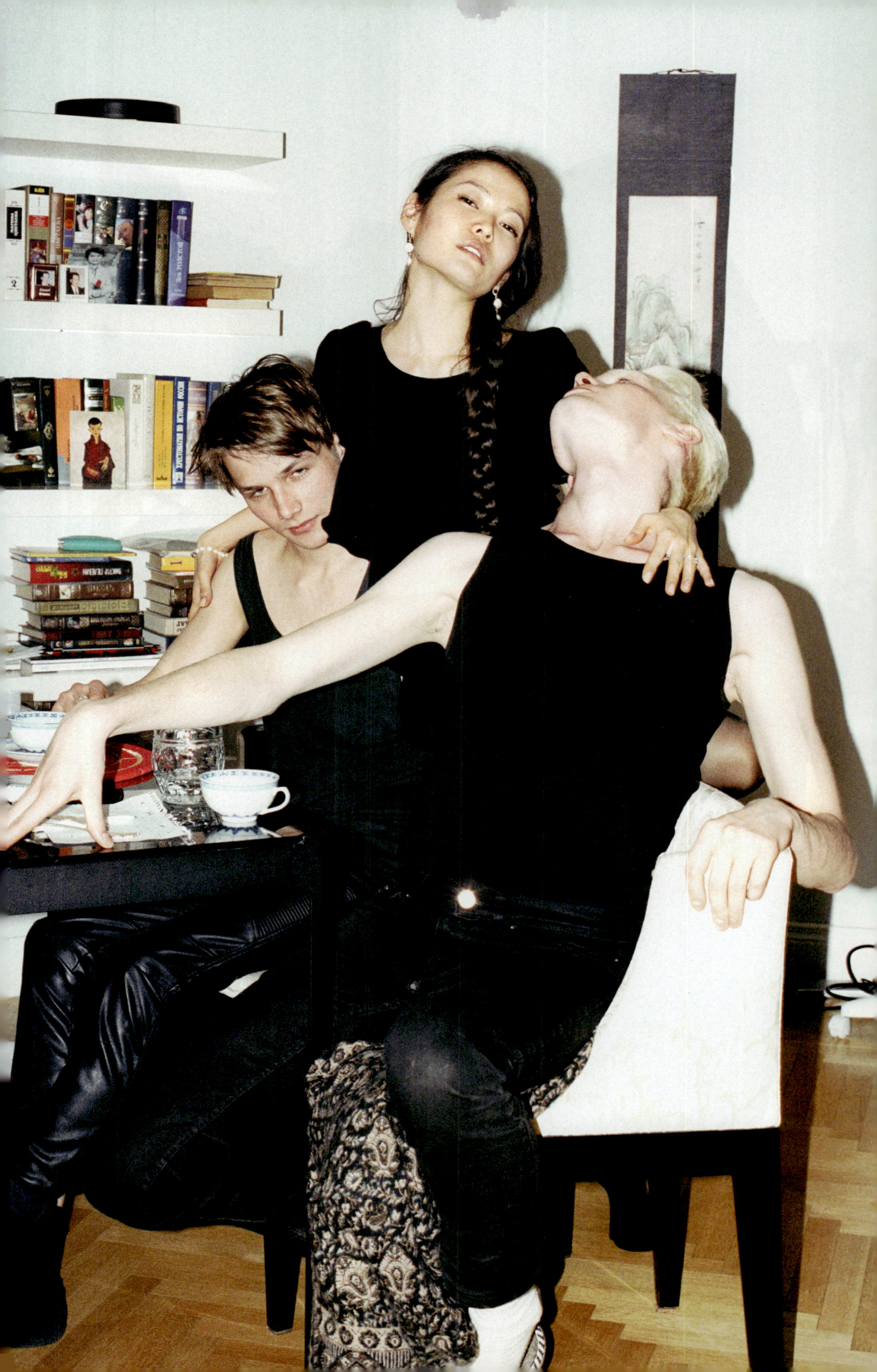

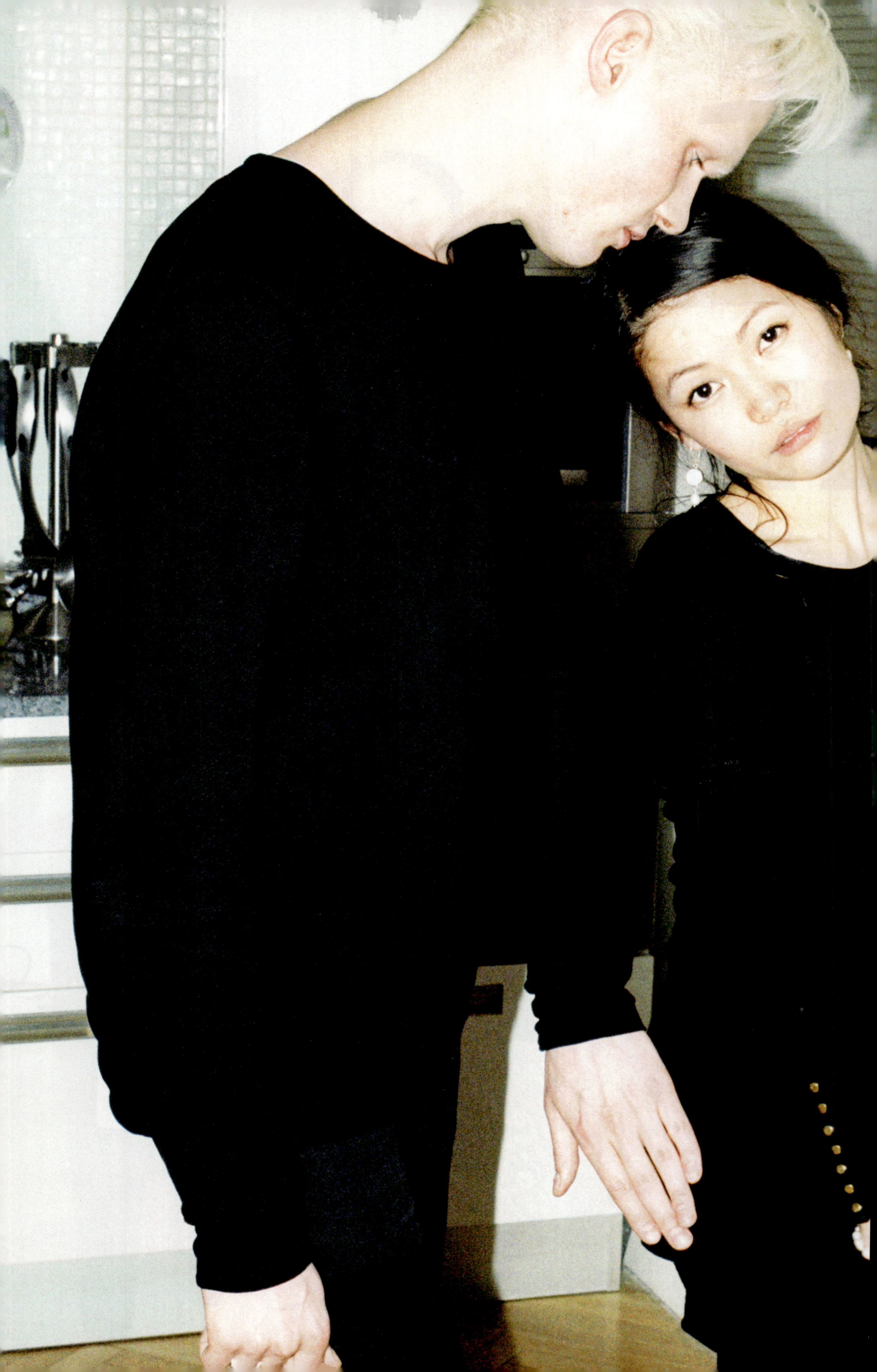

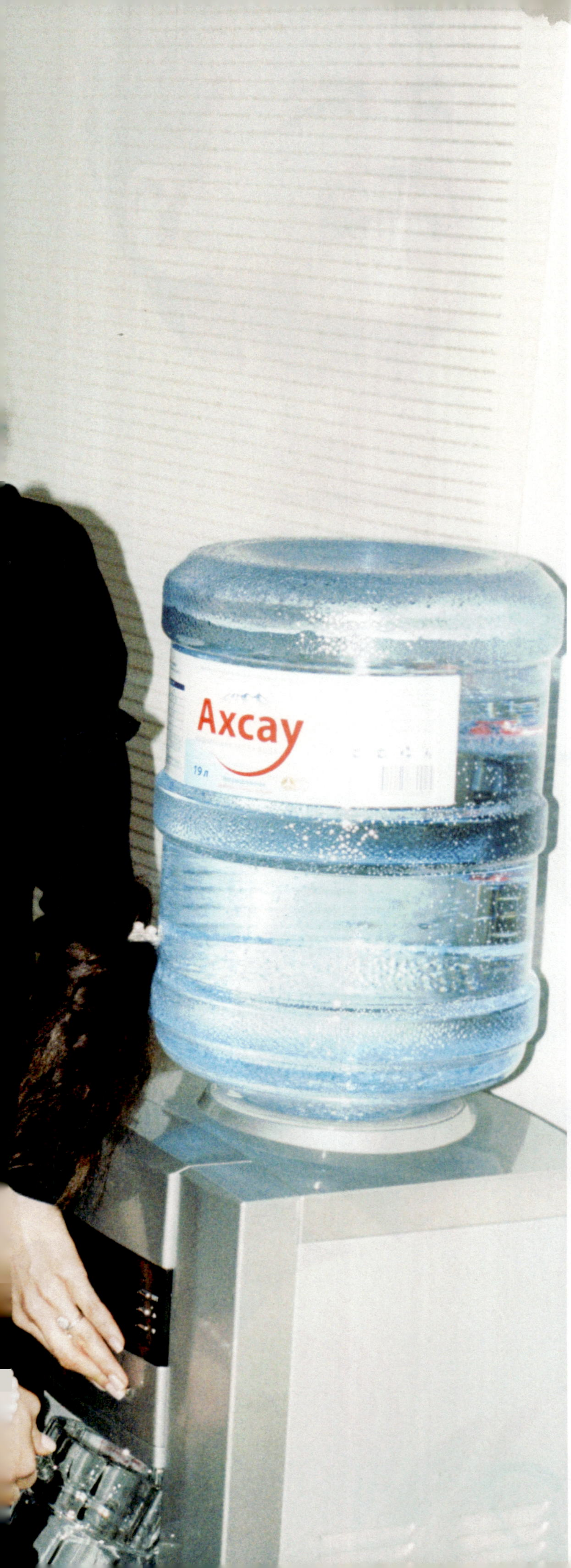
Axcay
19 л

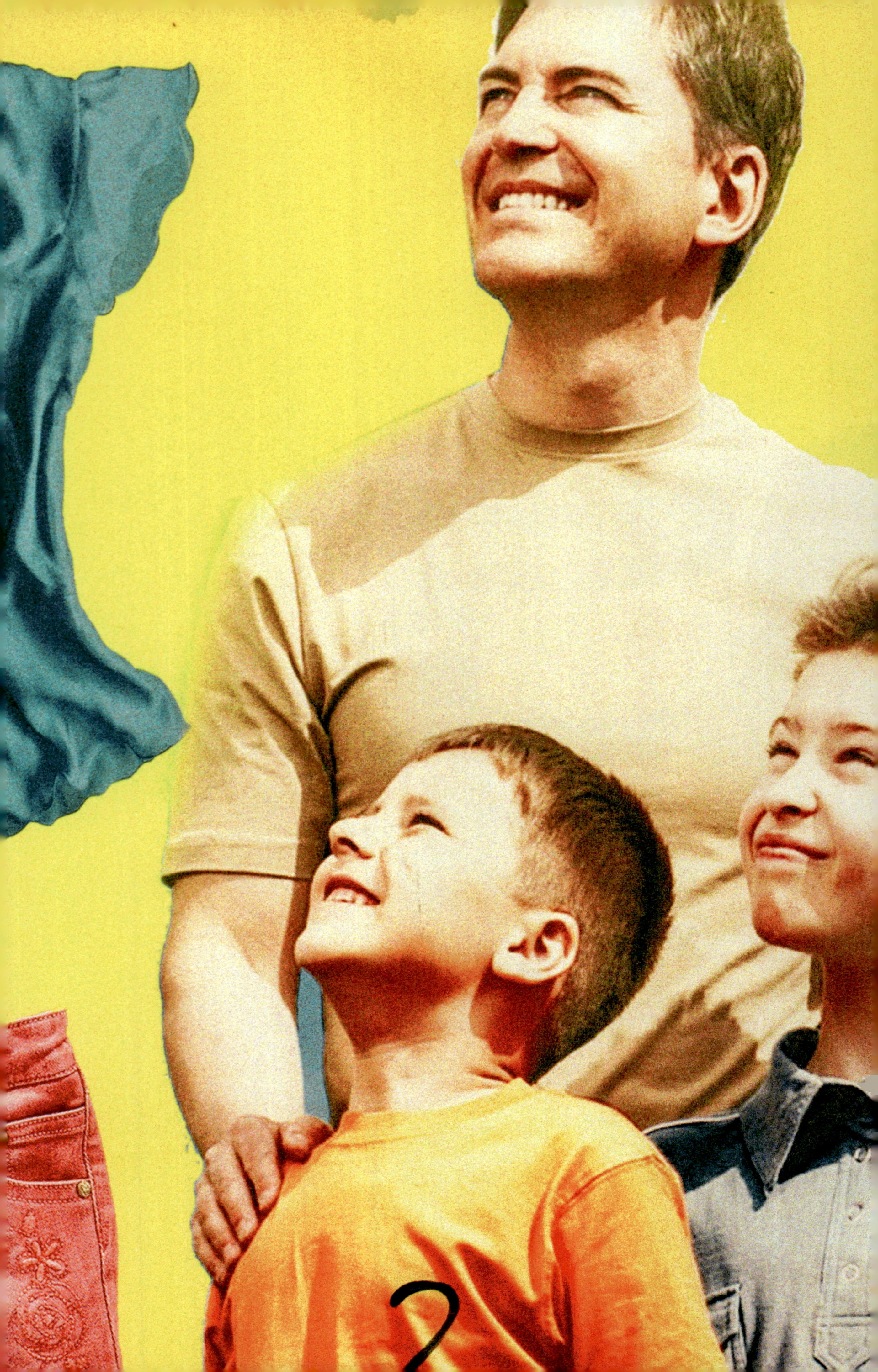

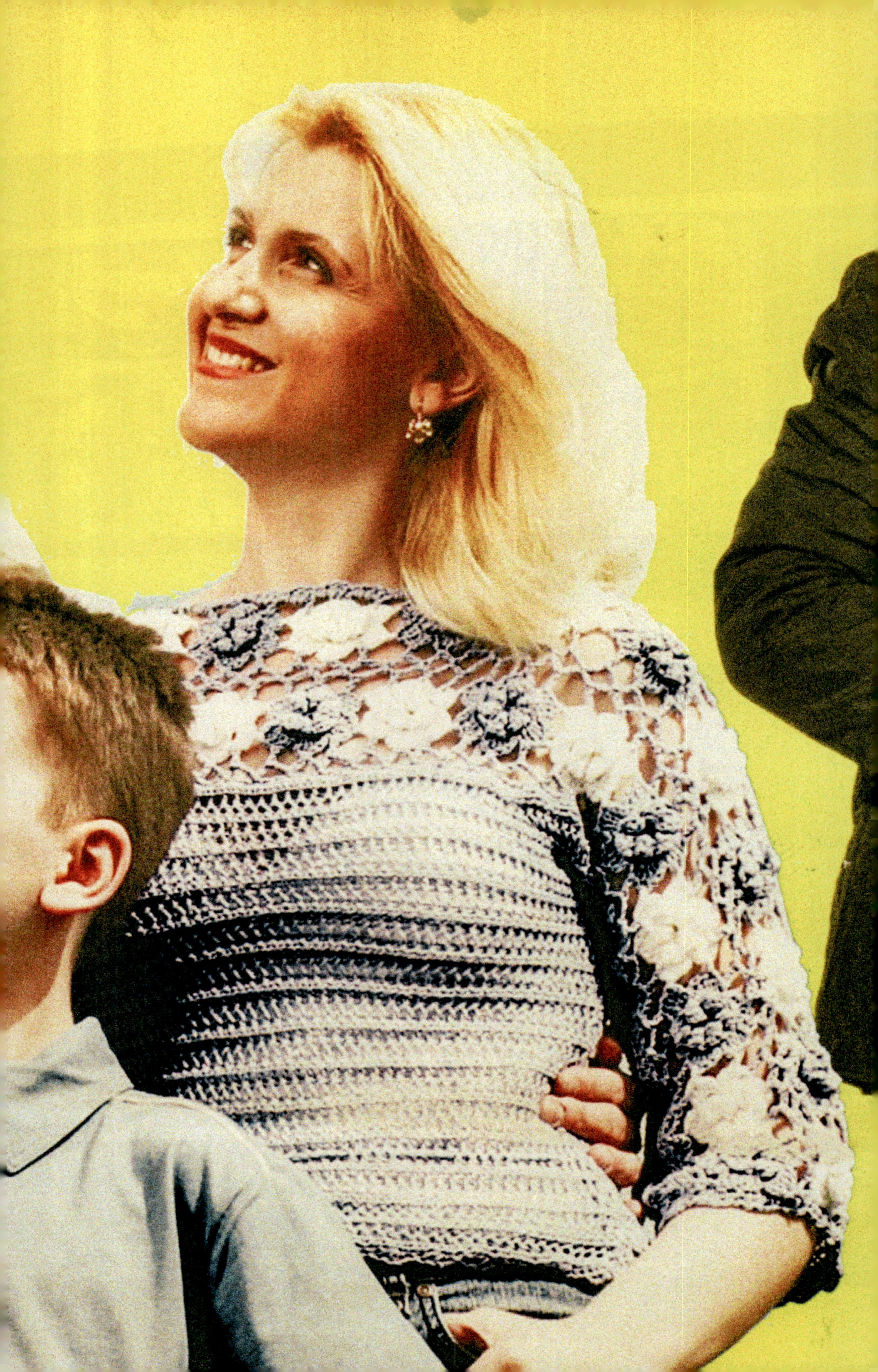

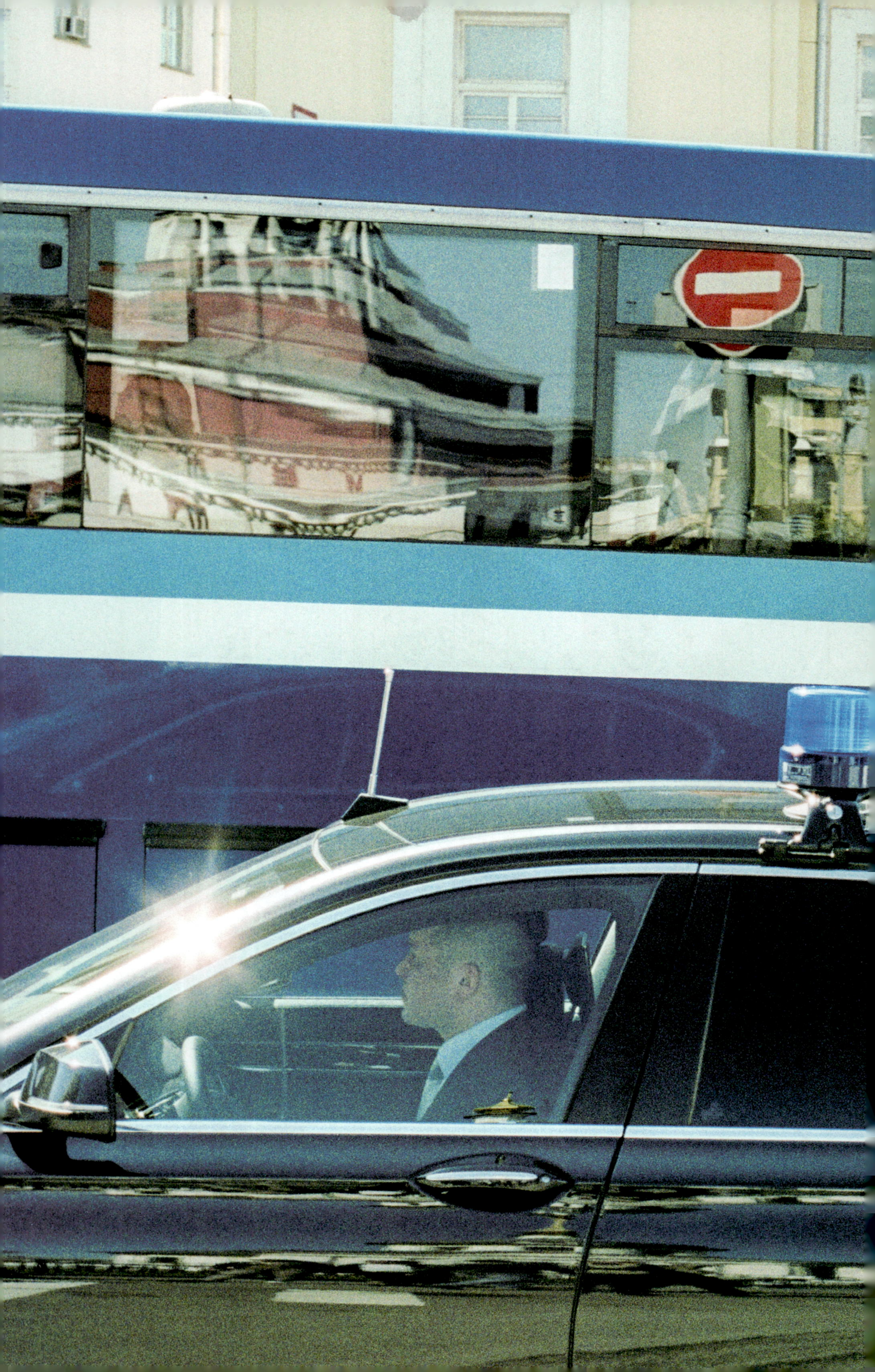

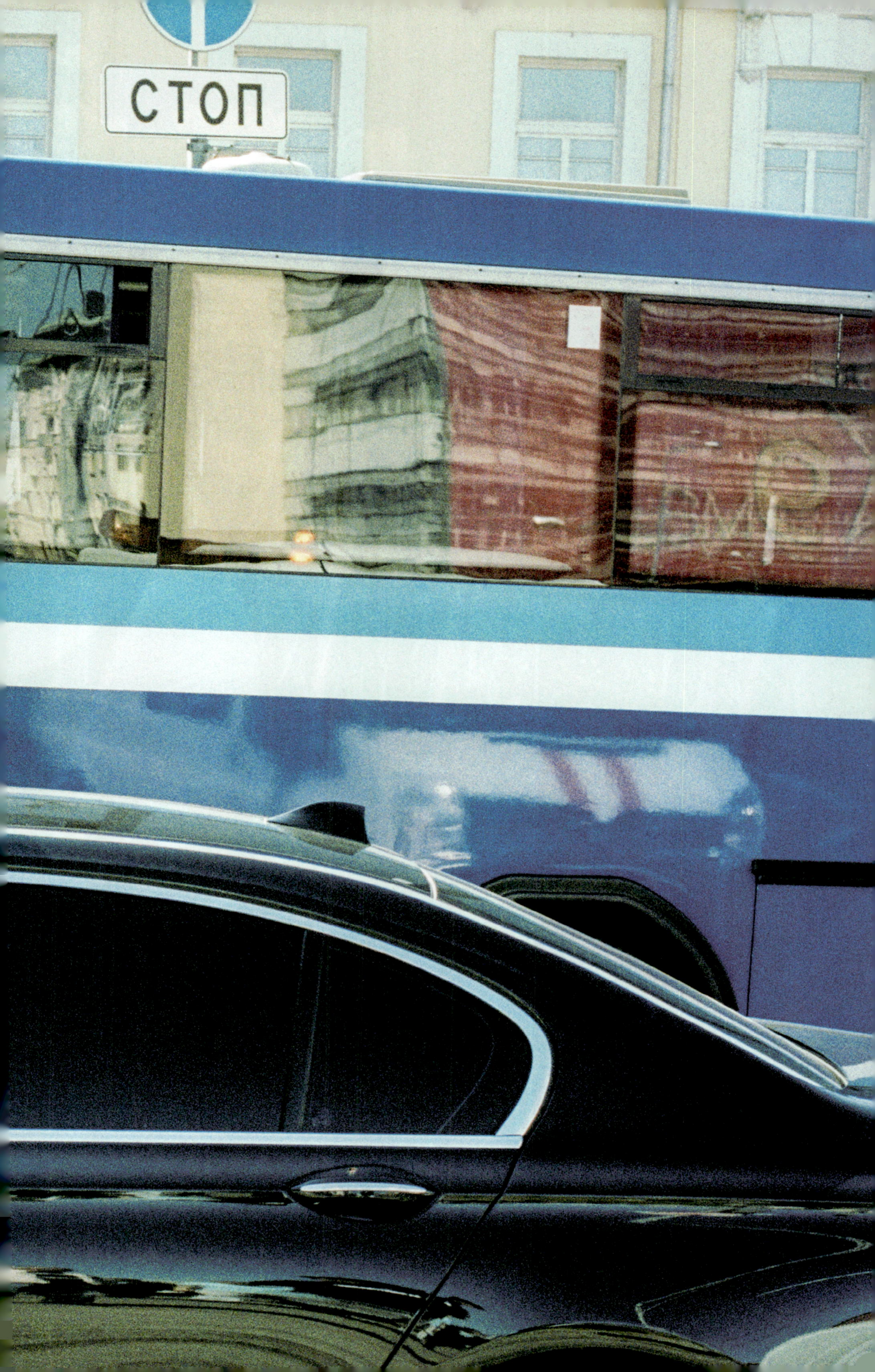
СТОП

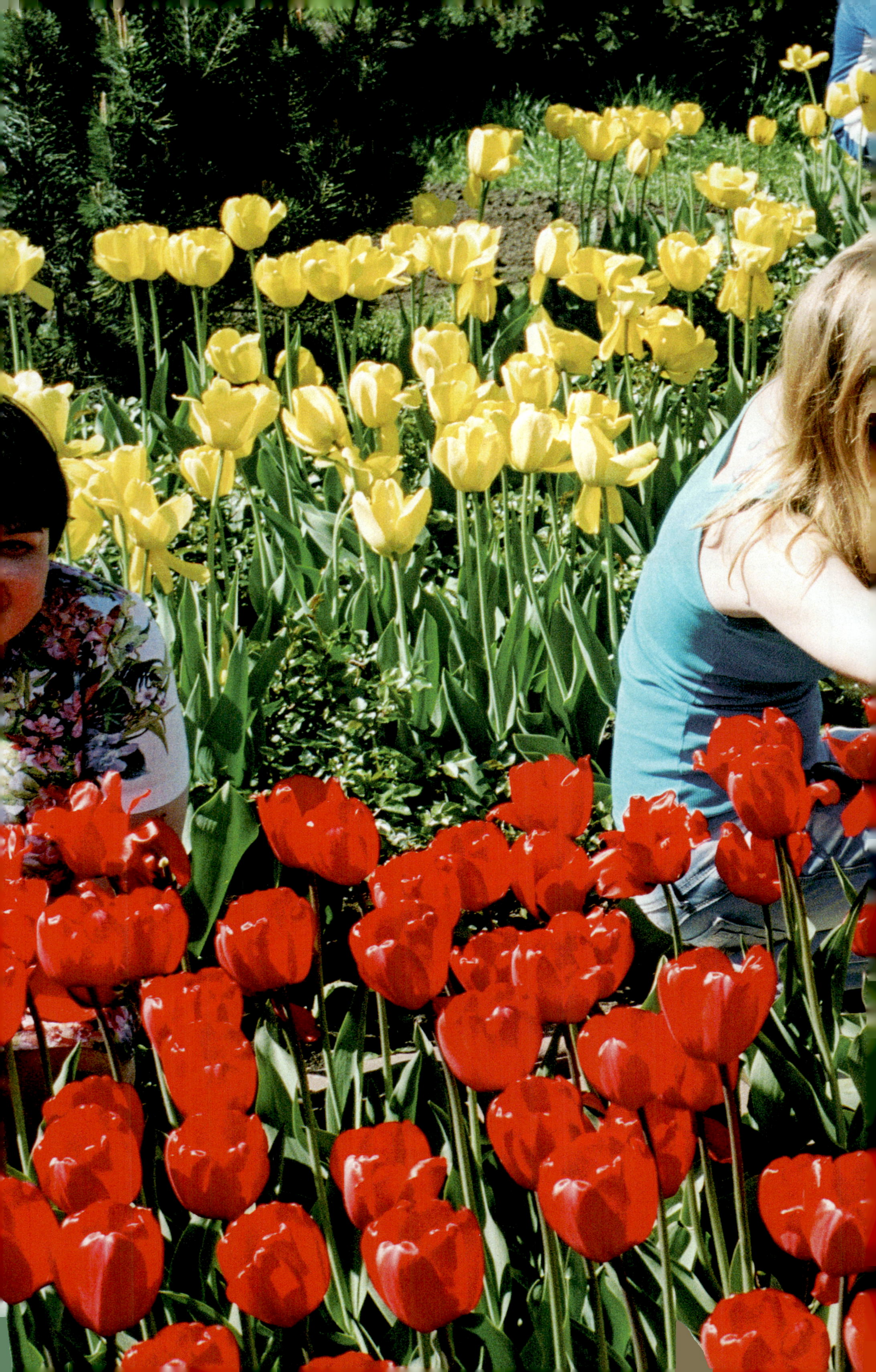

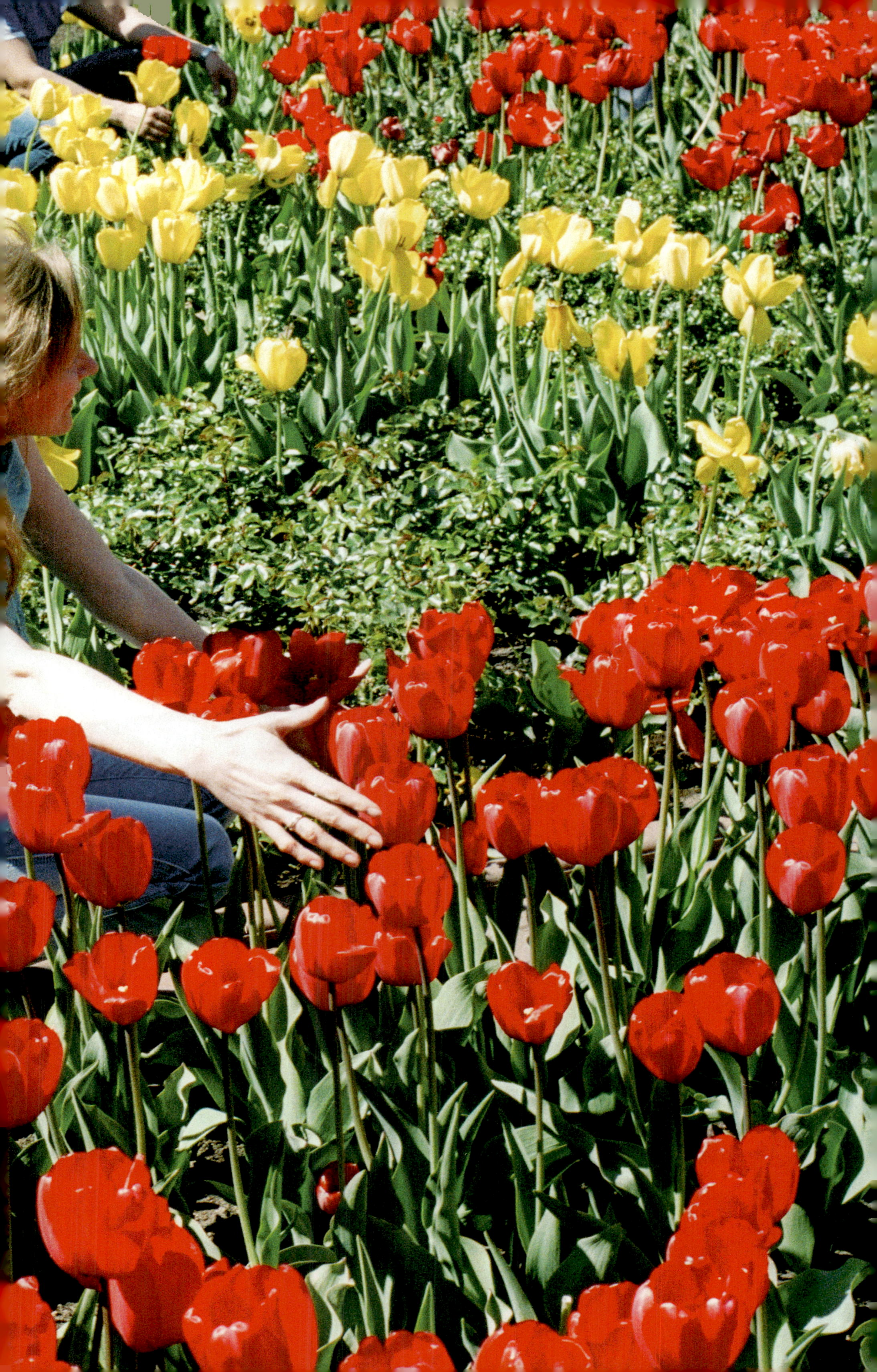

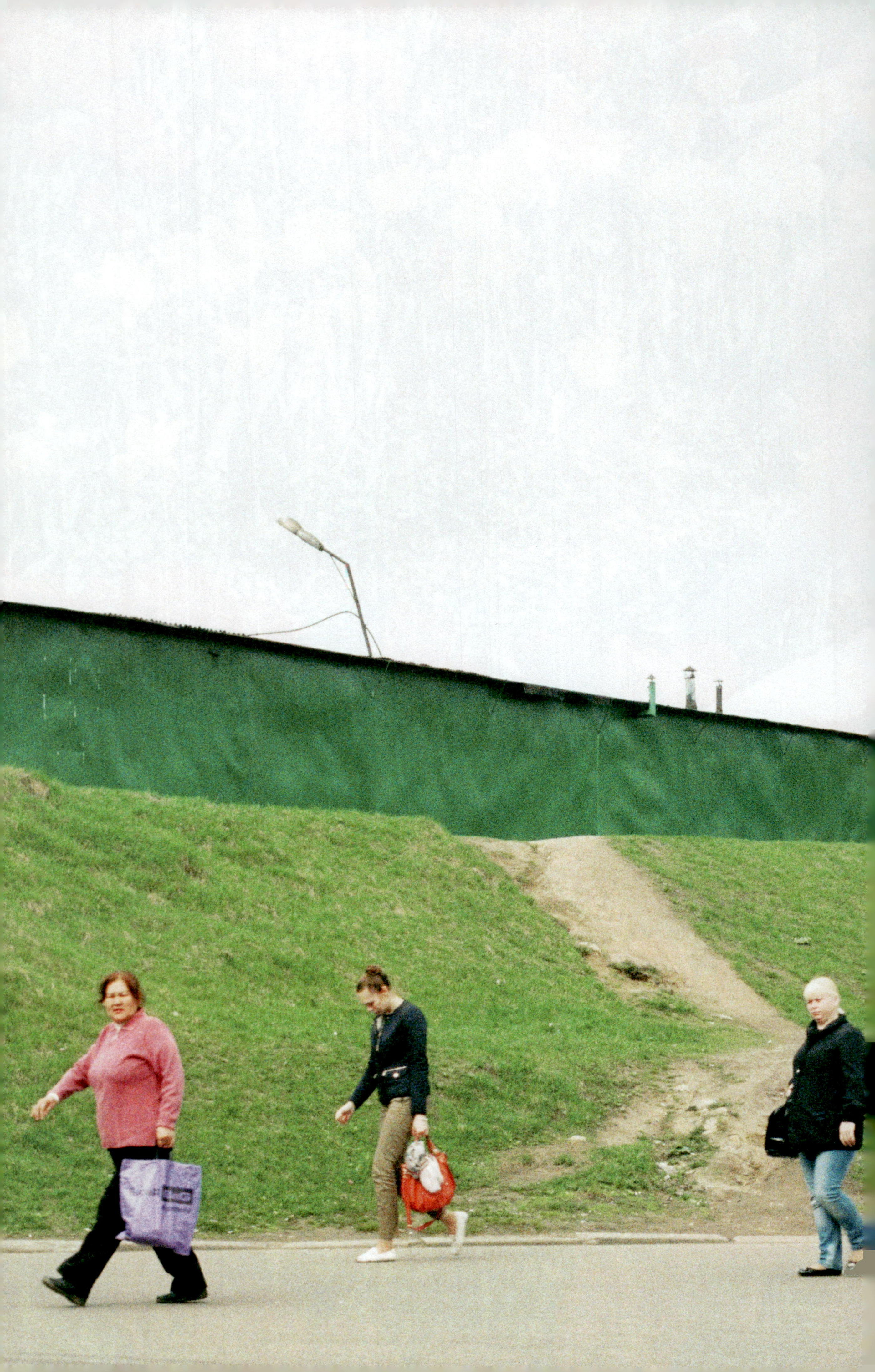

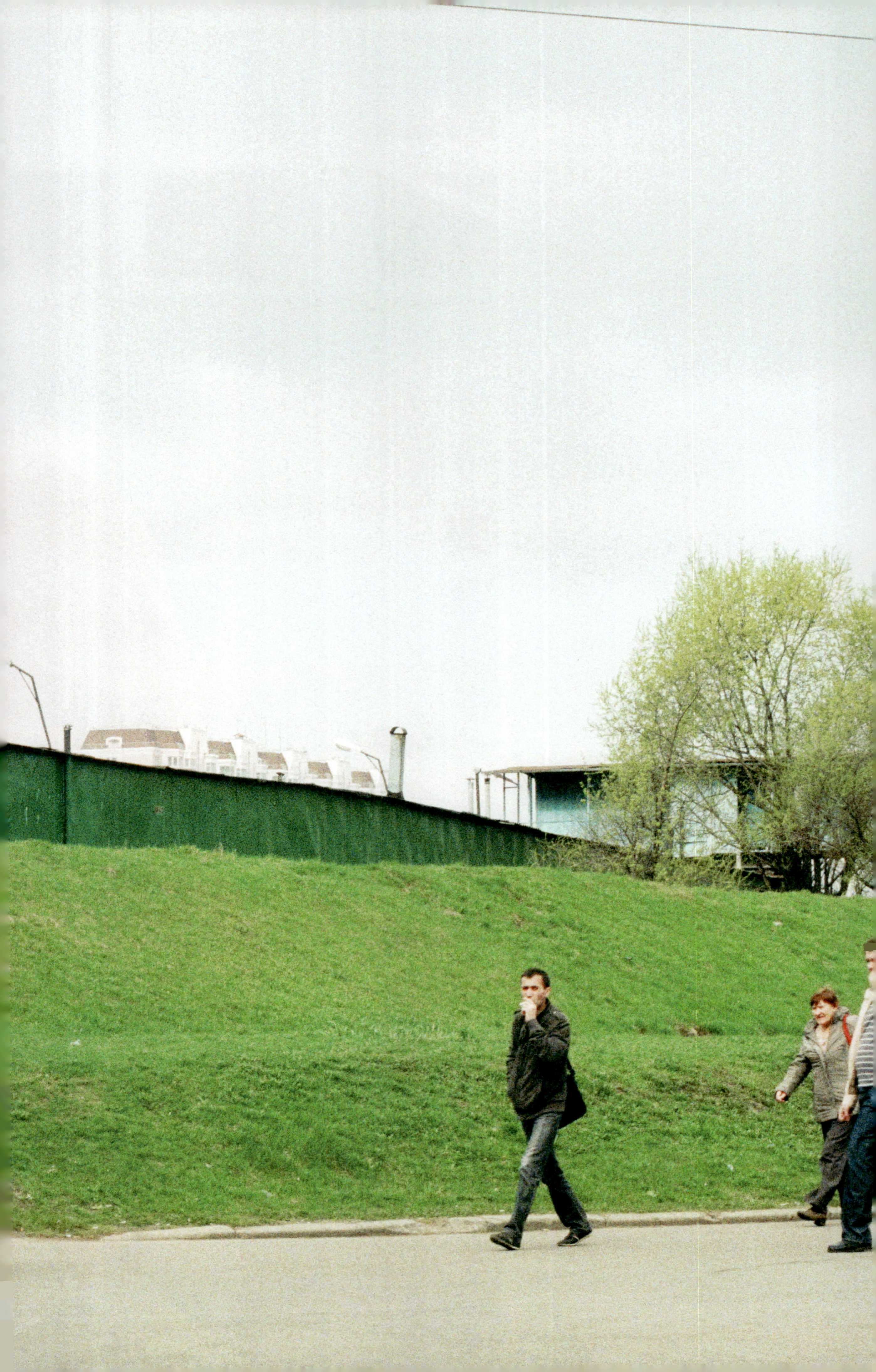

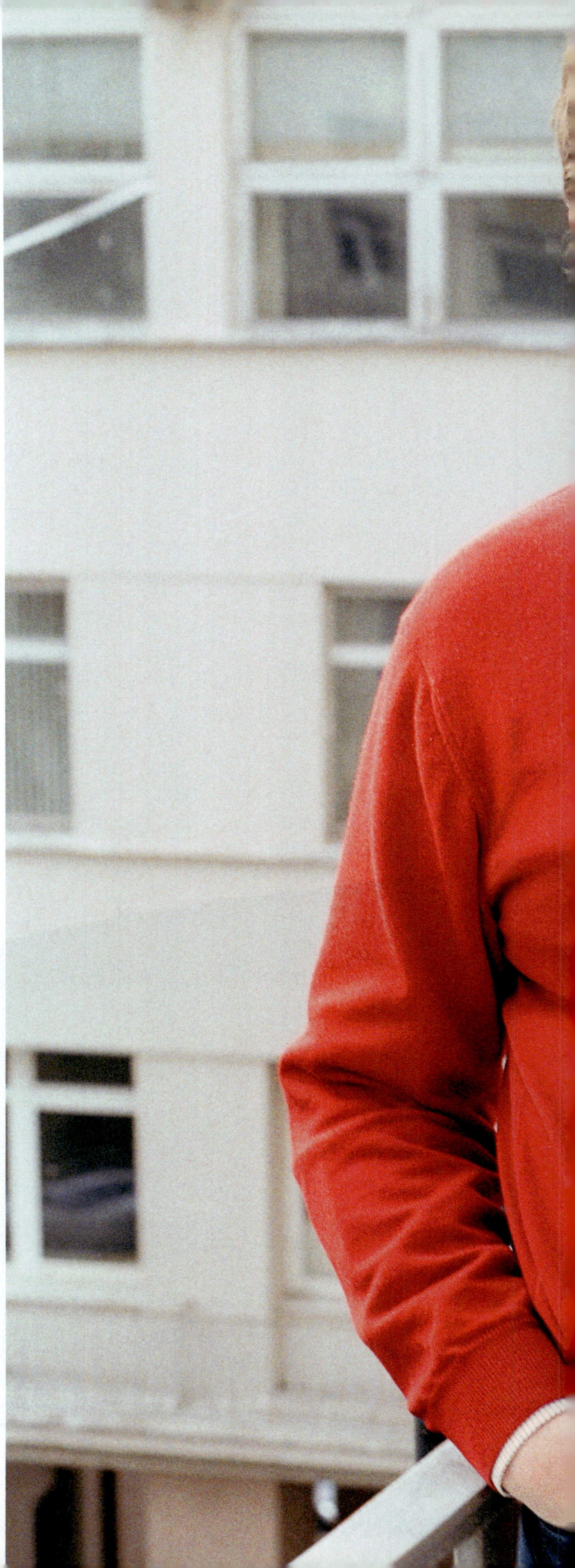

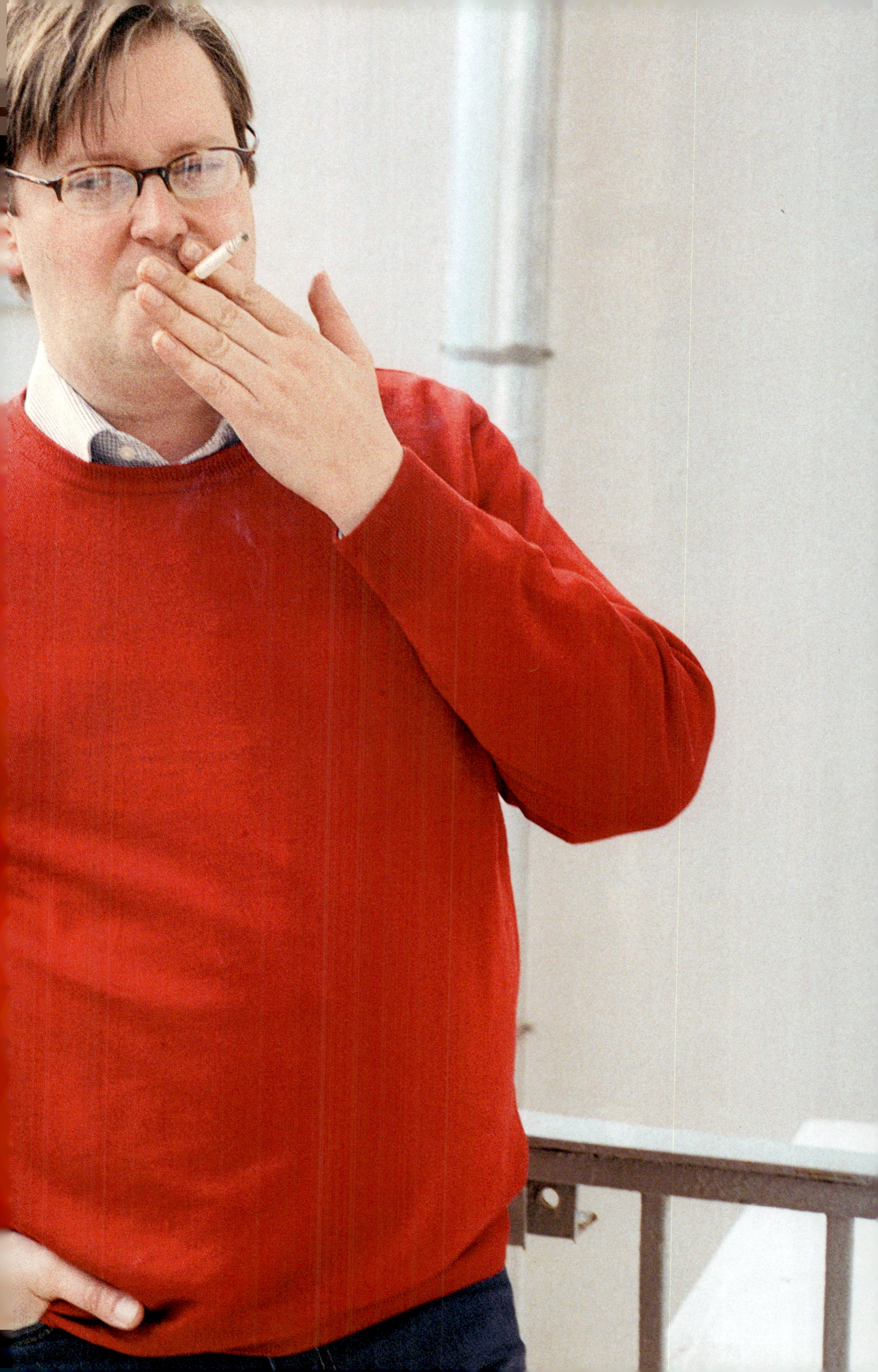

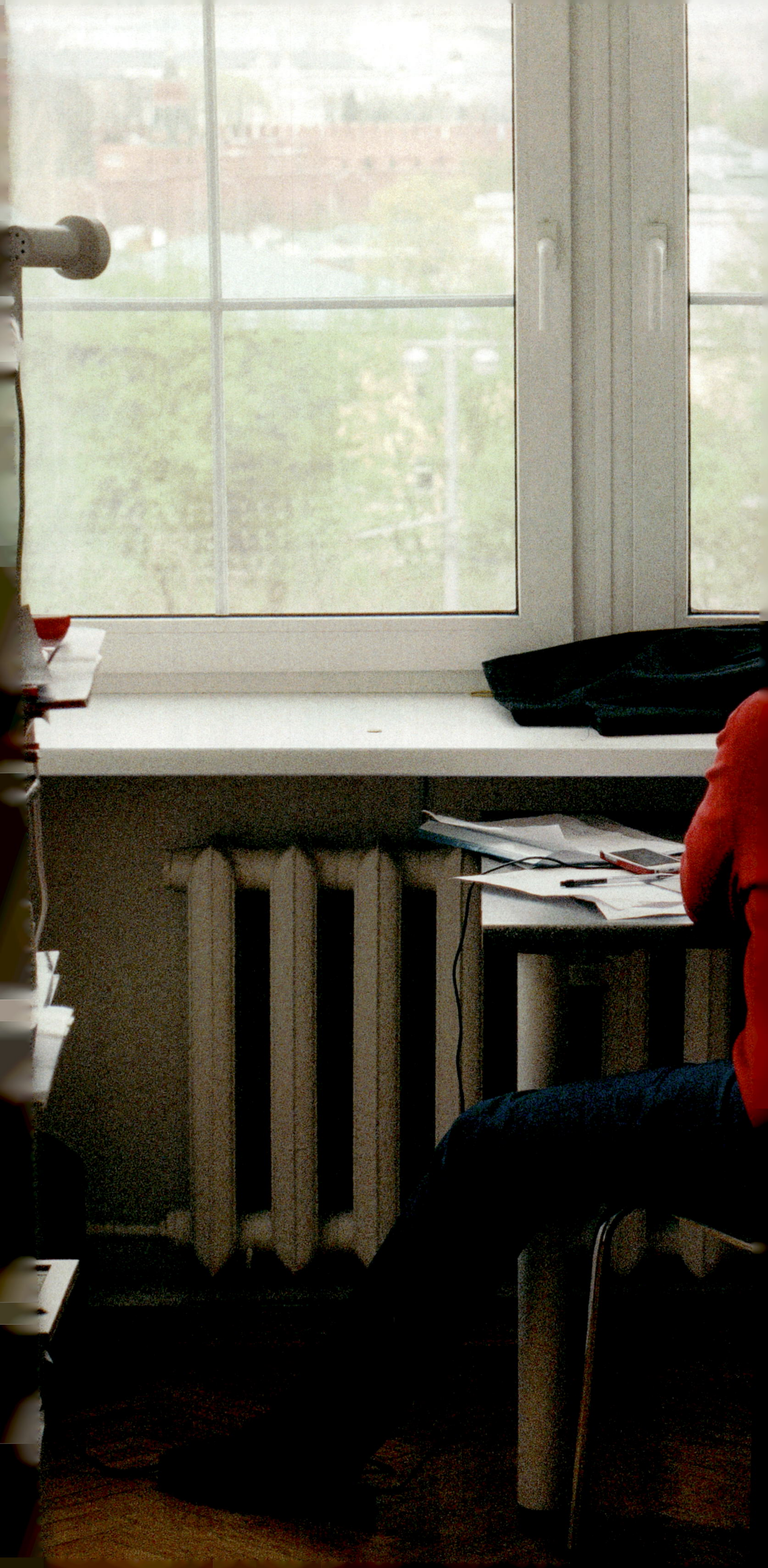

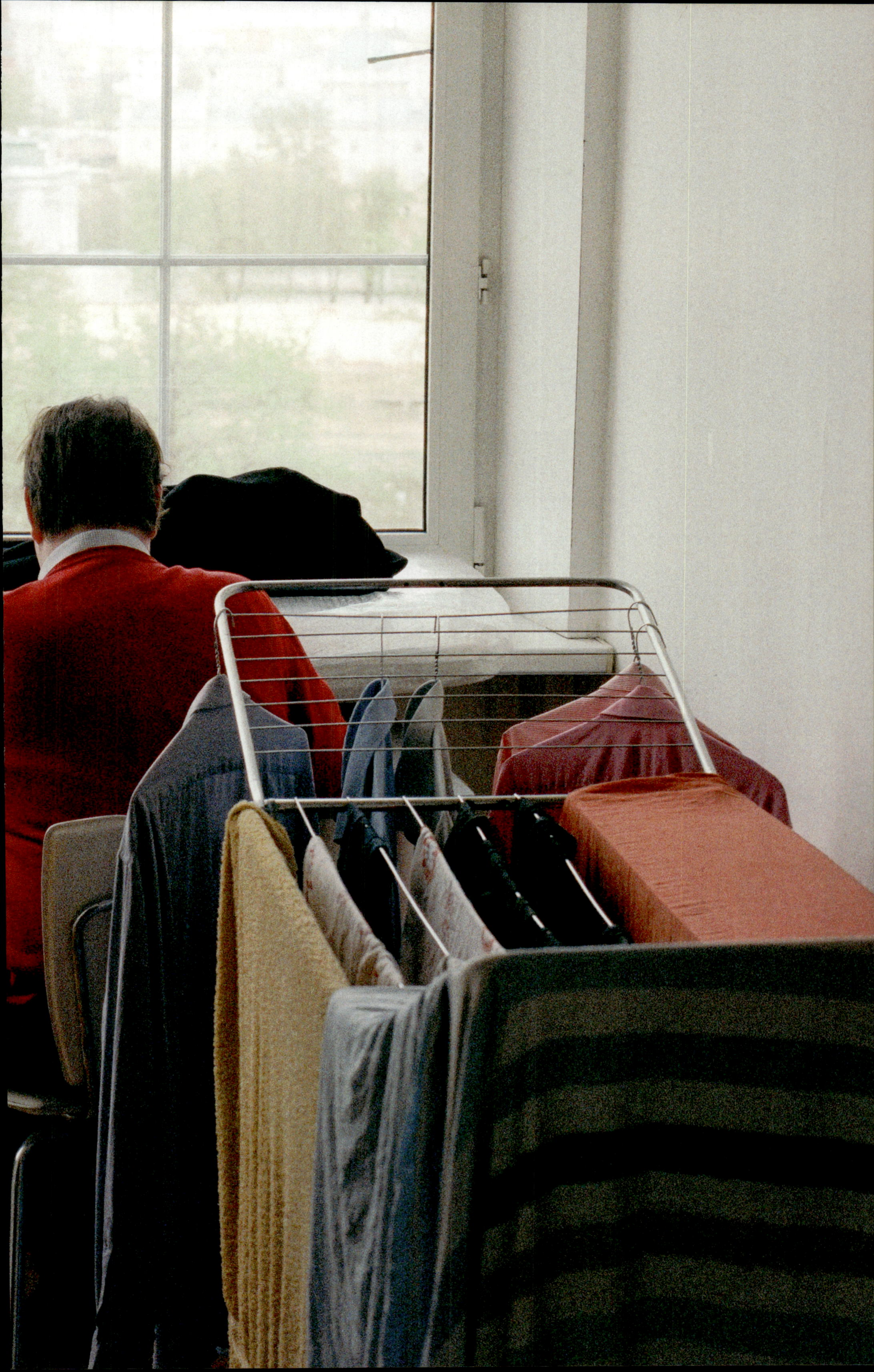

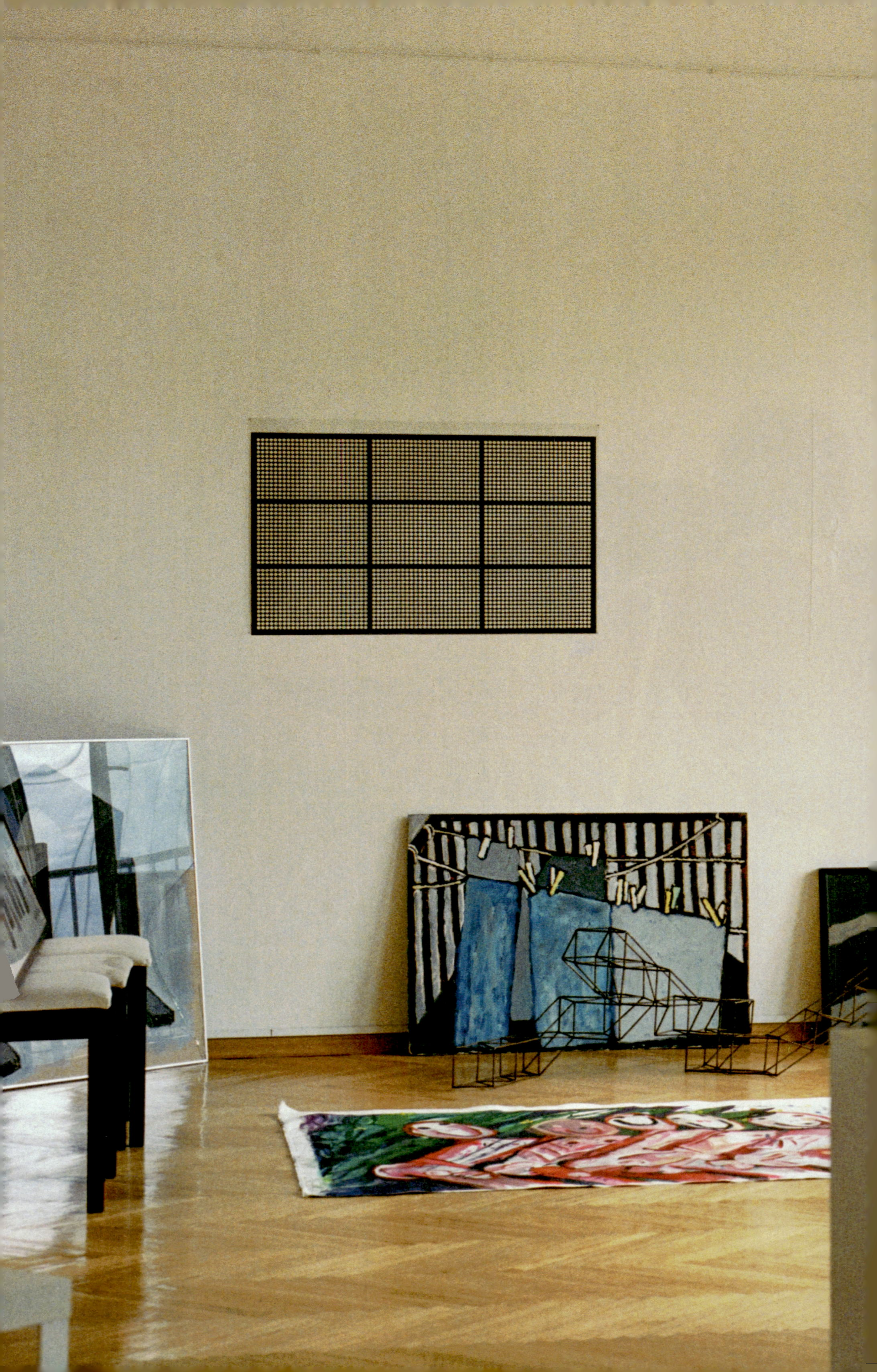

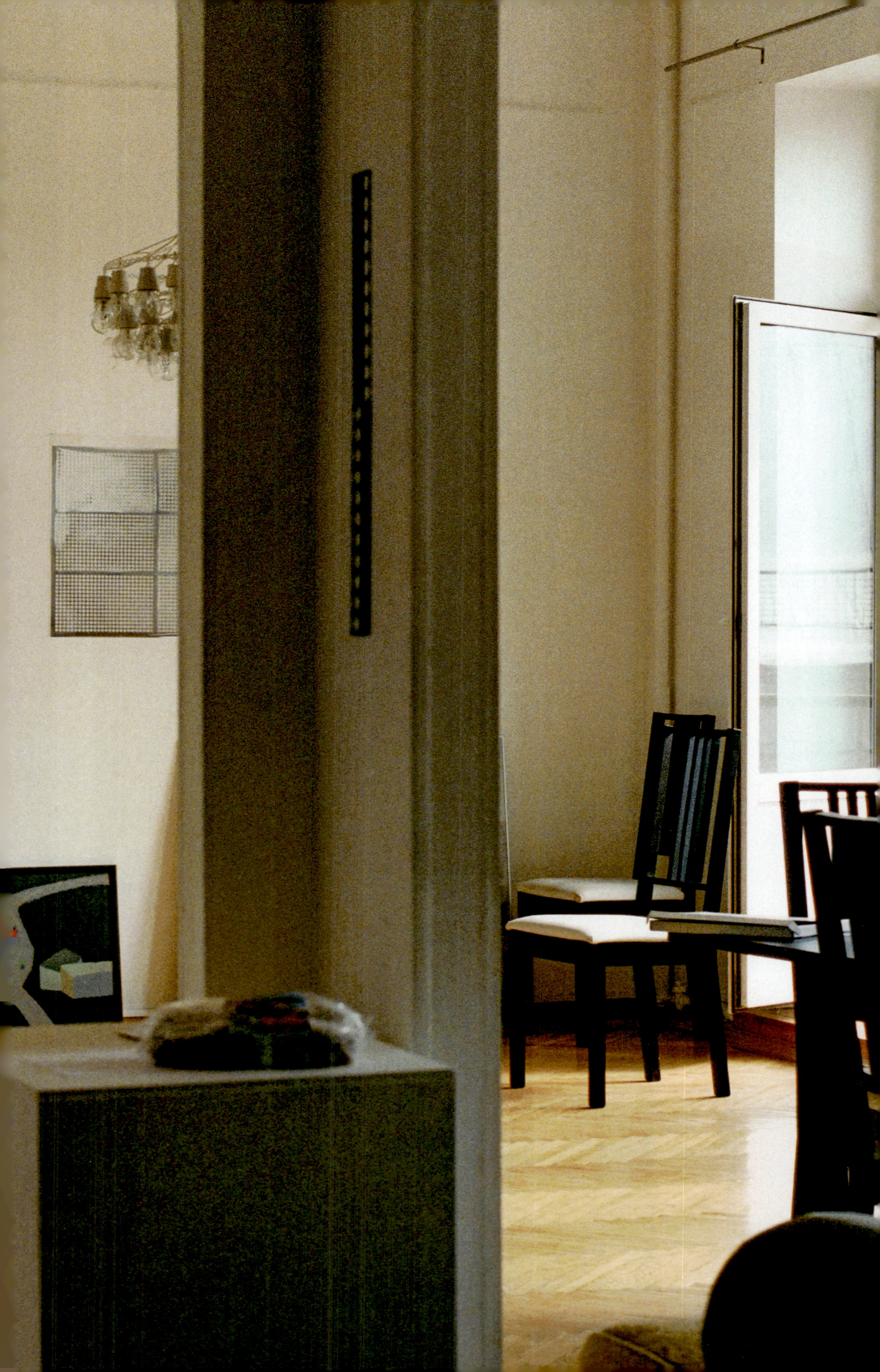

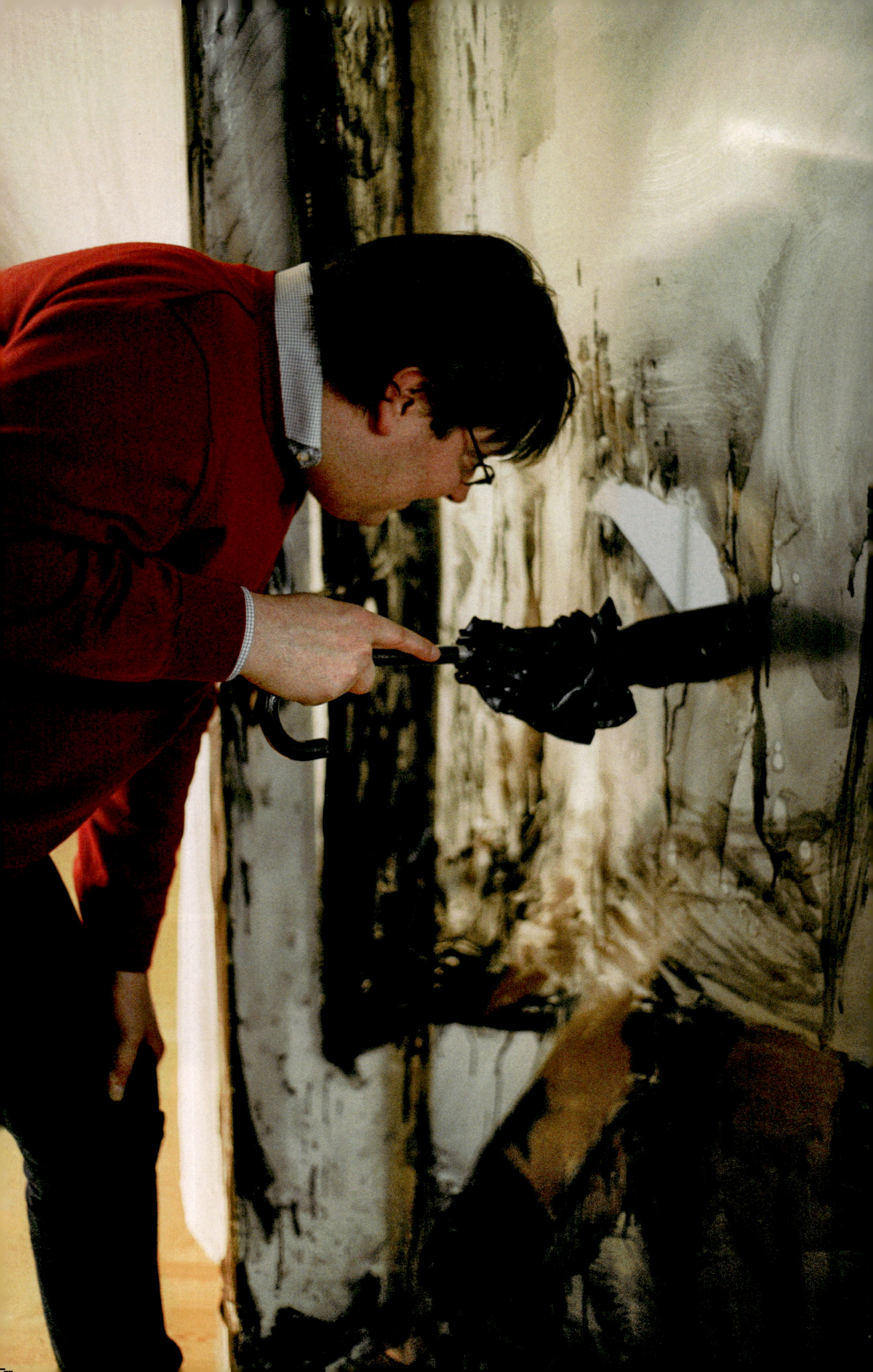

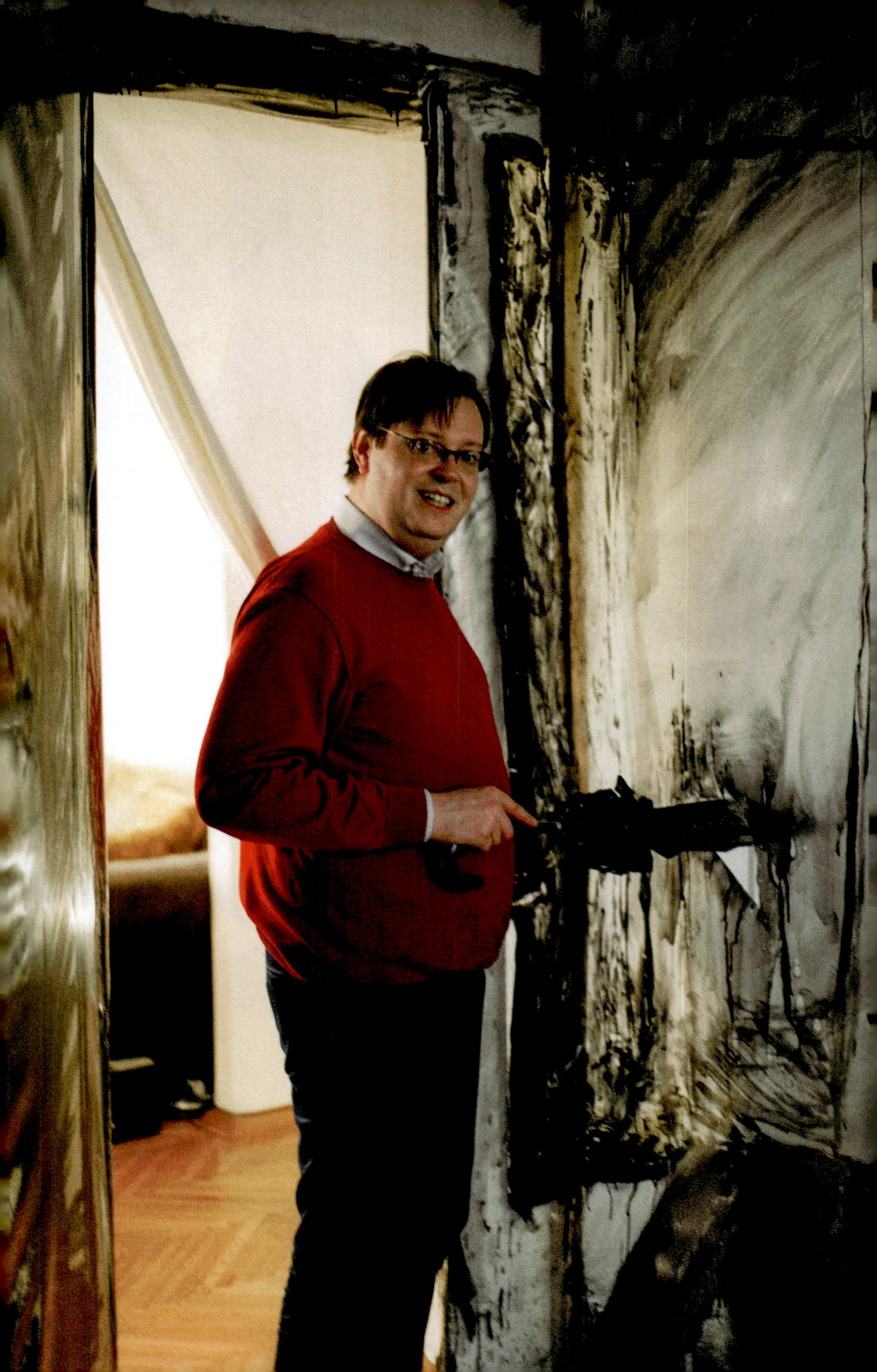

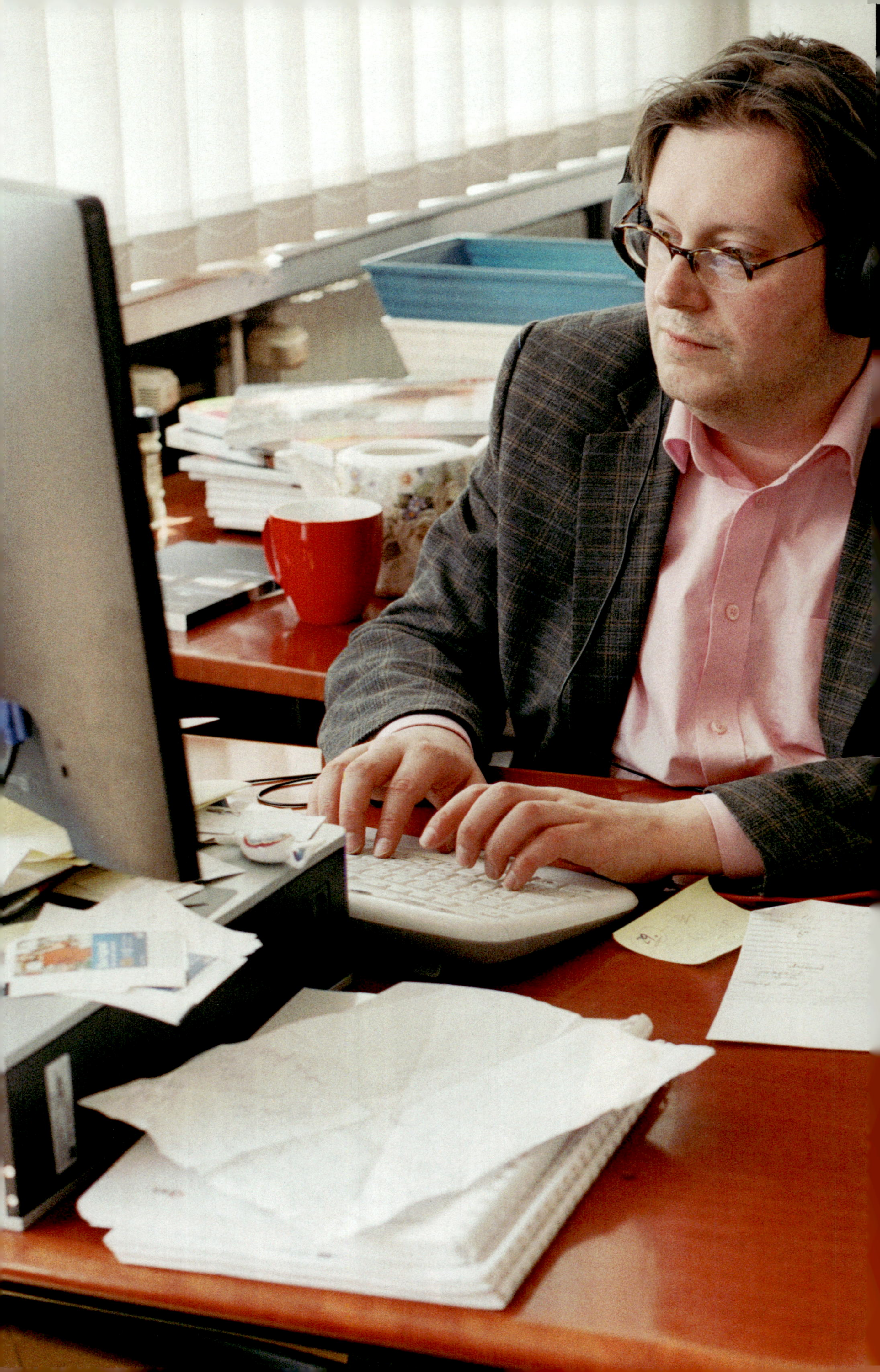

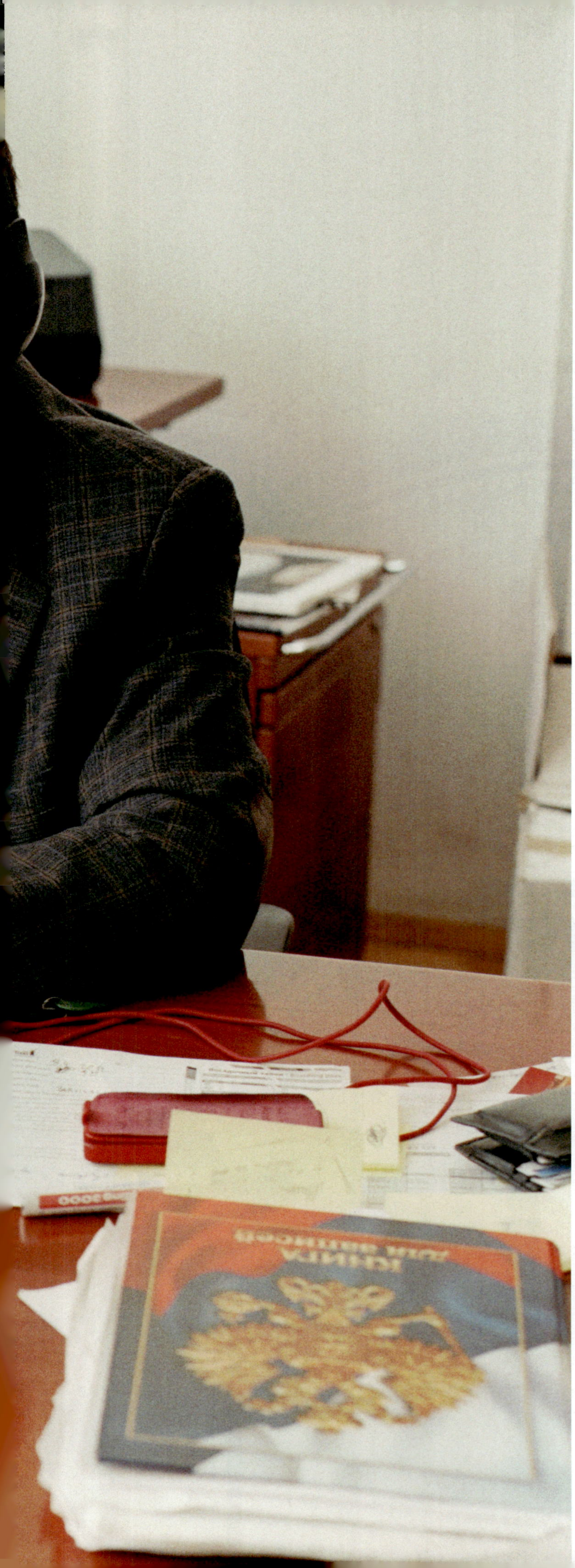
КНИГА
для записей

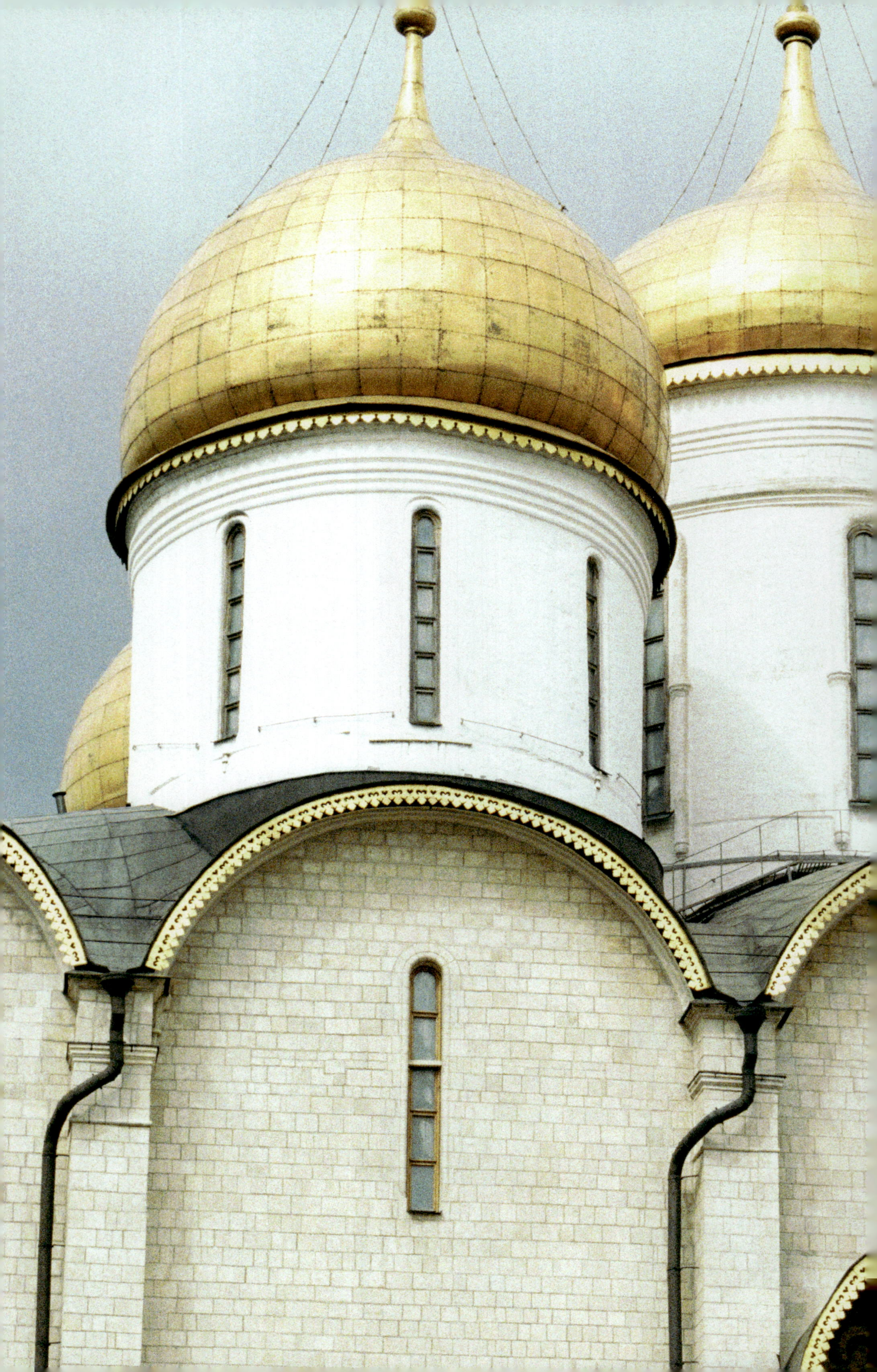

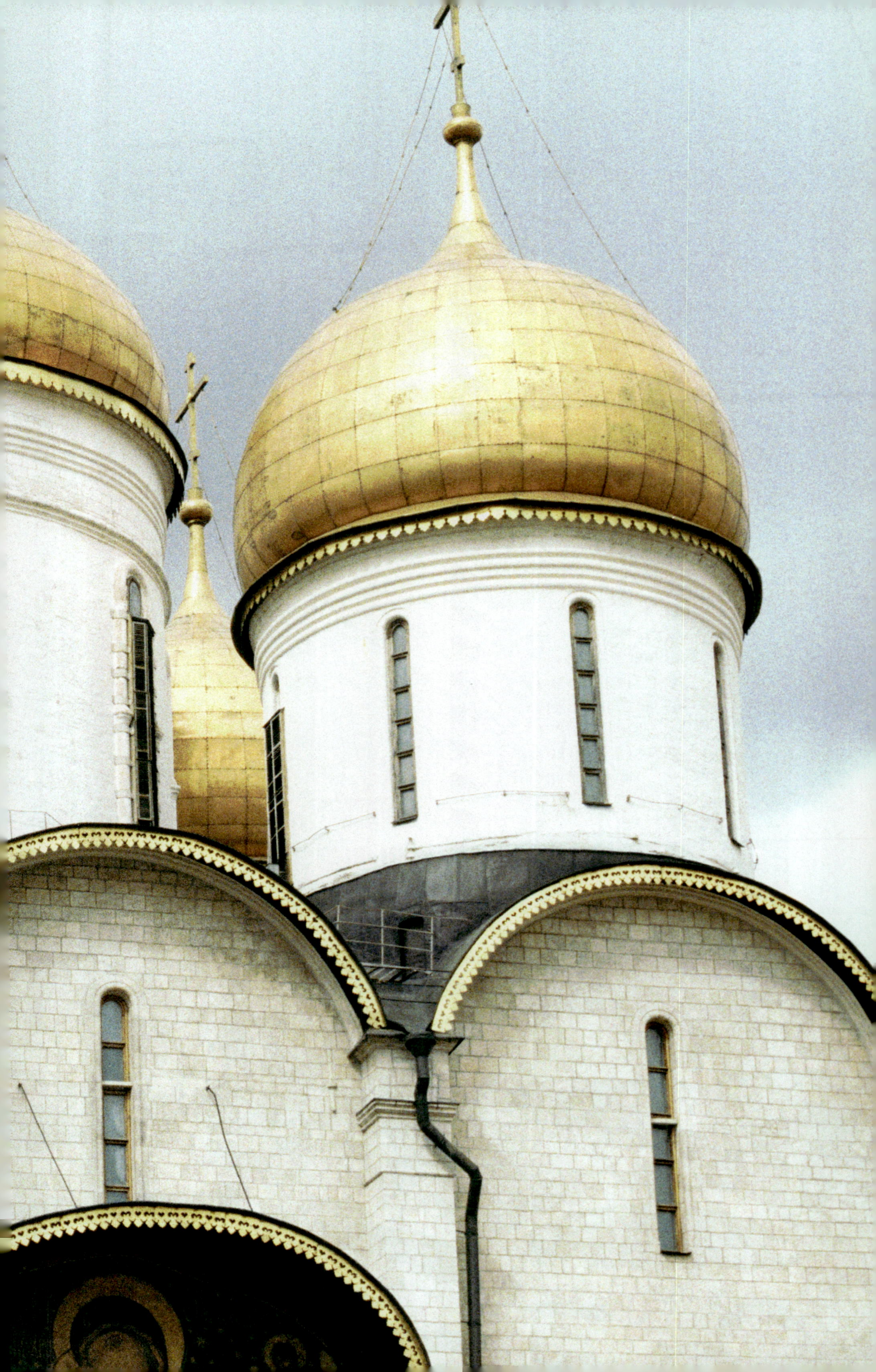

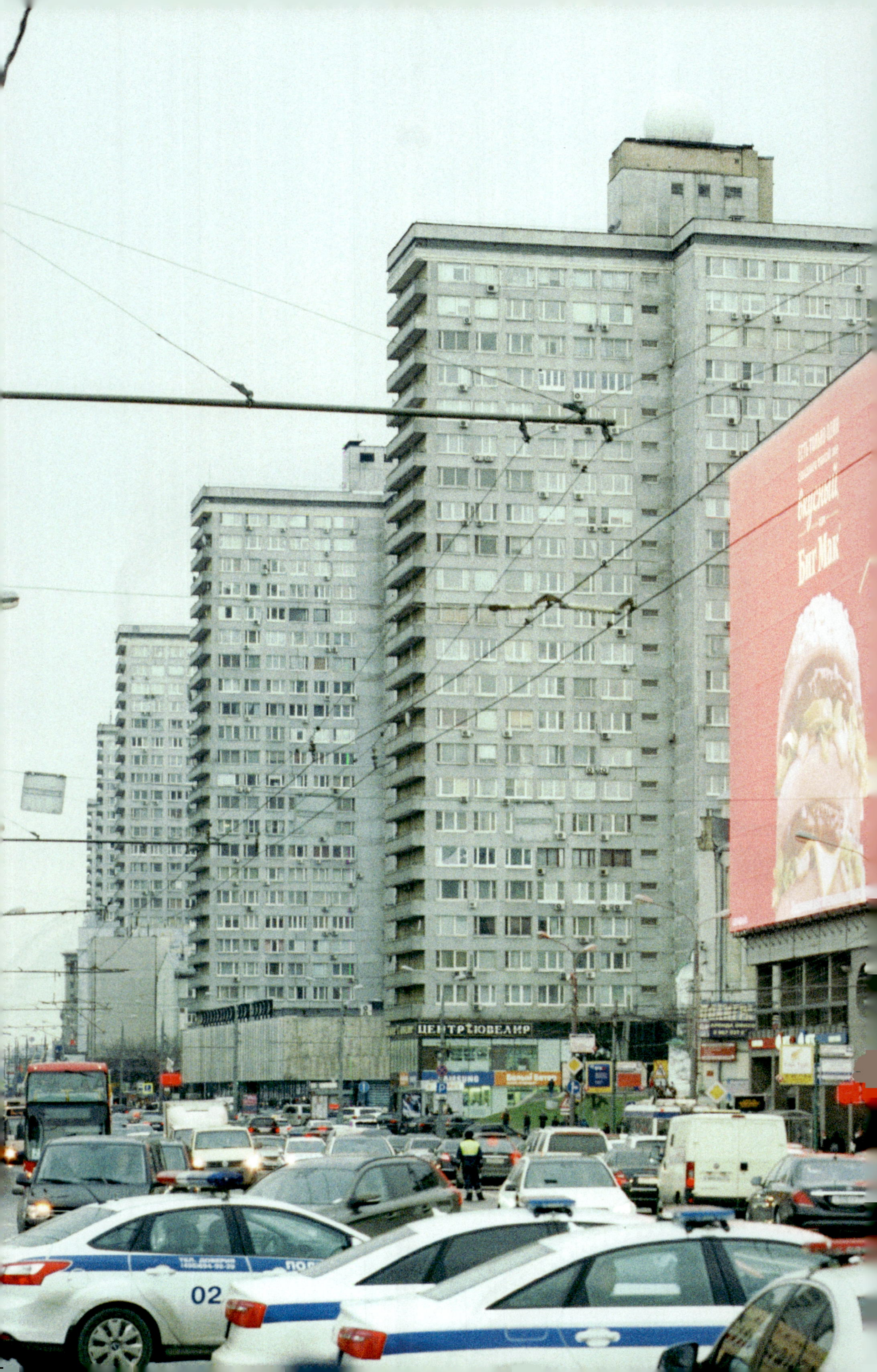
вкусный
Биг Мак
ЦЕНТР ЮВЕЛИР
02

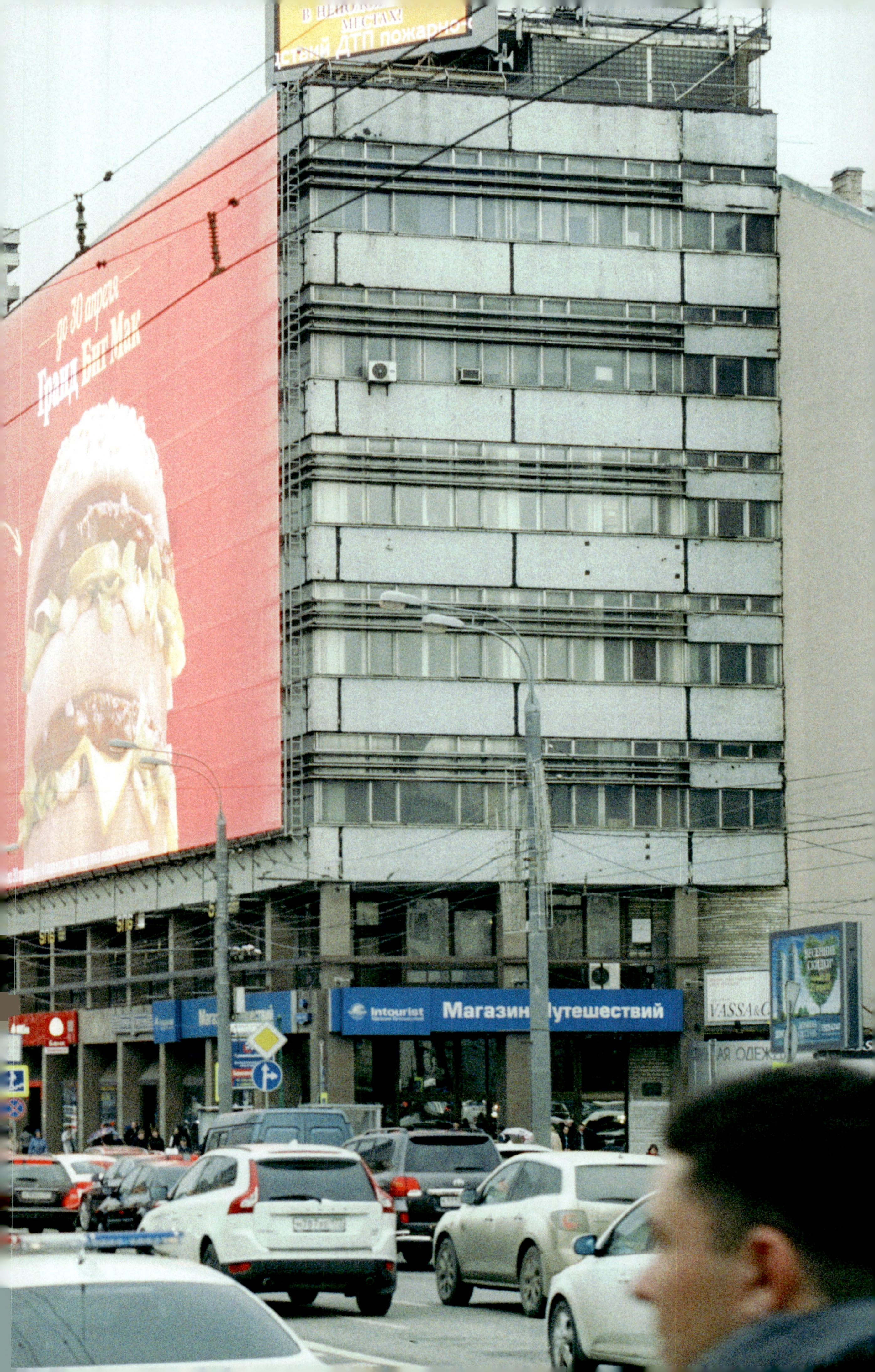
до 30 апреля
Гранд Биг Мак
Intourist
Магазин
утешествий

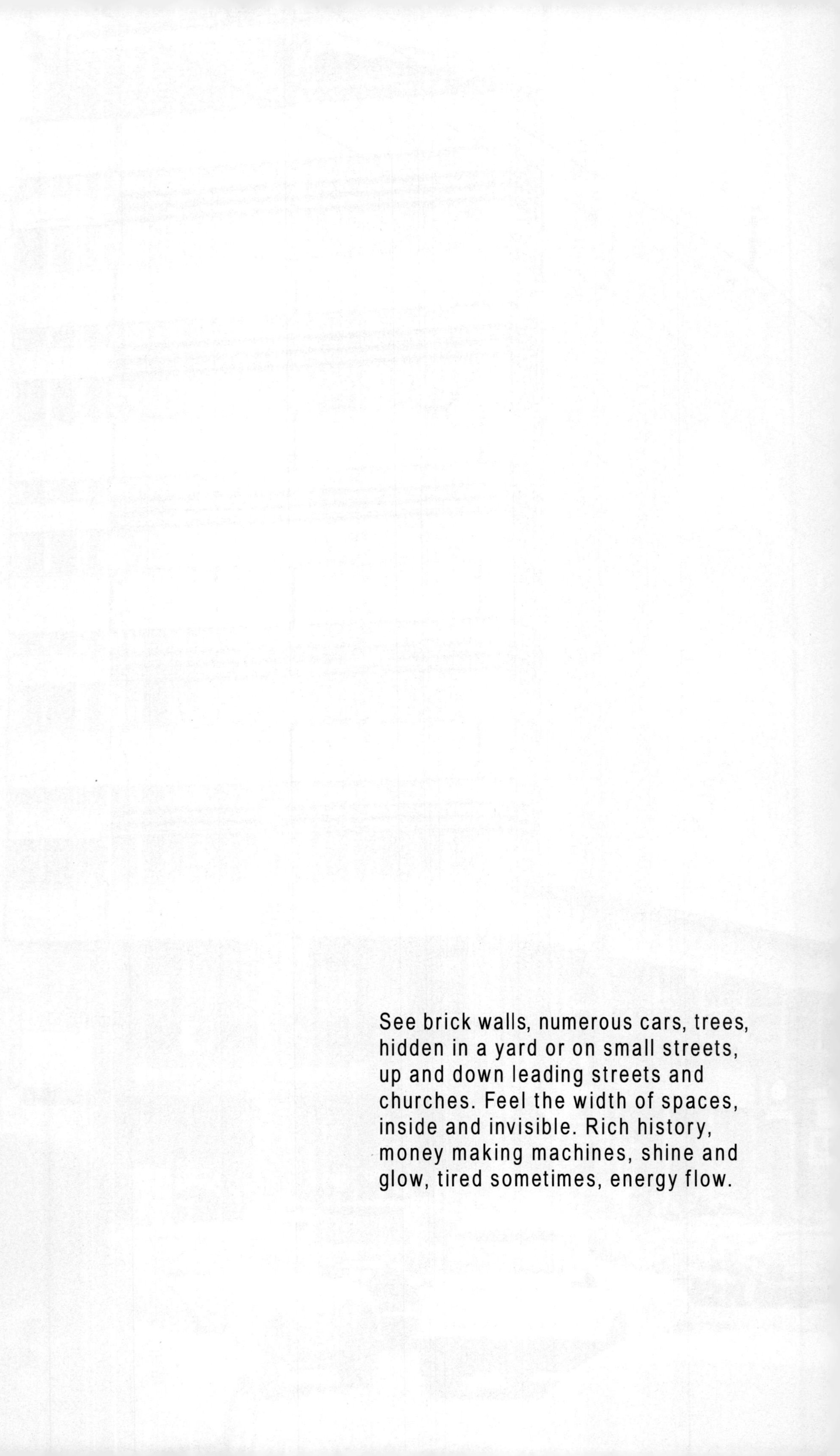

See brick walls, numerous cars, trees,
hidden in a yard or on small streets,
up and down leading streets and
churches. Feel the width of spaces,
inside and invisible. Rich history,
money making machines, shine and
glow, tired sometimes, energy flow.

LIKE A
LABYRINTH THAT
INVITES YOU IN
AND NEVER
LETS YOU GO

IF YOU TAME MOSCOW, LIKE A SNAKE, IT WILL BE ALL IN YOUR HANDS

HERE WE GO

I can say I have not been bored a single minute in my life and I do not know what that is. I think I can be very thankful about that. Lifetime is a big present and I do not know how long this lasts and I also believe that the time we have should be used in some way that it contributes to something. Within my conception and perception of life there is no place for boredom. Moscow indeed is a very intense city, but I must say life can be rich in whatever context, that is a question of mindset, not of environment.

When you take the rules of a game, it works better and easier. I am new to this kind of state thus now life is not that easy. Moscow is the city of opportunities so if it suits you and you are totally into it, it is not hard to achieve a good life. All the difficulties are in your head.

I enjoy long walks in the city. Almost all of the time it feels like you are trying to transcend the void, moving through wide prospects or some lost streets in the center. Moscow is huge.There are different kinds of people, places and, surely, ways of living. Everything depends on what are you looking for, what is good for you personally. Definitely you can't be bored in Moscow, because a lot of interesting things happen every day. If you're dark inside it doesn't matter where you are. And to be honest, every winter can immerse you in a real vanity of existence. But it ends.

ARTISTS ARE SMART, ARTISTS ARE BRAVE AND THERE IS NO ALTERNATIVE TO GO THE WAY ONE NEEDS TO GO

I FOCUS ON THE LANDSCAPE AND THE PEOPLE

Life here is a constant struggle – with the weather, with traffic, sometimes with other people. It is a city powered by money, and you can achieve a very good lifestyle here, but it will cost you a fortune. Moscow is very convenient and pretty enjoyable for rich people and offers them the most exquisite things. If you are not rich, you can still enjoy it, but in a different way –there are good museums, art institutions, theatres and concert halls here which are affordable. What is difficult here is to have a healthy lifestyle – healthy food is expensive, sun is a rare guest, the weather is very changeable and the level of pollution is high. Outside sport activities such as jogging can hardly be realized in winter.

My Moscow this spring-summer was very active with a lot of friends, fun and work. We were painting all the time and had nice days out of the city. Few times a week we had many guests and dinners with friends. In may I was invited to participate in a group project where we were working on one piece all together. There was a round table with a canvas that was turning around all the time because it was connected to a huge wheel. All the time people should go inside this wheel and work like a hamster walking or running inside. Few days later there was a night of museums and until 6 a.m. there was a huge line of visitors in front of the gallery. After visiting the gallery, I went to a club to meet my friends who gave a party and an exhibition there. And we danced until the morning.

LIFE IS MORE LIKE A DREAM

I do not use the word 'career'. For me every person has his or her own preferences, hobbies and something what he or she may do better than most people. But it depends what you choose – risk or not. I choose risk, so for me 'career' – it is like extreme sport, like riding your bicycle down a mountain. You may fall down and break yourself, or you may reach the beginning of it and feel how ALIVE you are!

ALL DISCUSSIONS ABOUT OIL, GAS, RUBLES AND CRAZY POLITICS LOSE ANY IMPORTANCE FACING WHAT WE TALK ABOUT HERE

Russia is the most stunning and artistically fascinating country I have ever seen. Not only because of its size, but because of its incredible diversity of cultures, historic places and stories. A lot of these places and histories have not yet been discovered by artists as a source of artistic inspiration. There is incredibly lot to do, enough for many lives, so I at least try to use the time I have to dedicate myself to the work I am doing. I have to focus on what is important, I don't know how much time I have here.

I ACTUALLY LIKE THIS FEELING

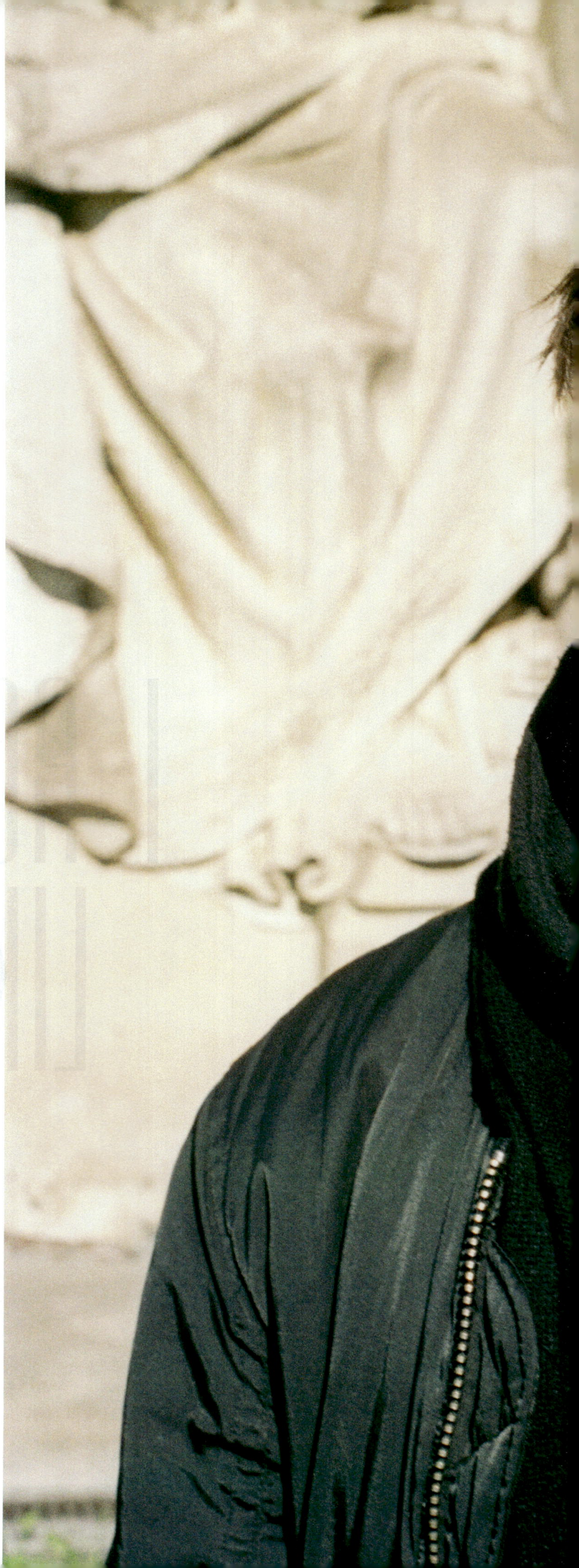

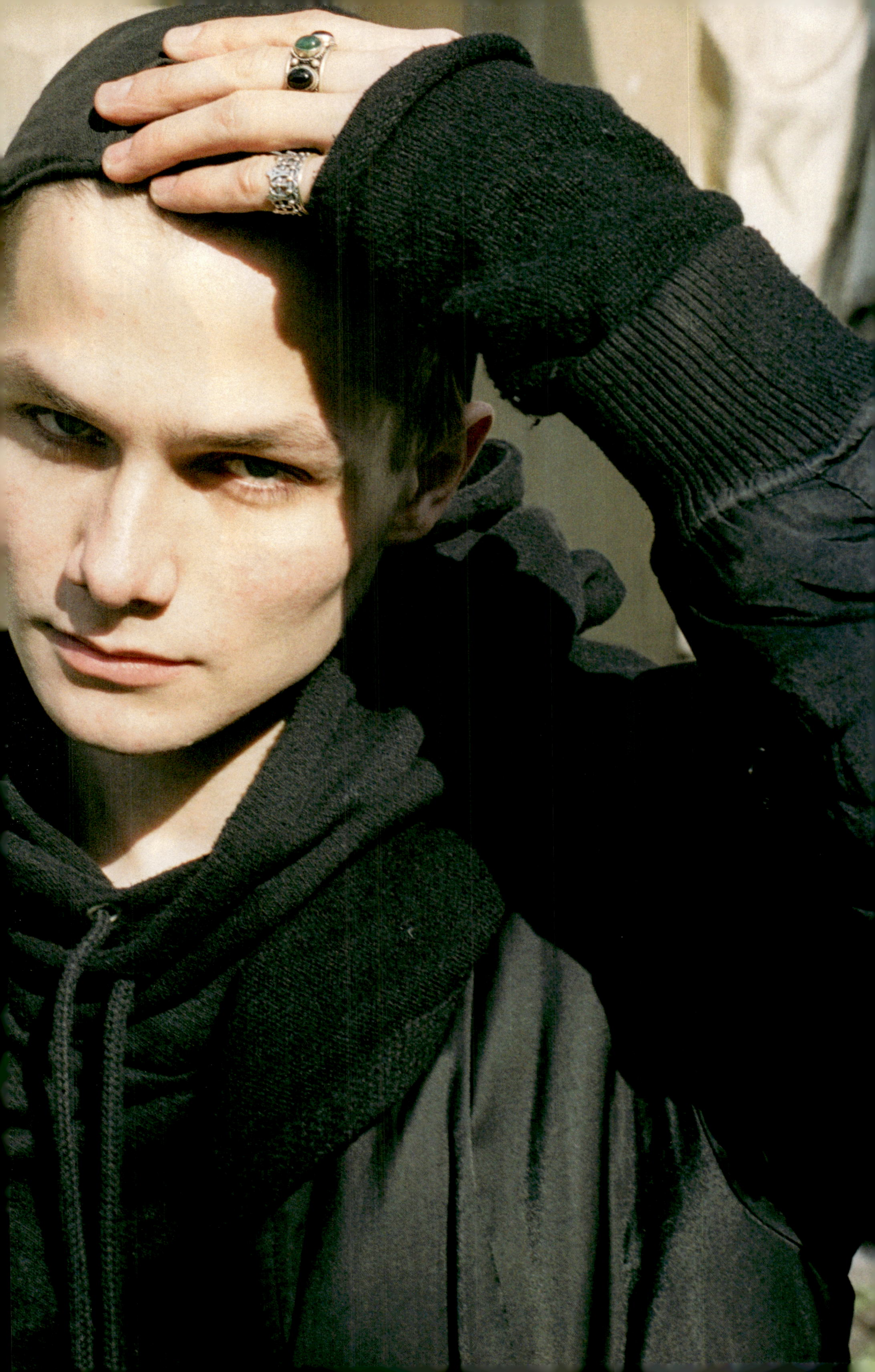

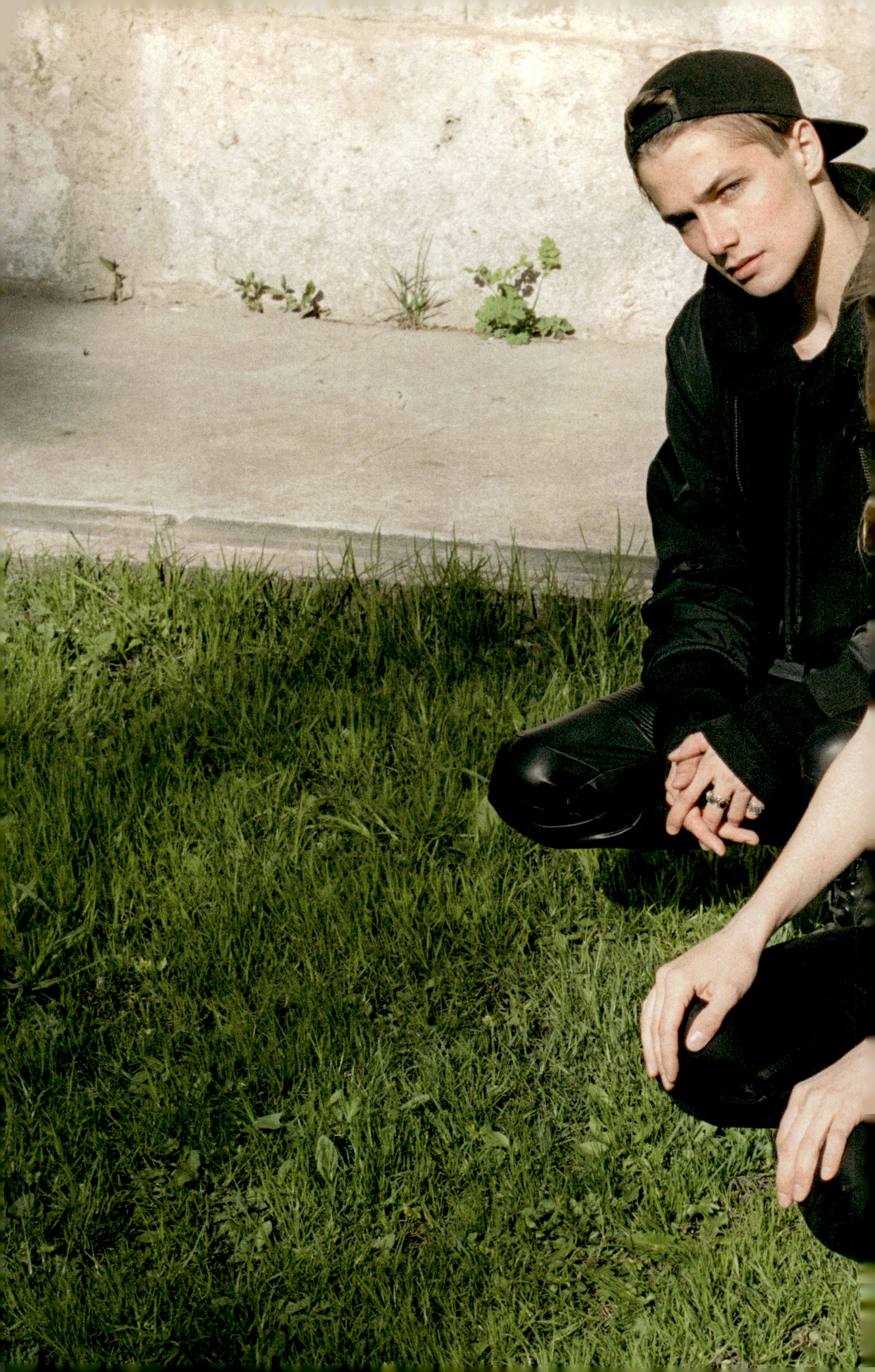

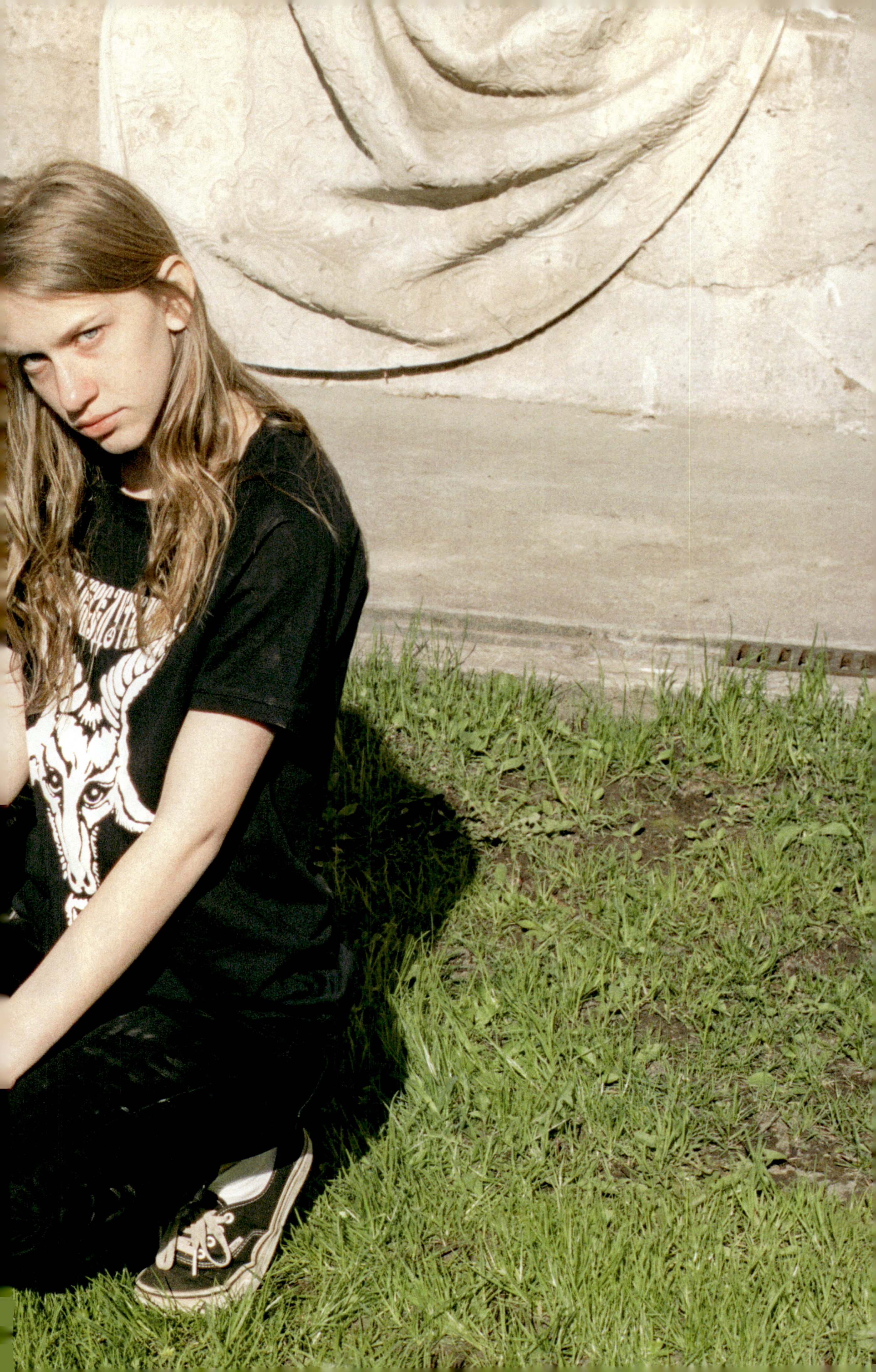

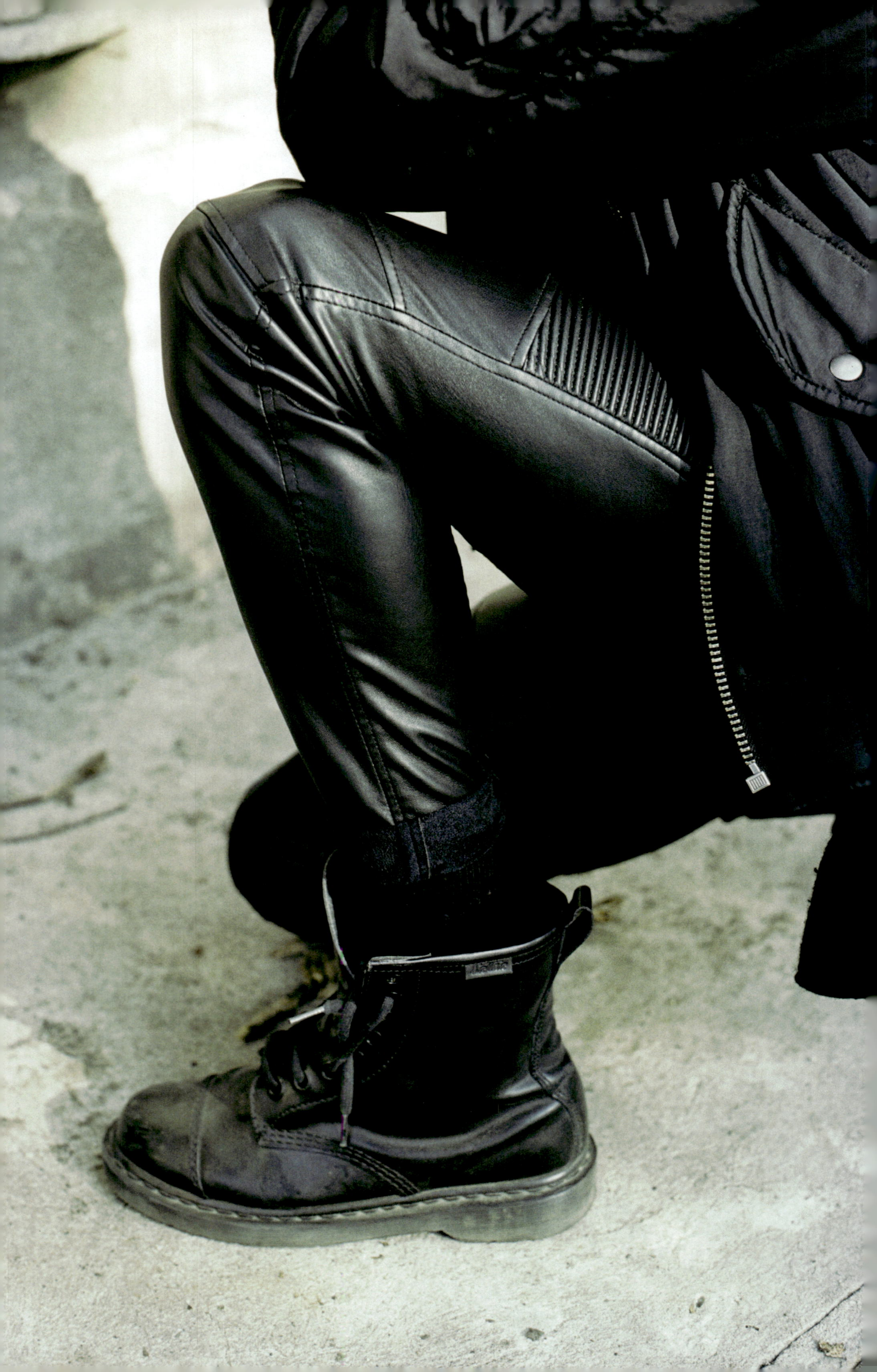

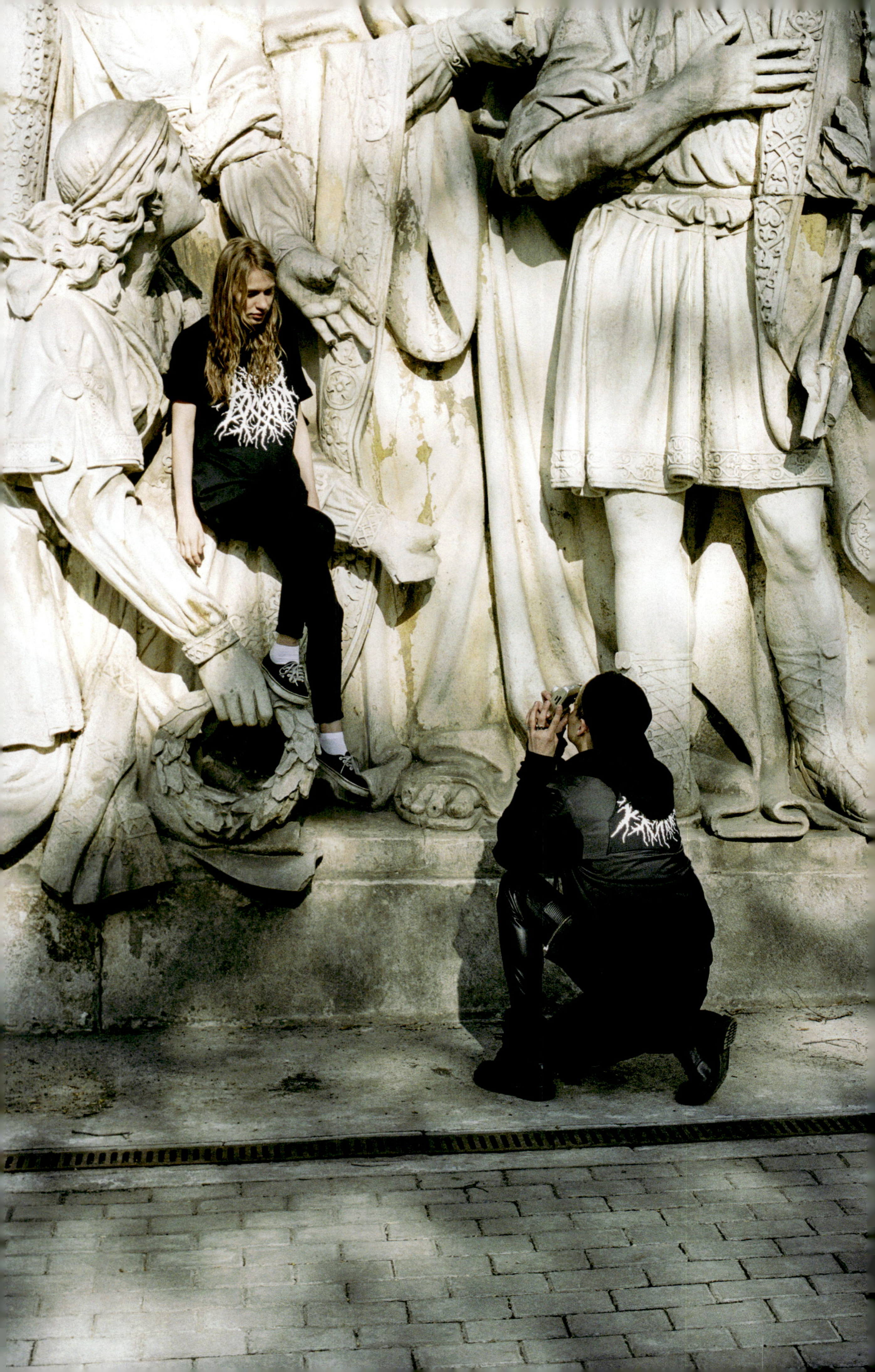

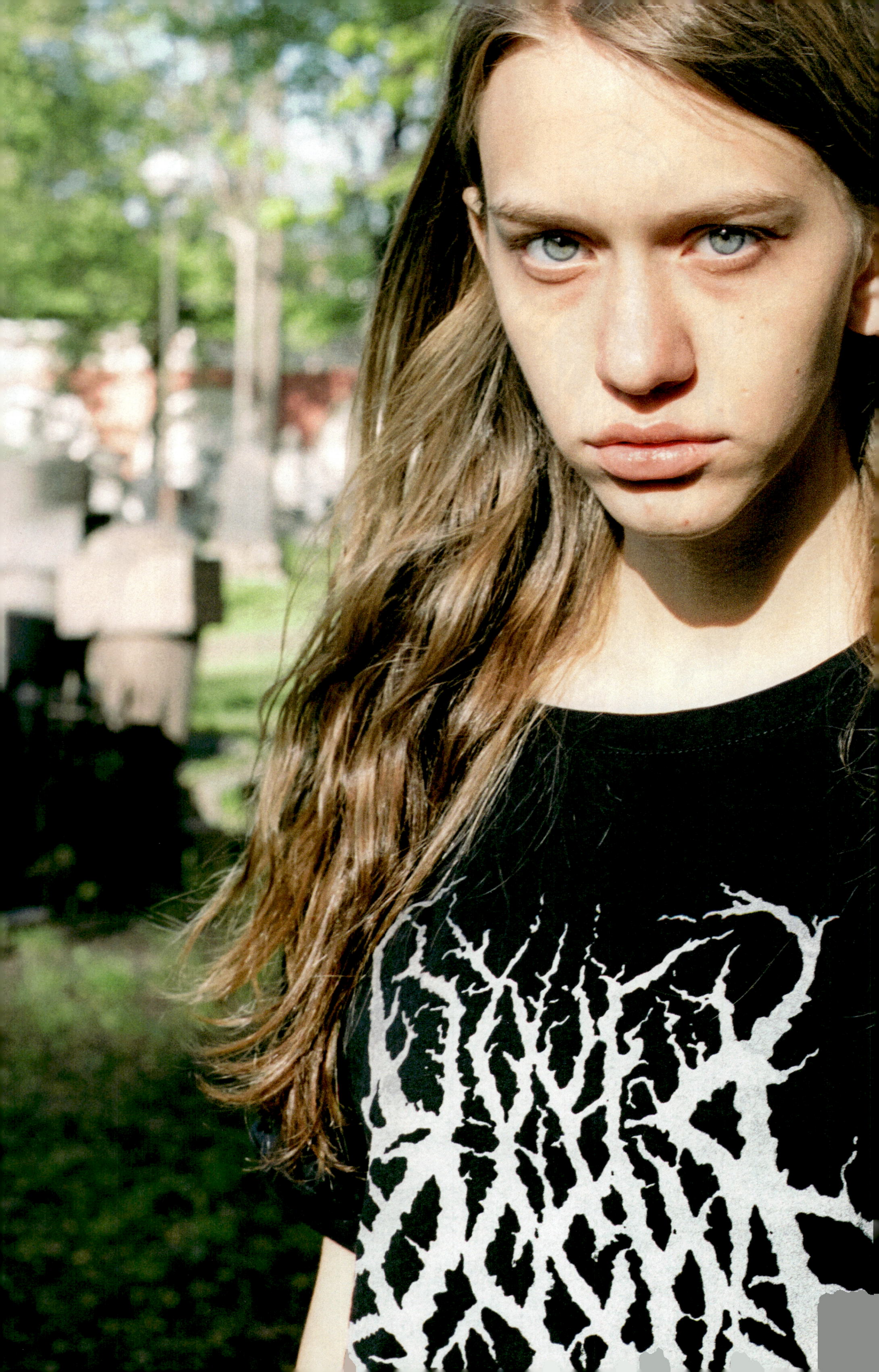

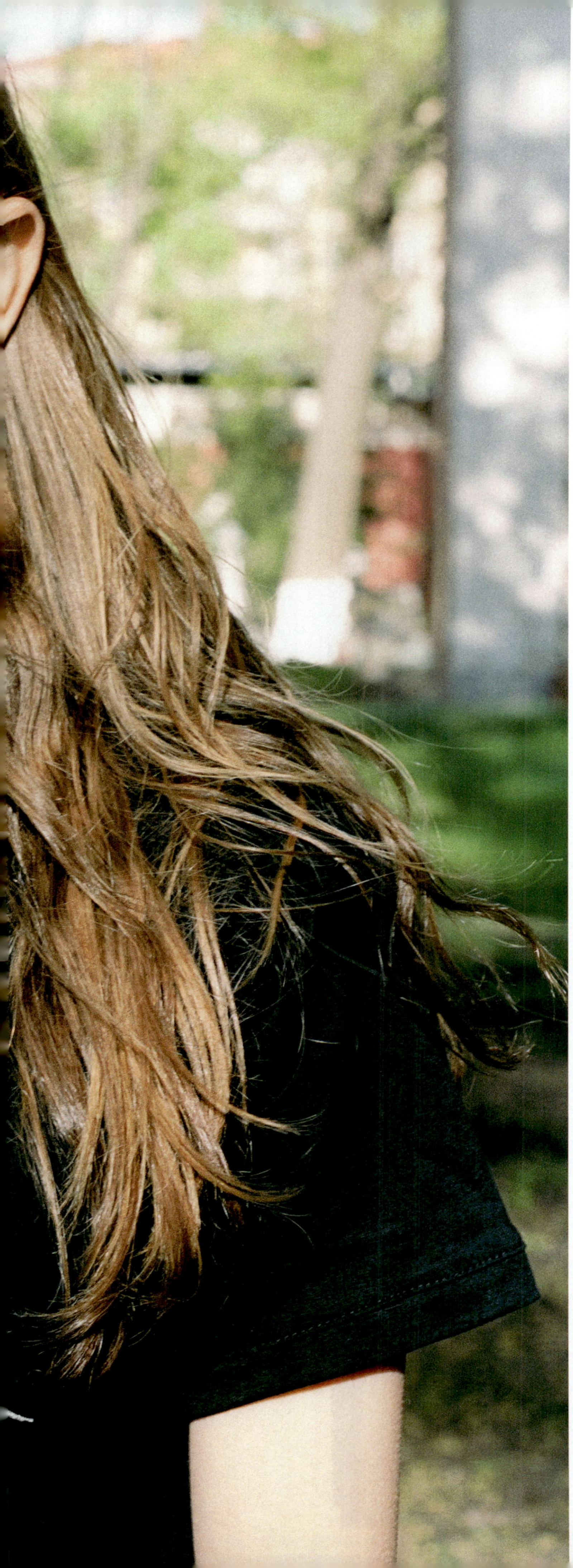

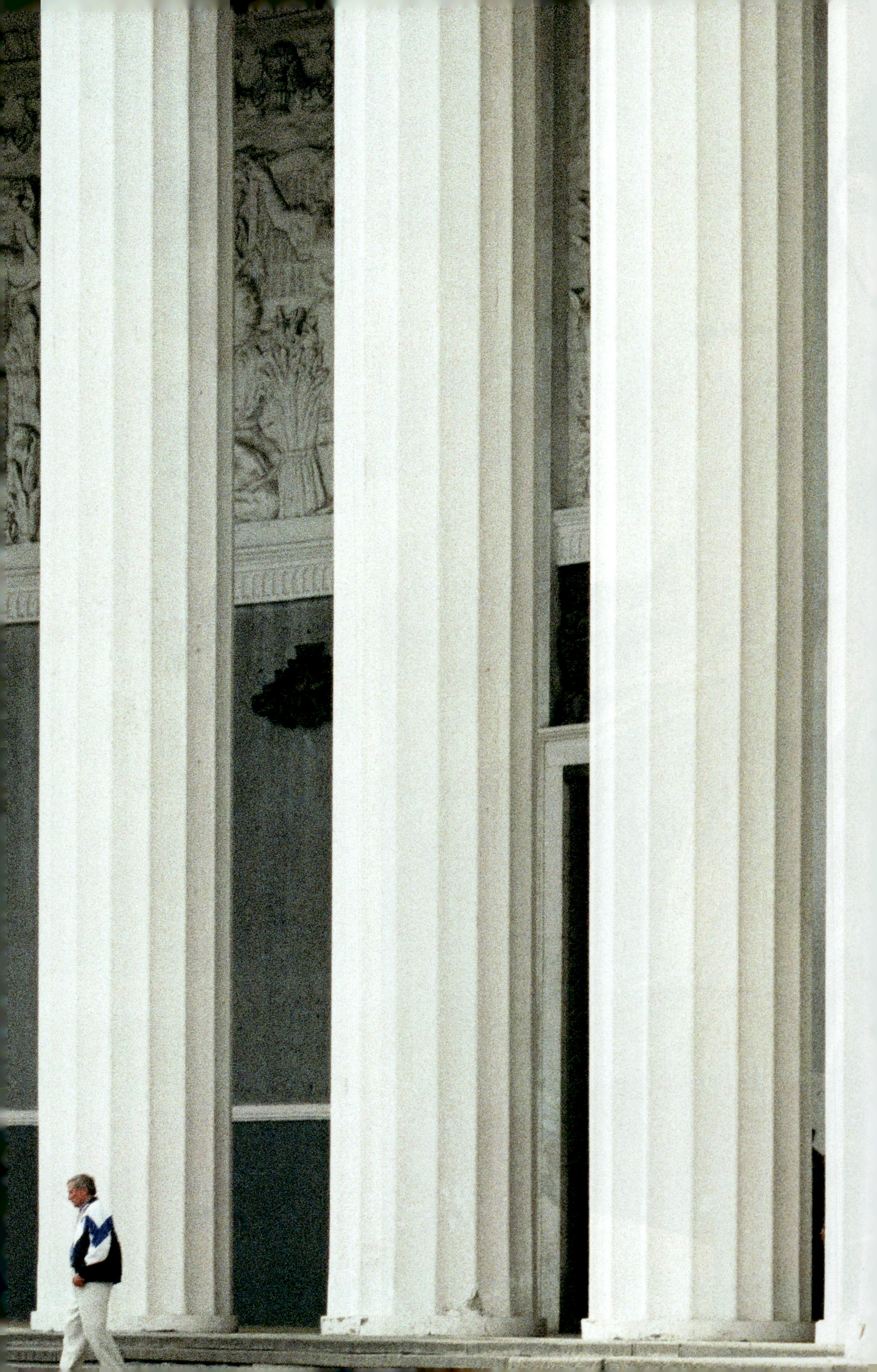

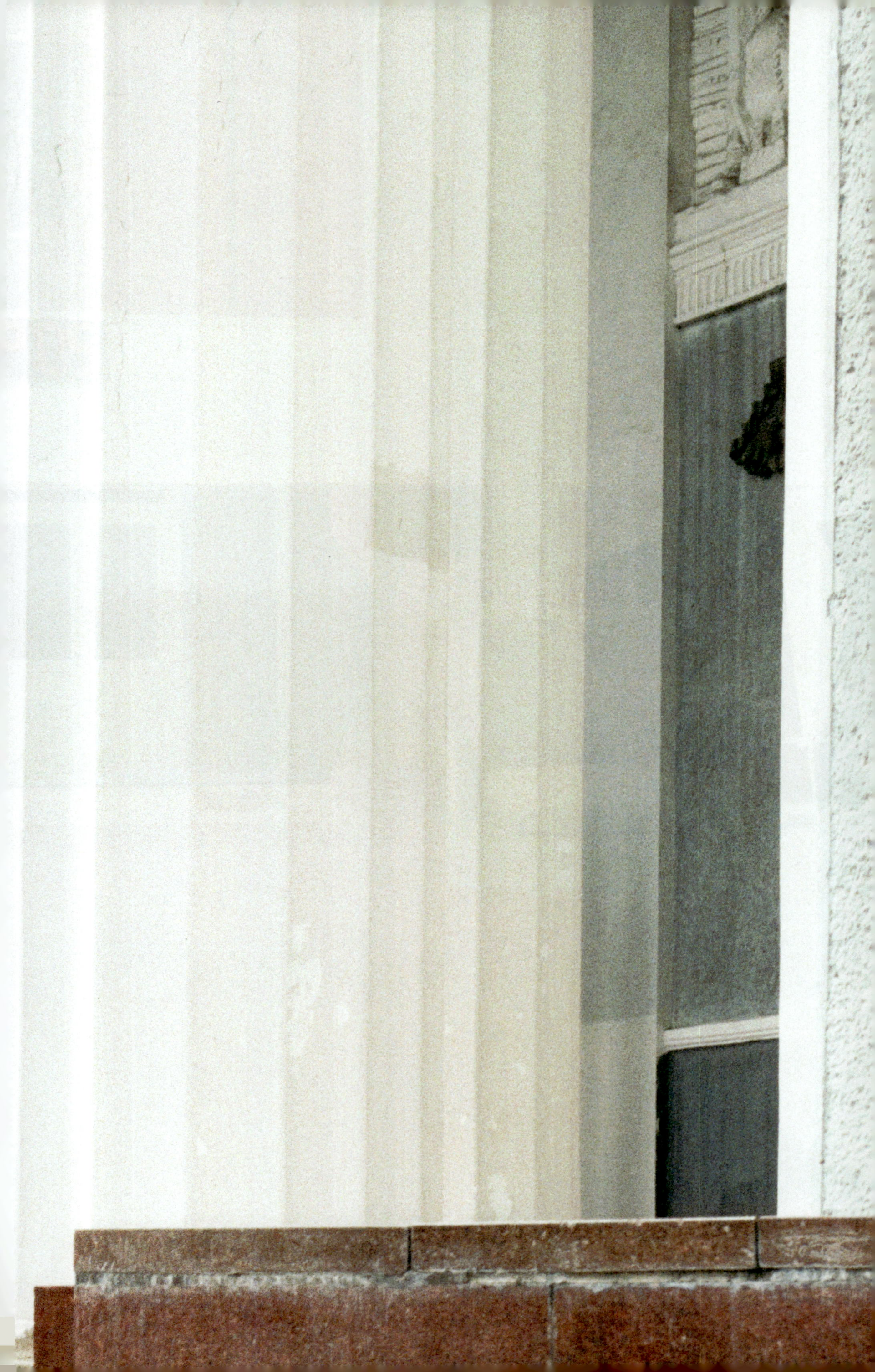

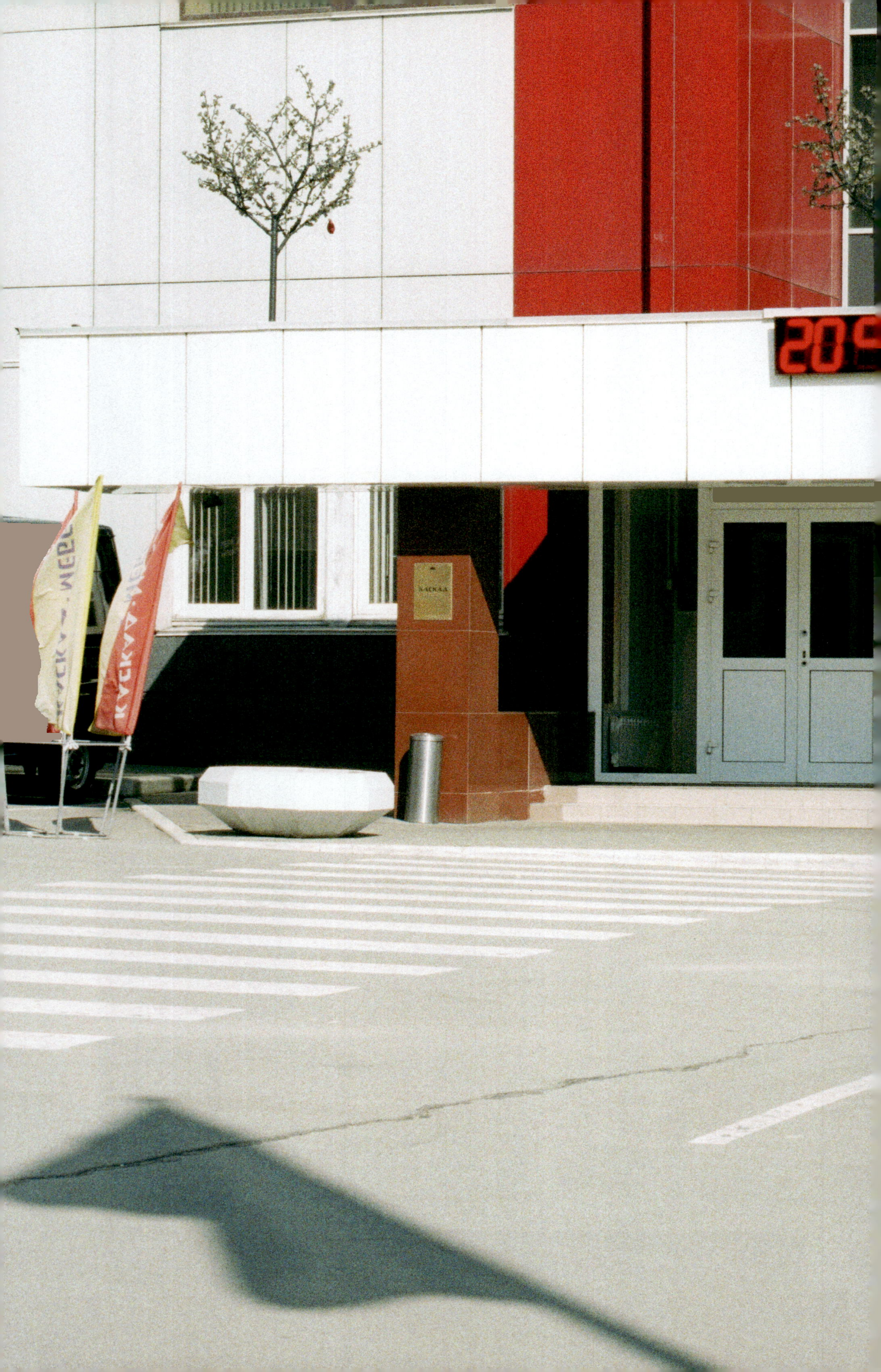
20

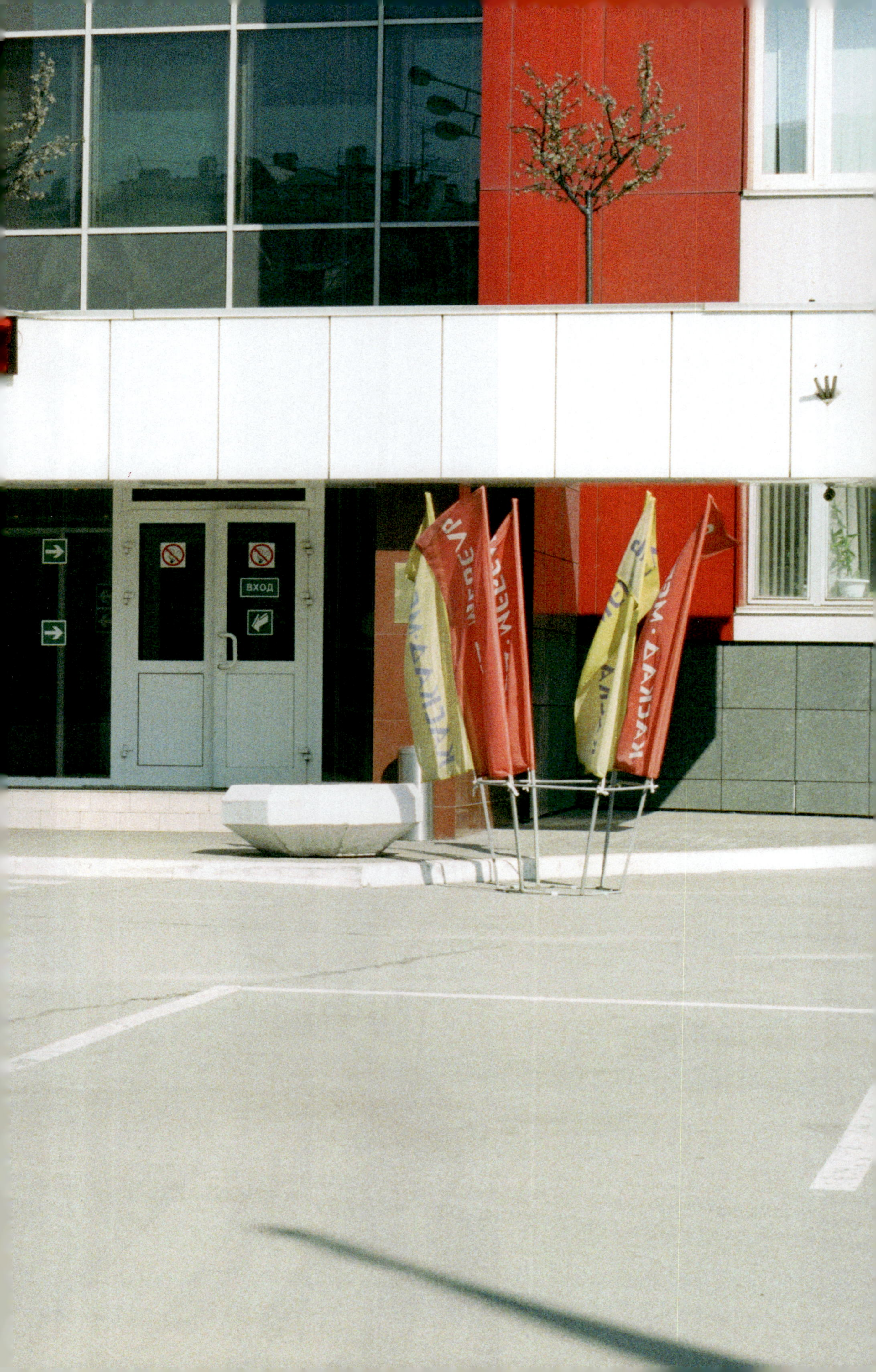
ВХОД

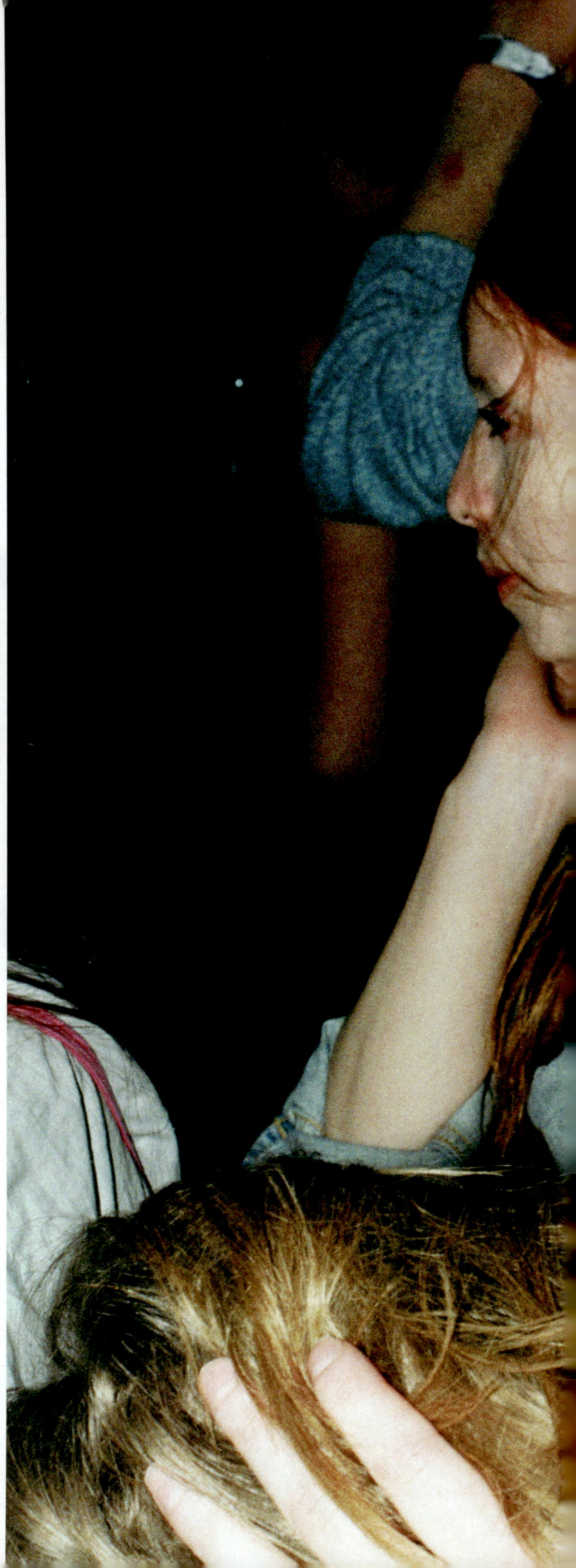

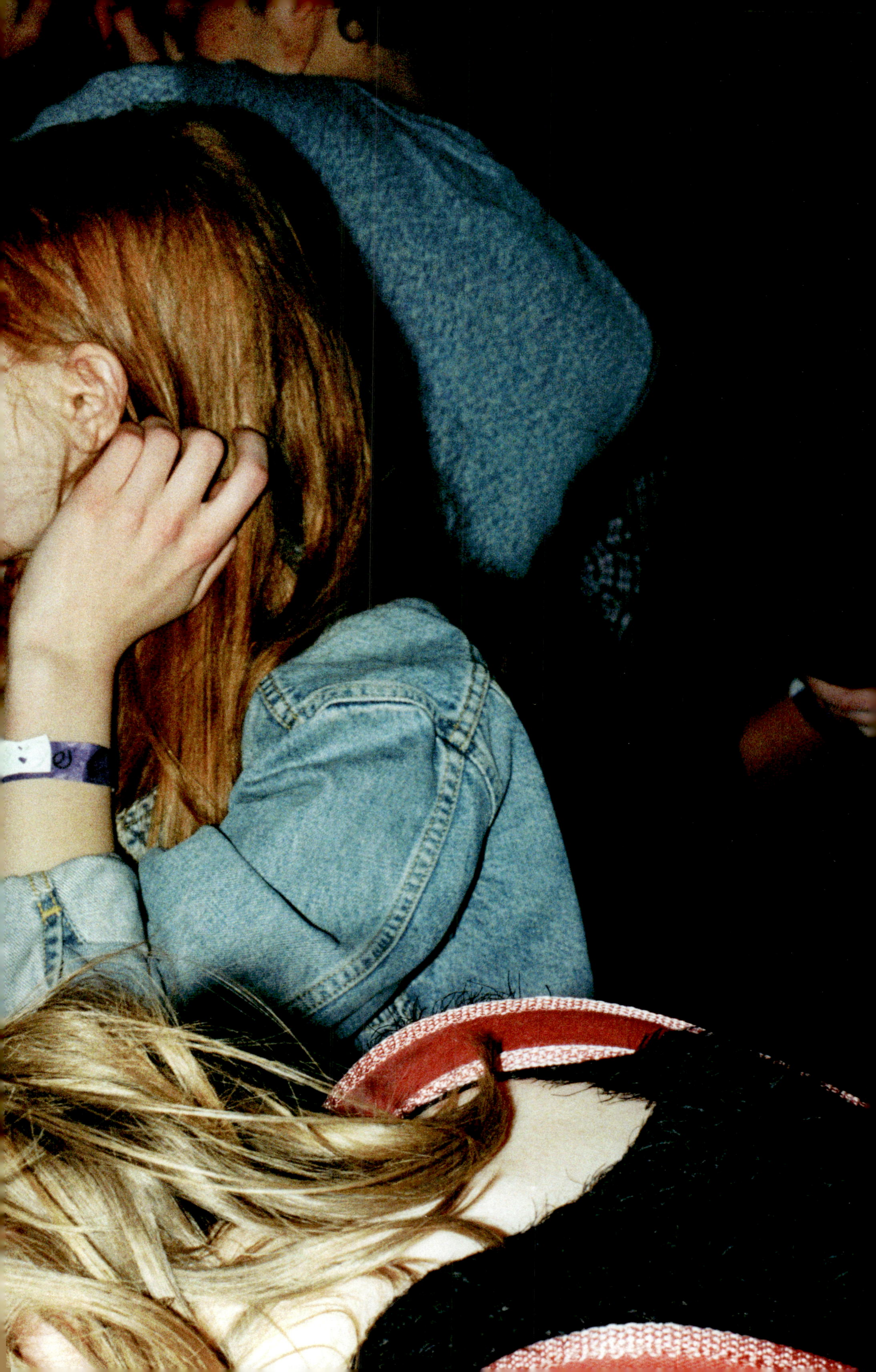

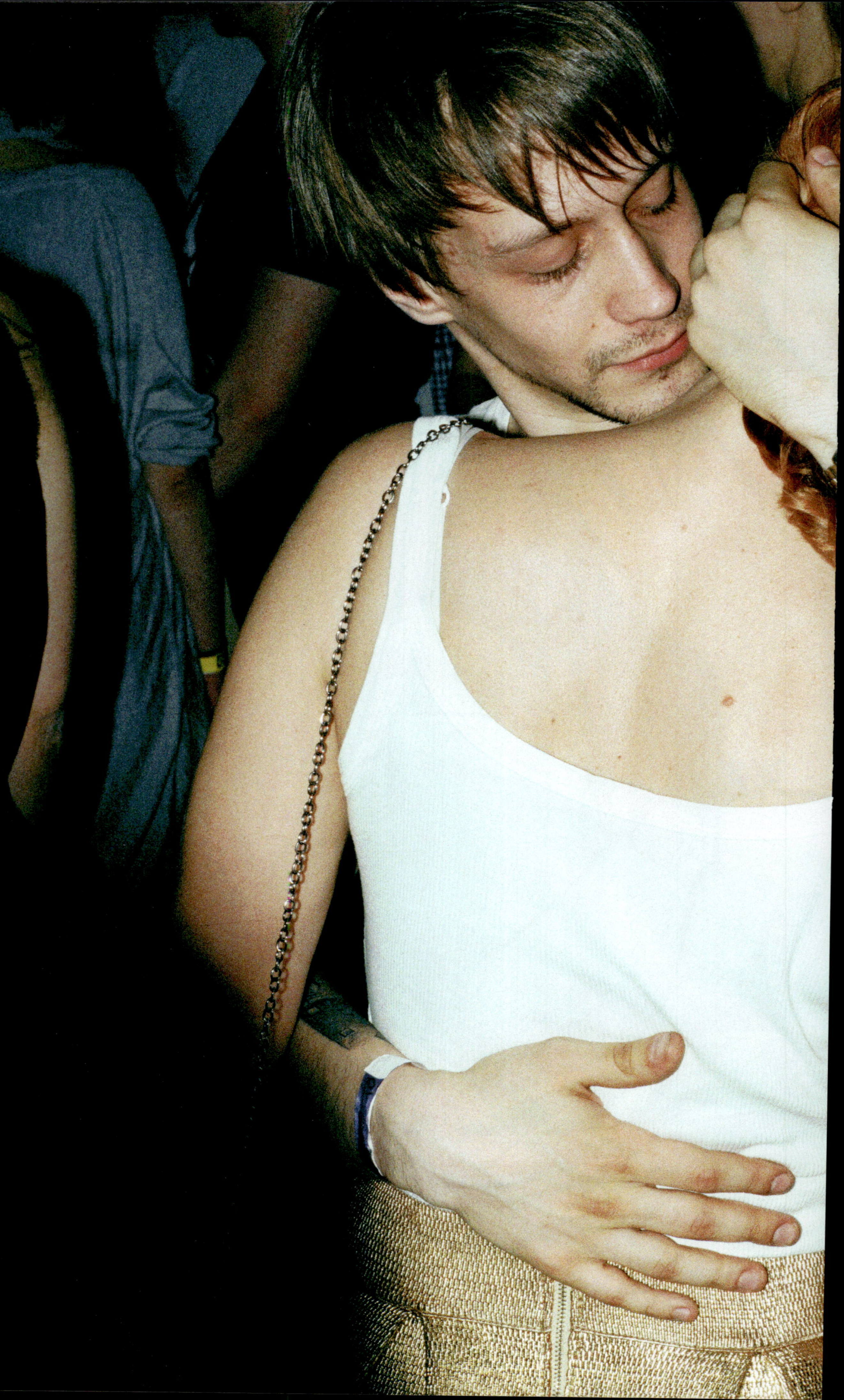

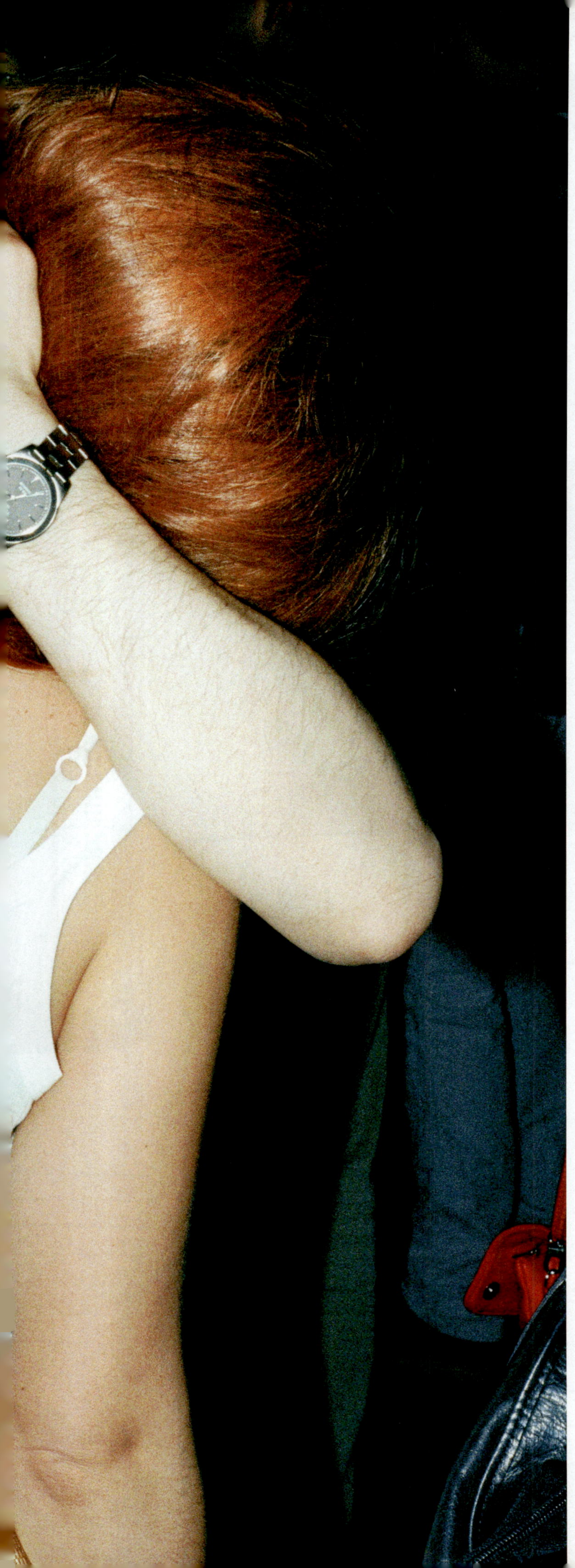

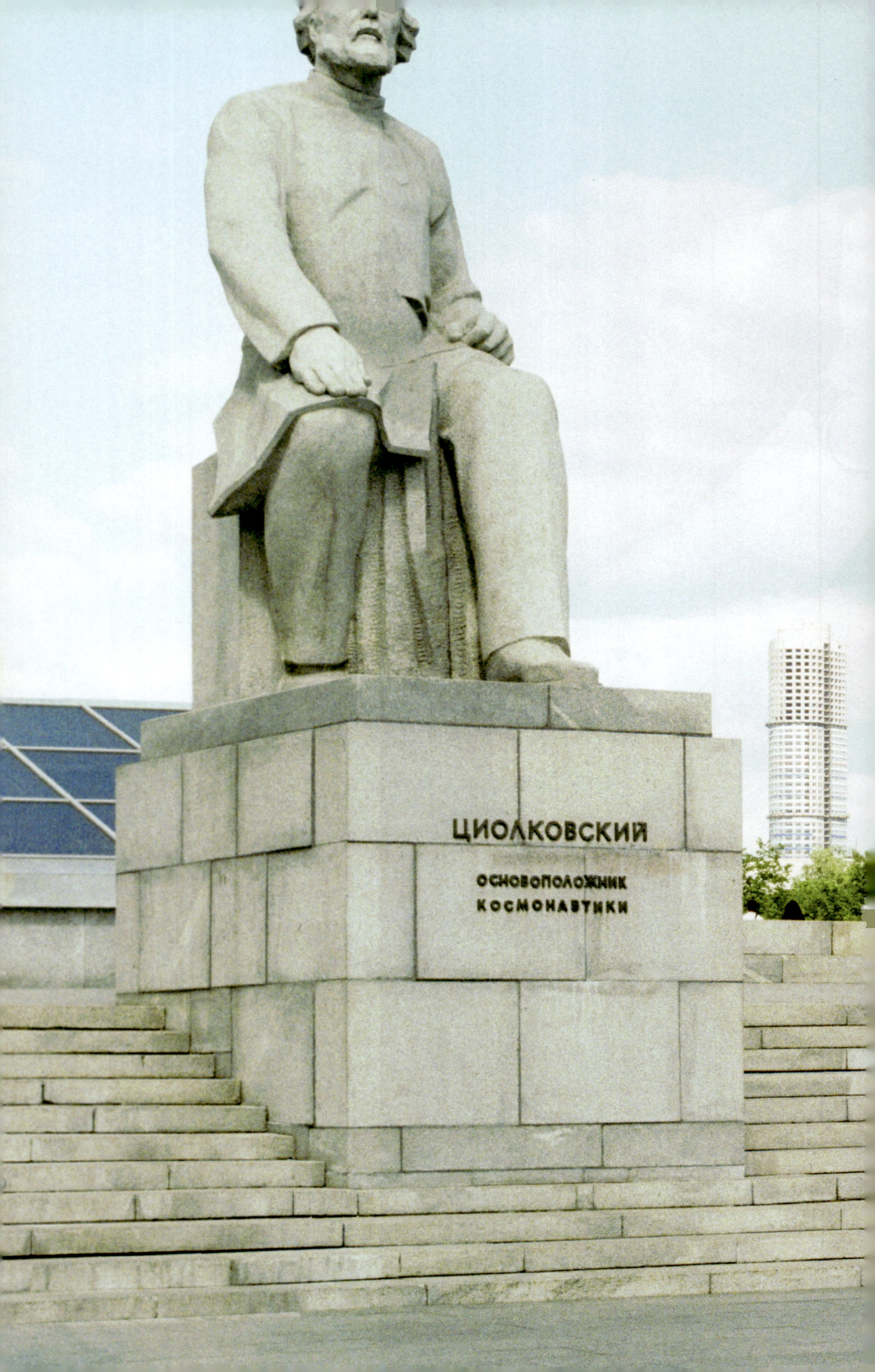
ЦИОЛКОВСКИЙ
ОСНОВОПОЛОЖНИК
КОСМОНАВТИКИ

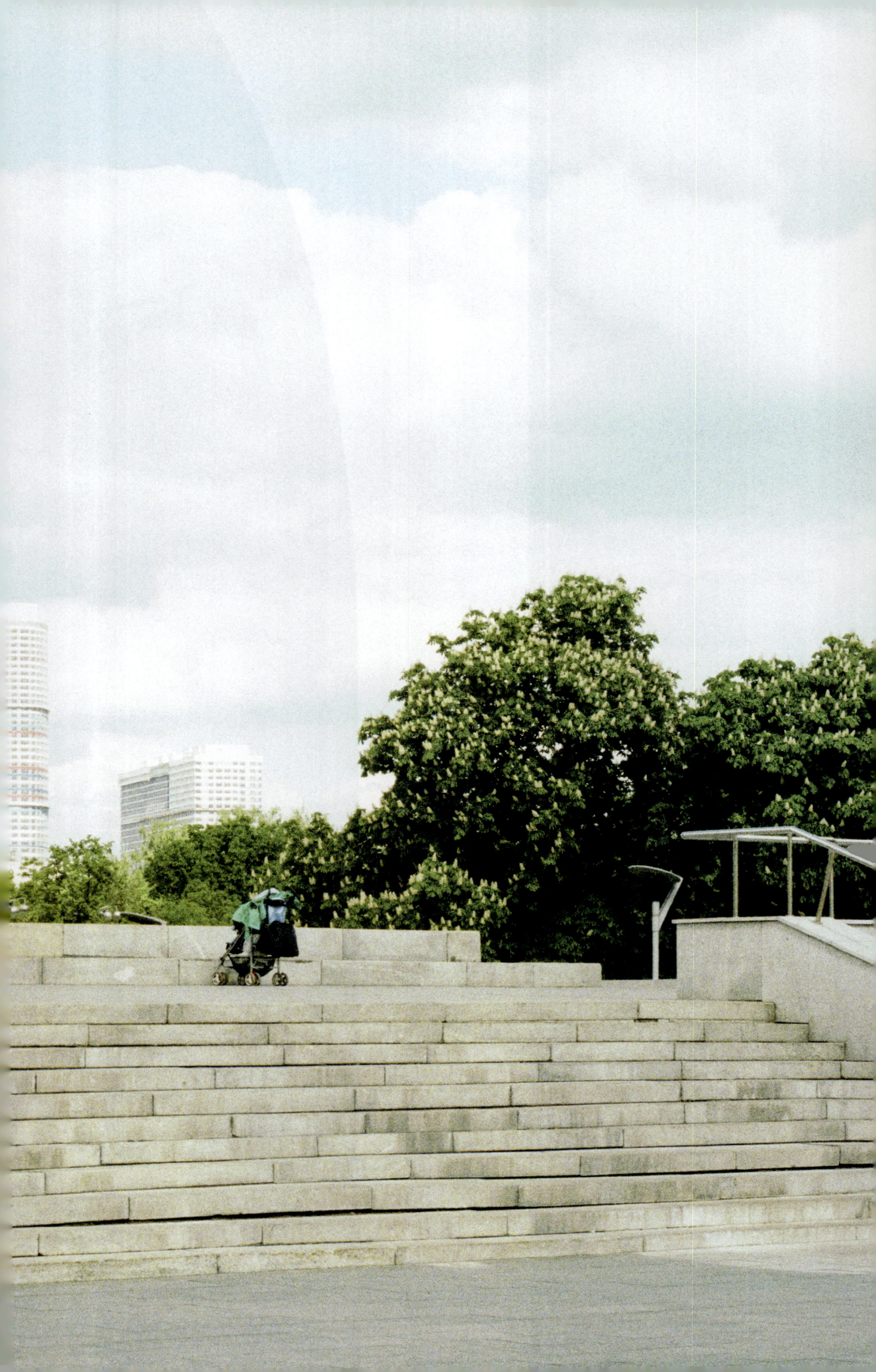

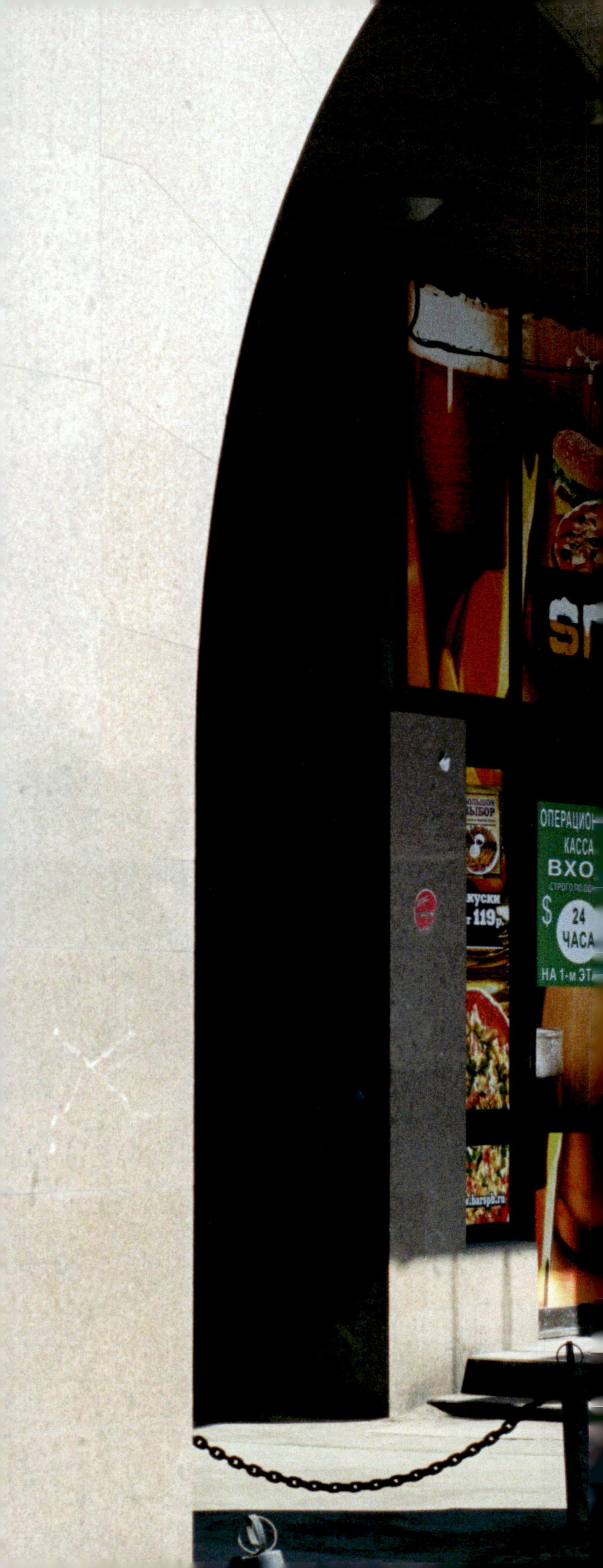
КАССА
24
ЧАСА

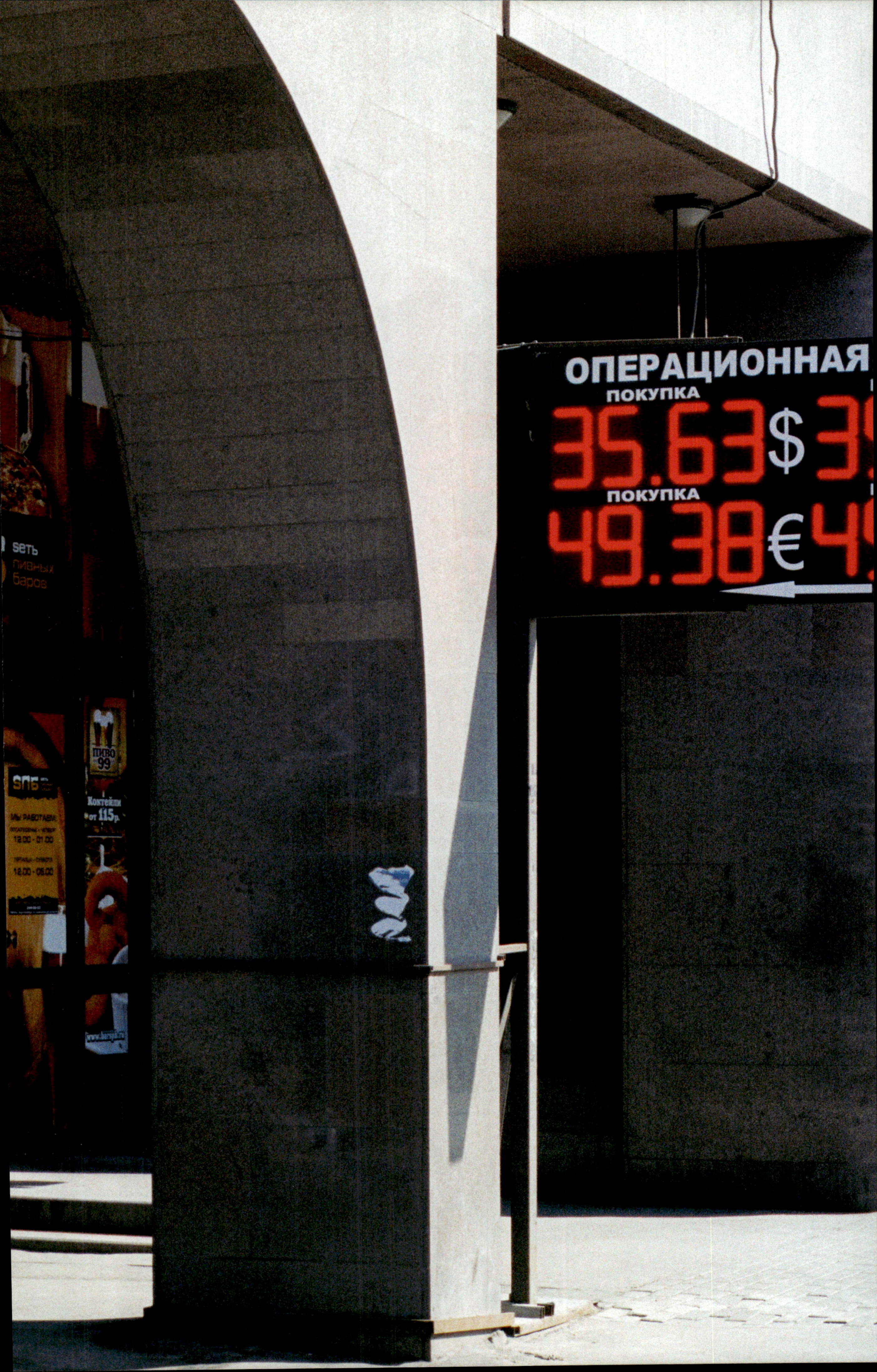
ОПЕРАЦИОННАЯ
ПОКУПКА
35.63 $
ПОКУПКА
49.38 €
сеть пивных баров
ПИВО 99
Коктейли от 115р.

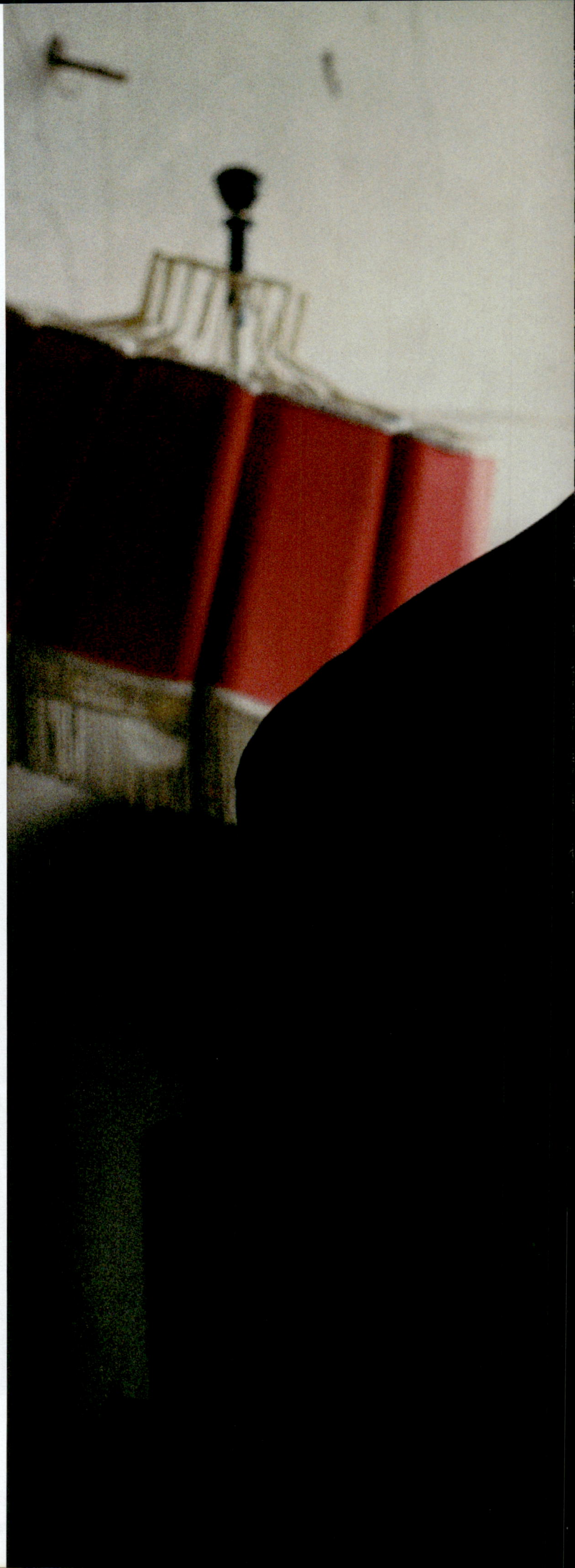

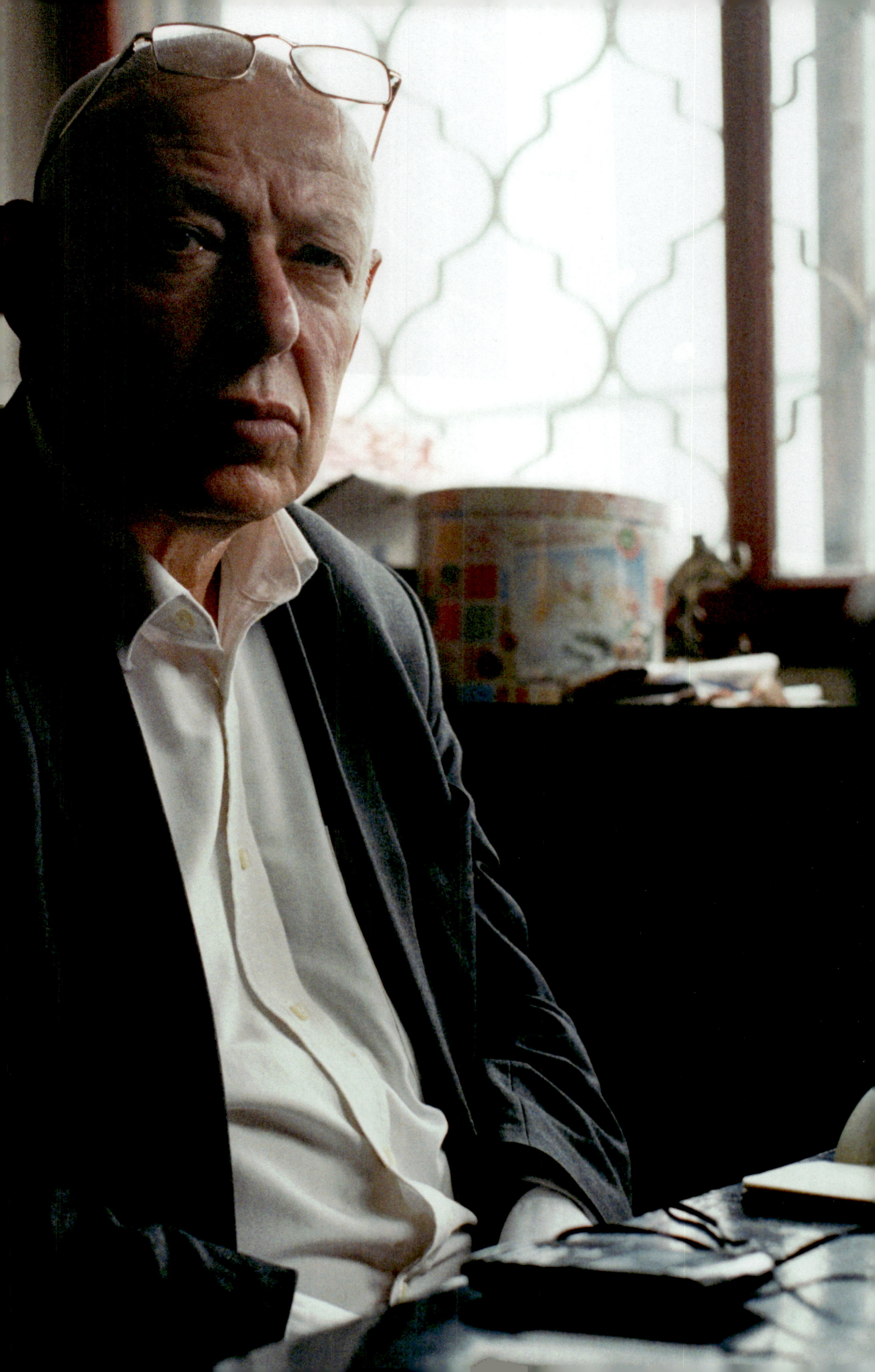

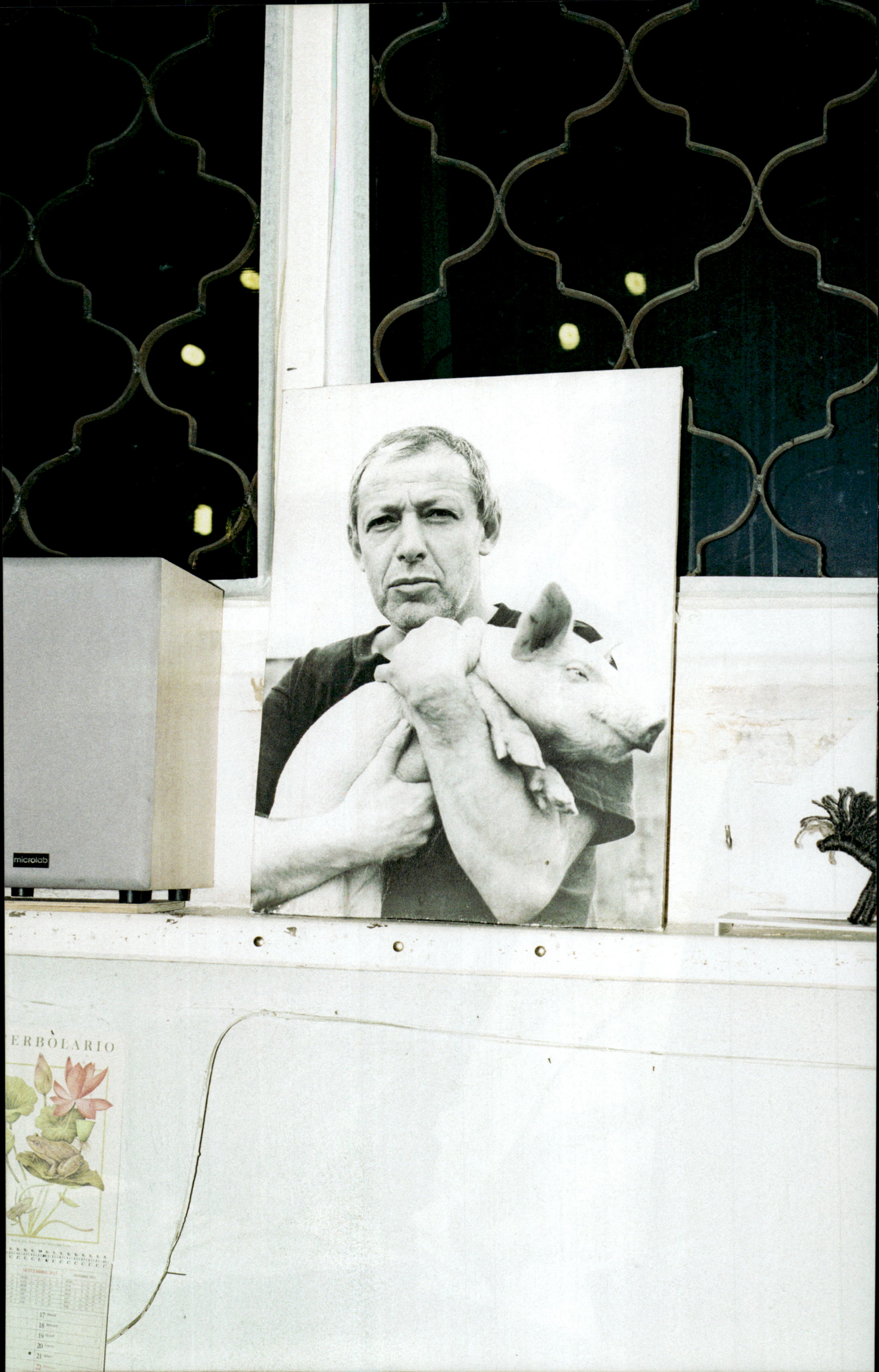
microlab
ERBOLARIO

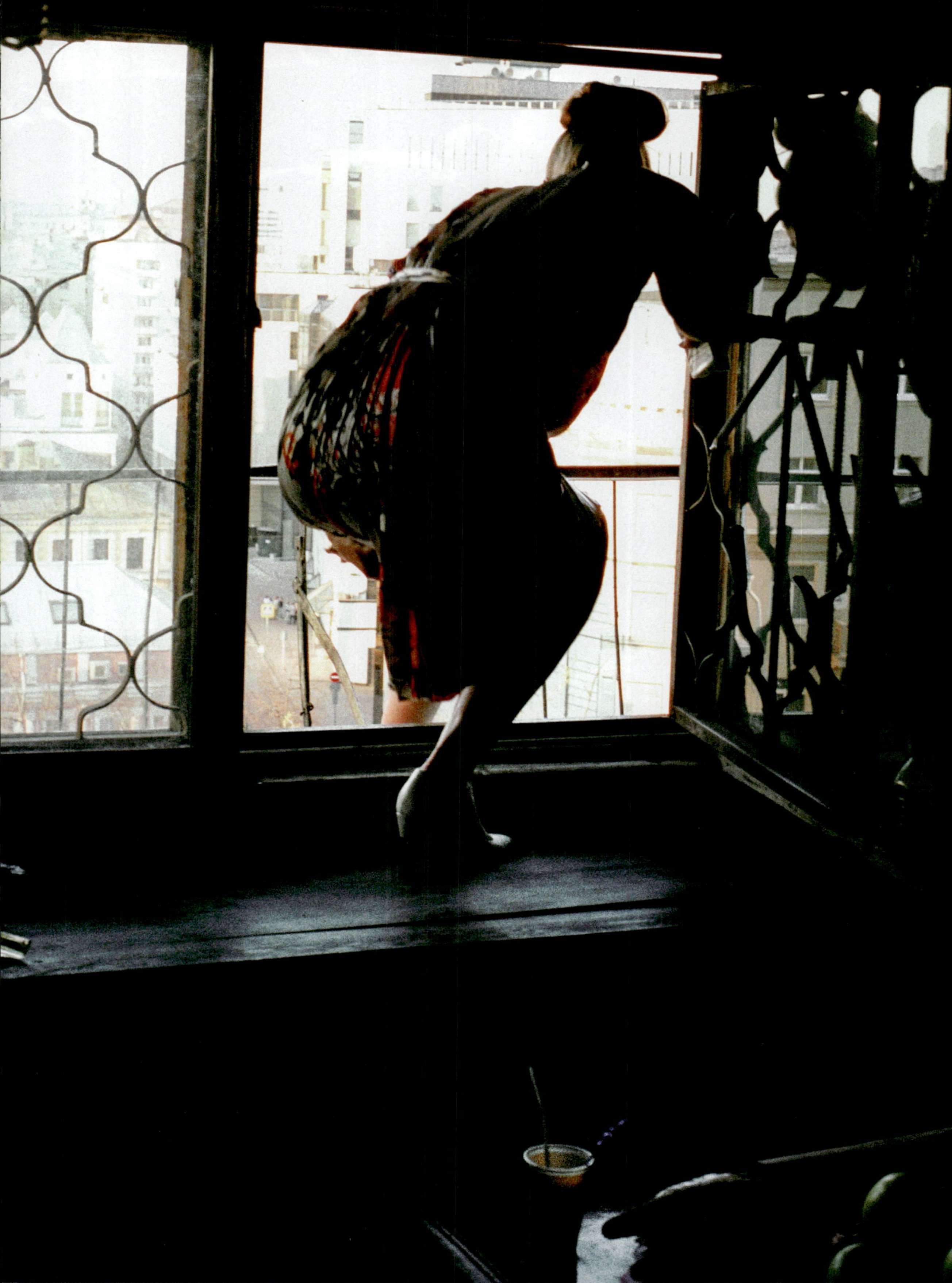

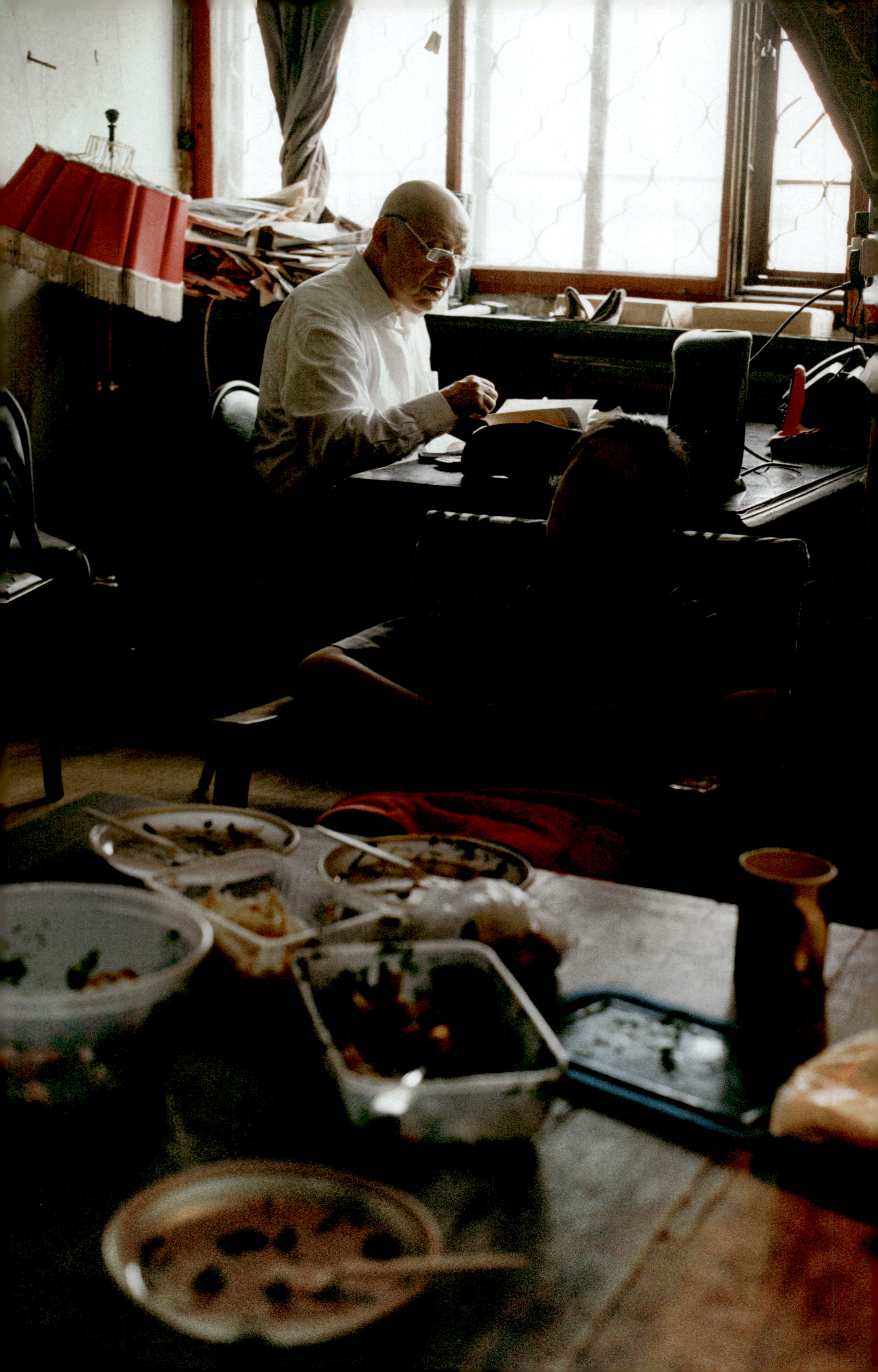

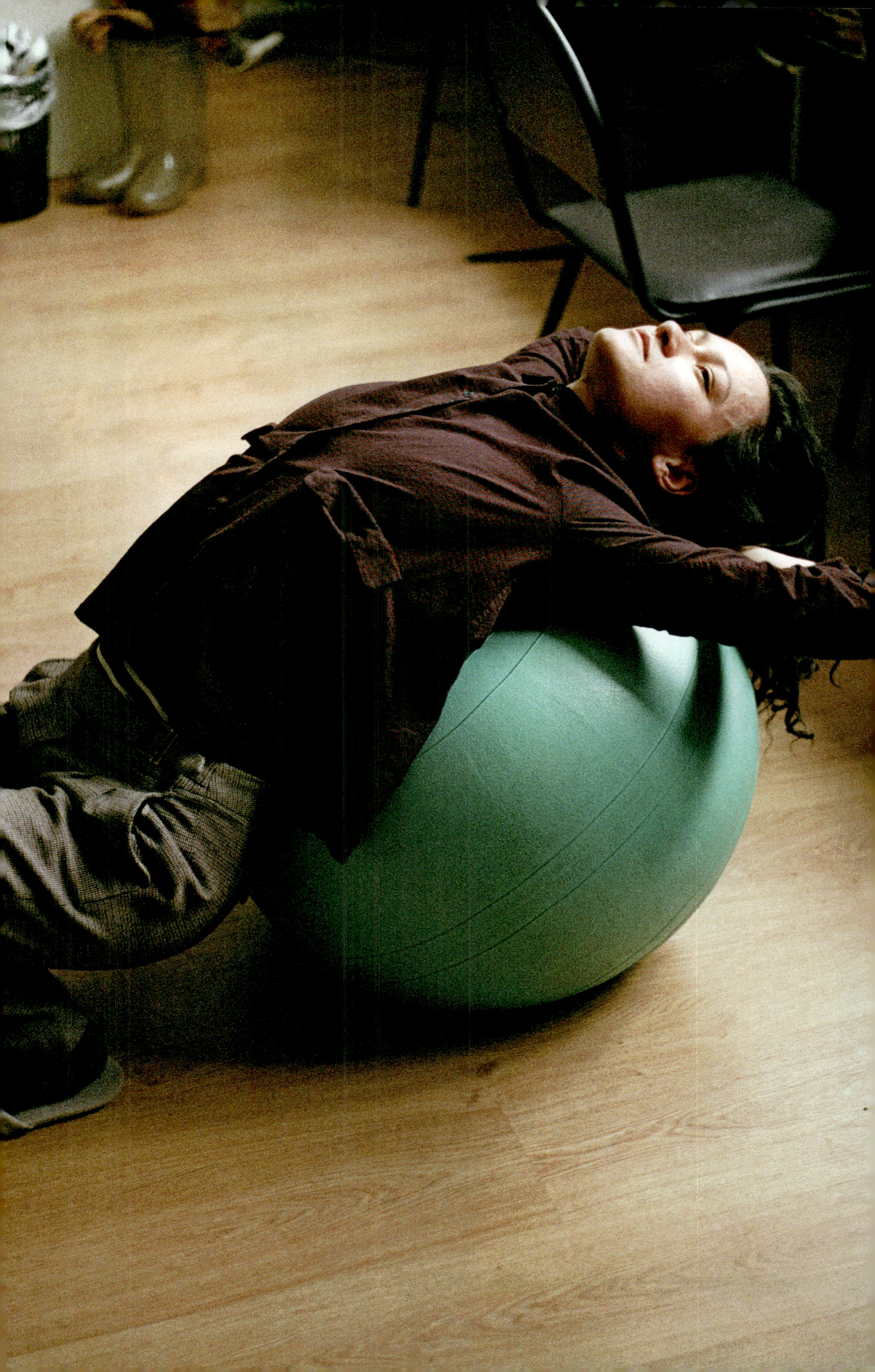

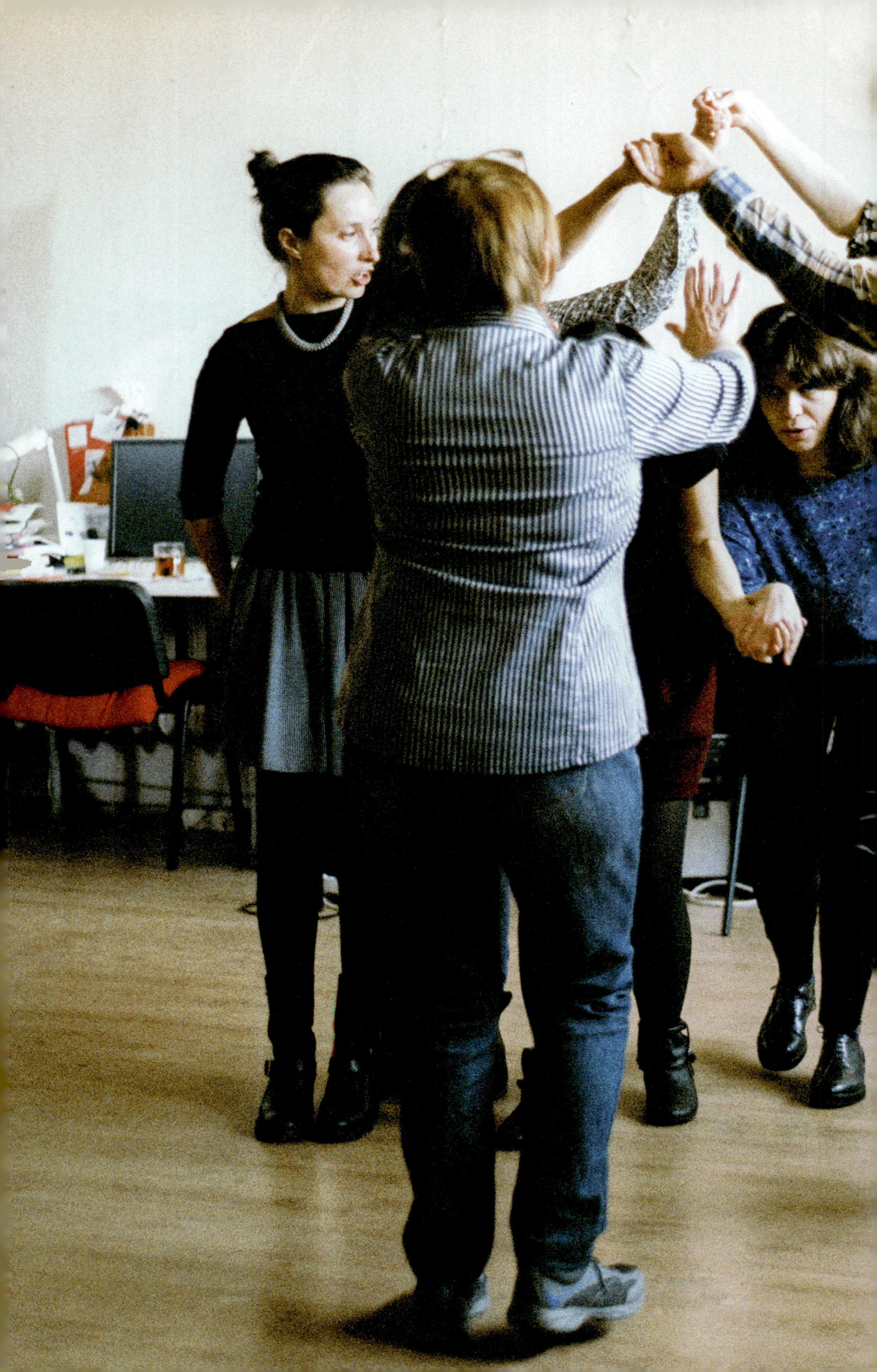

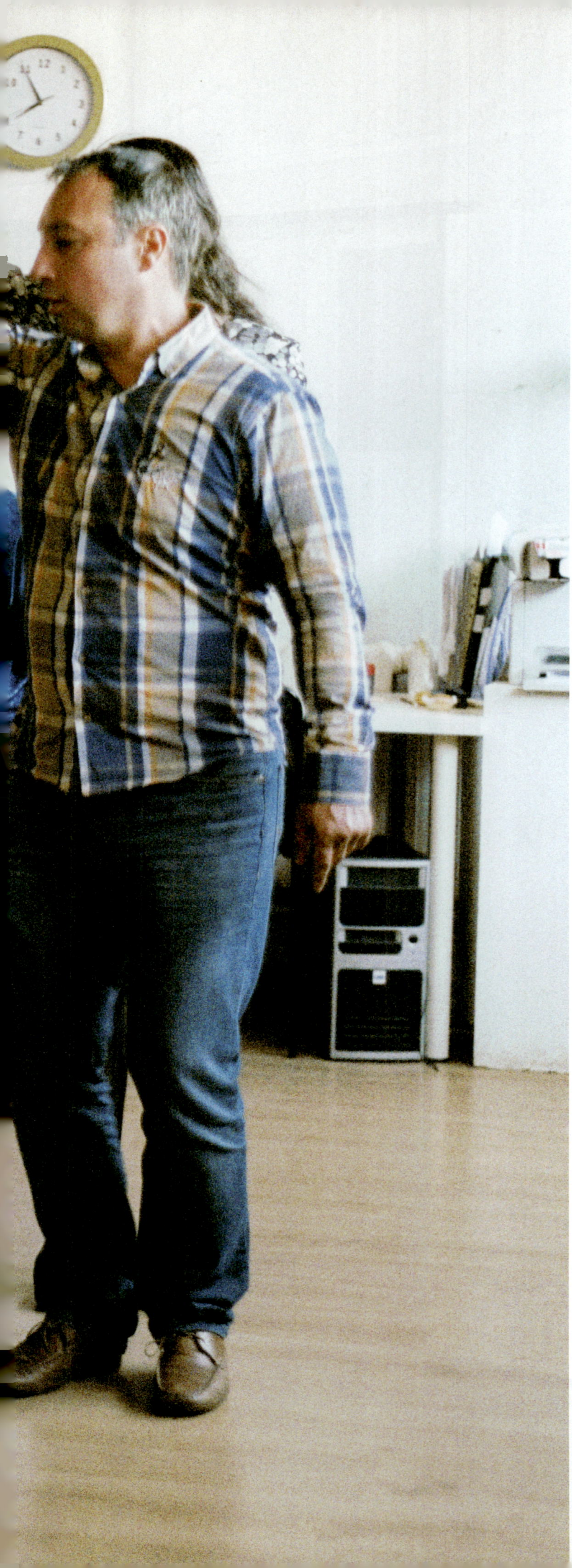

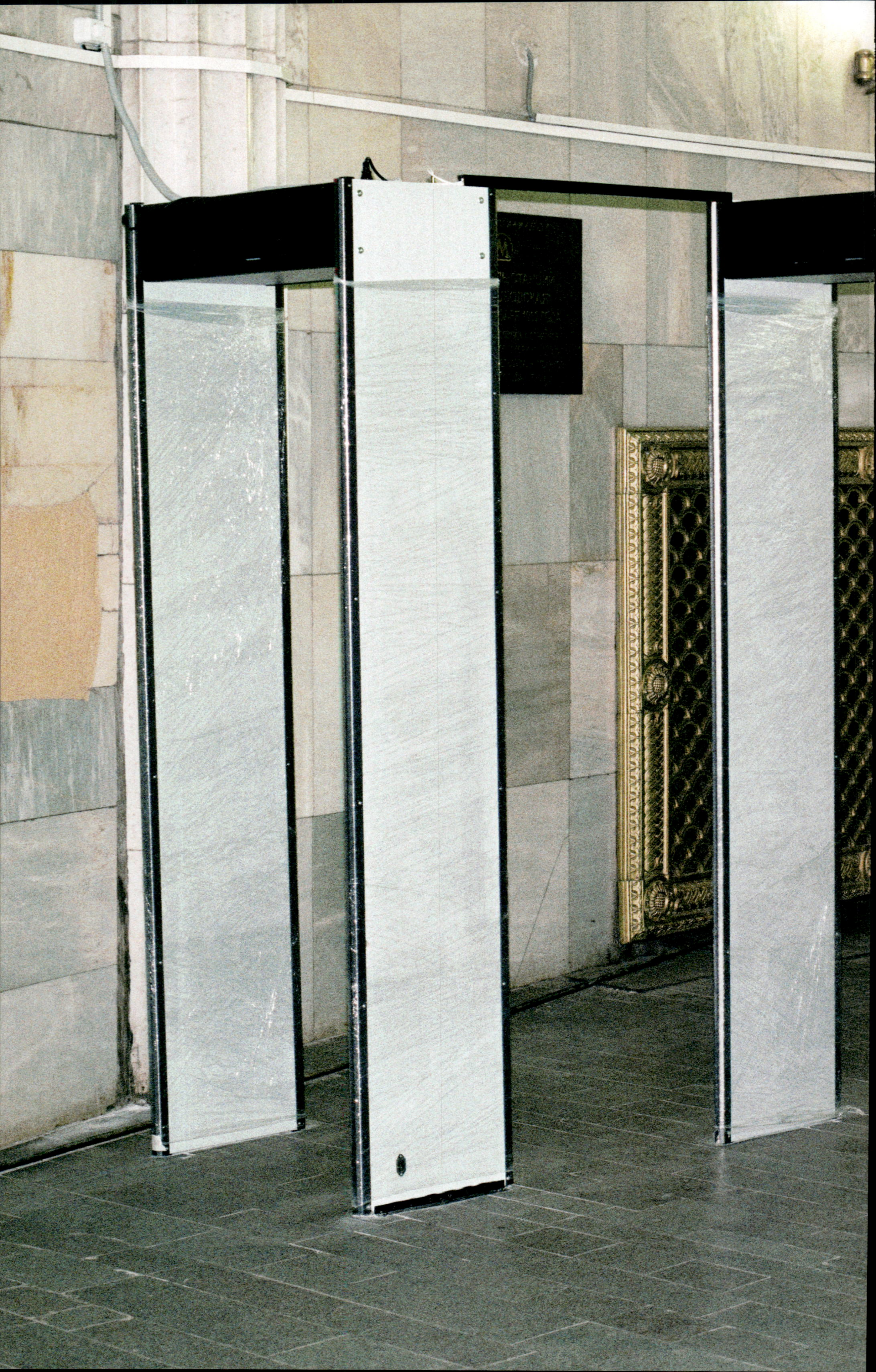

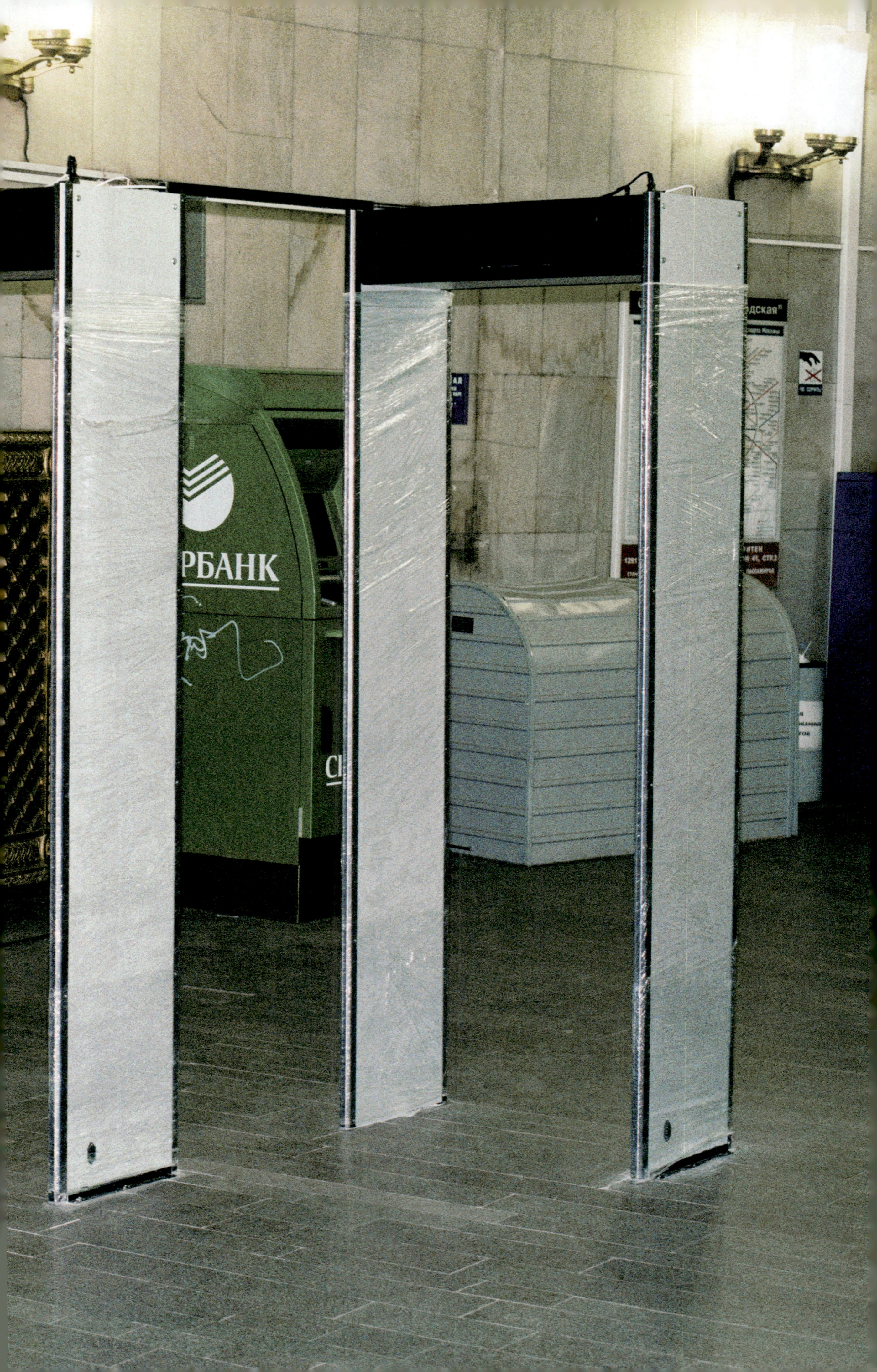
РБАНК

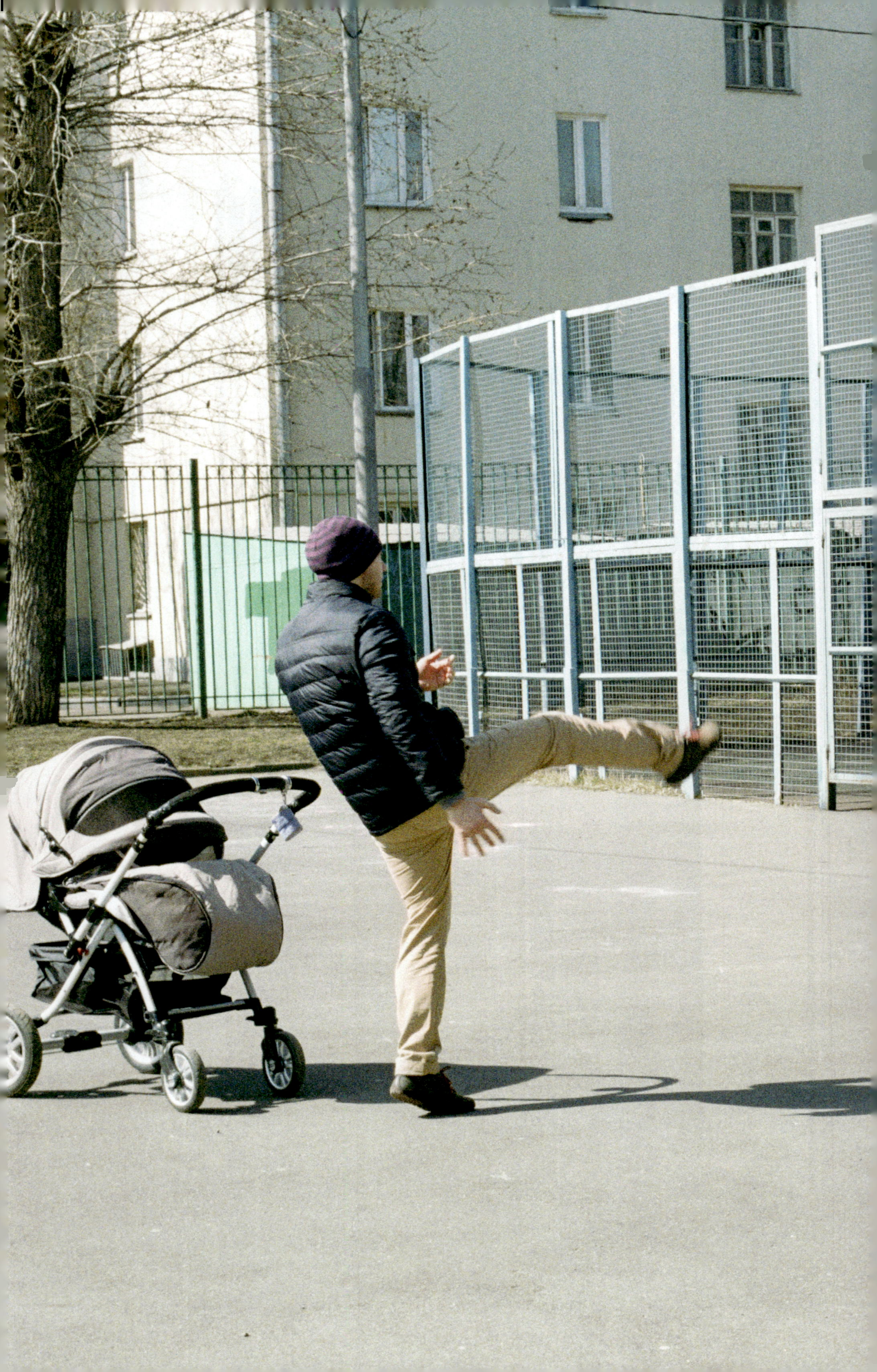

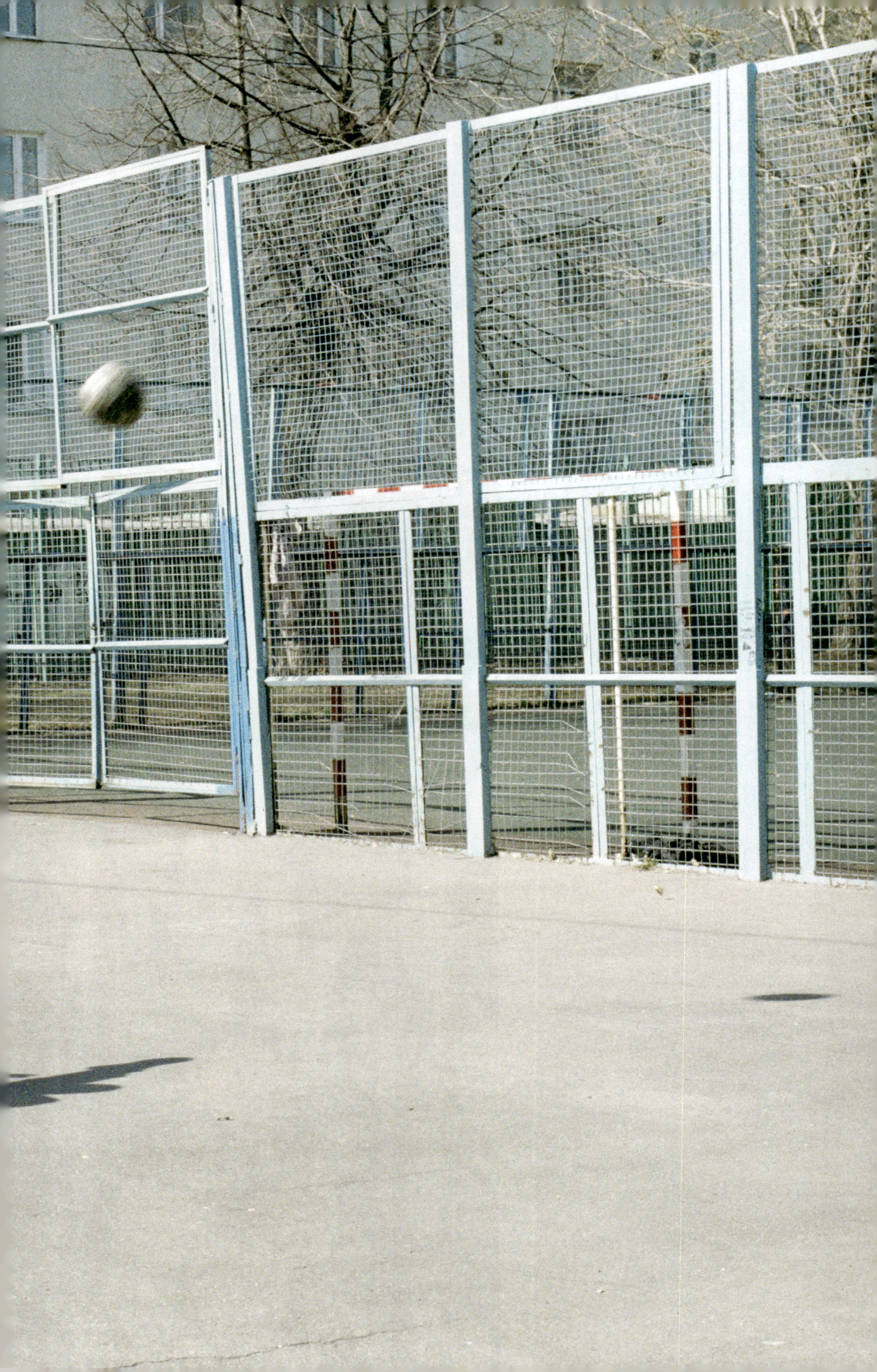

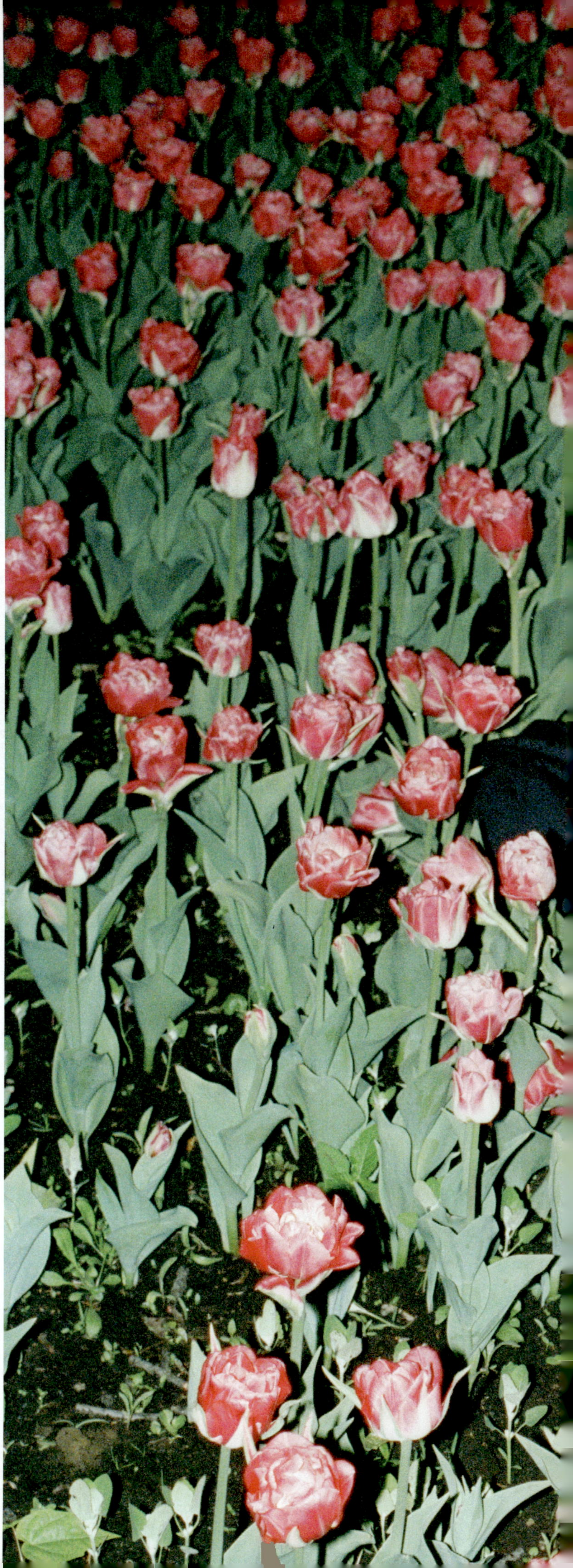

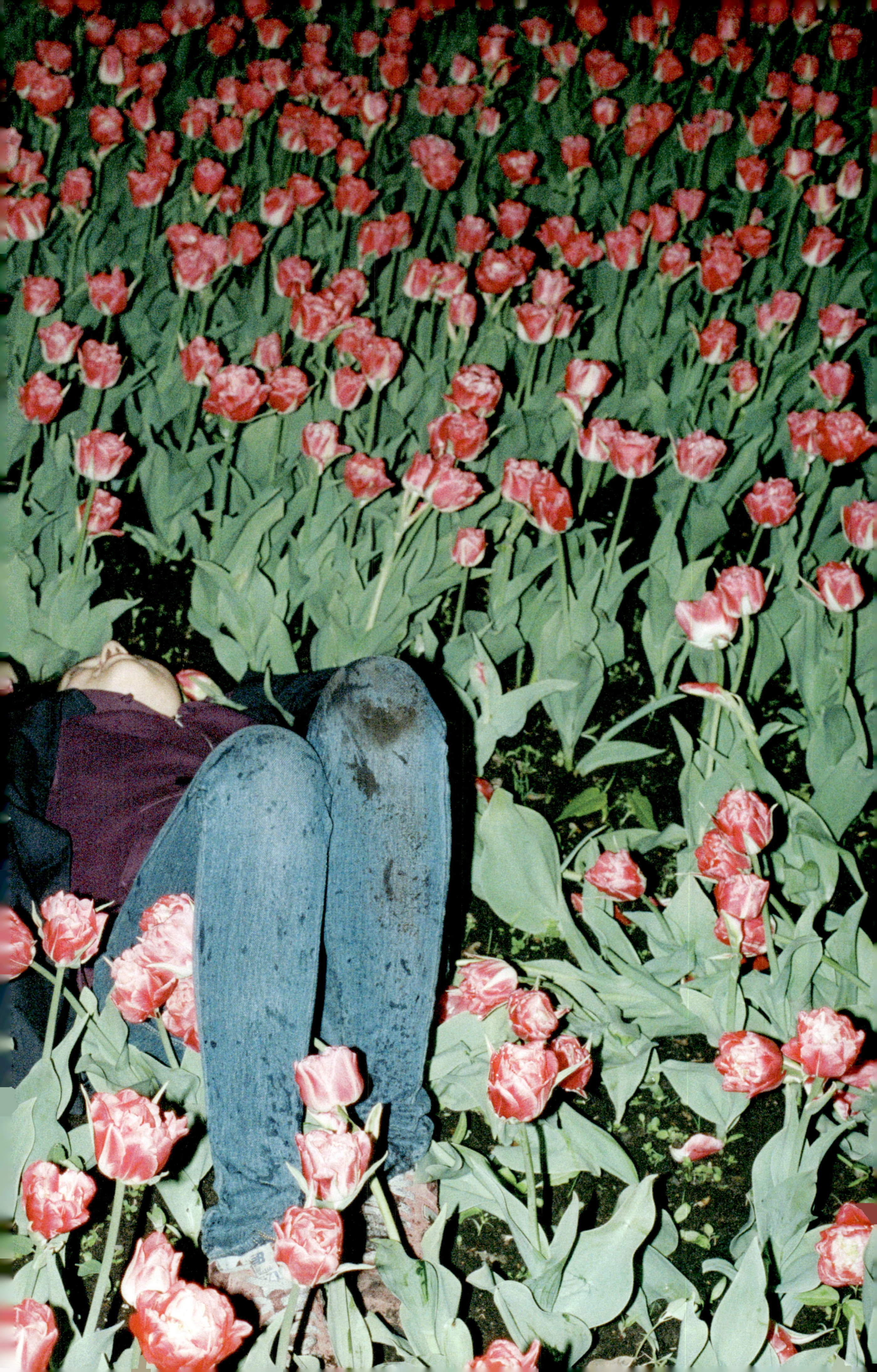

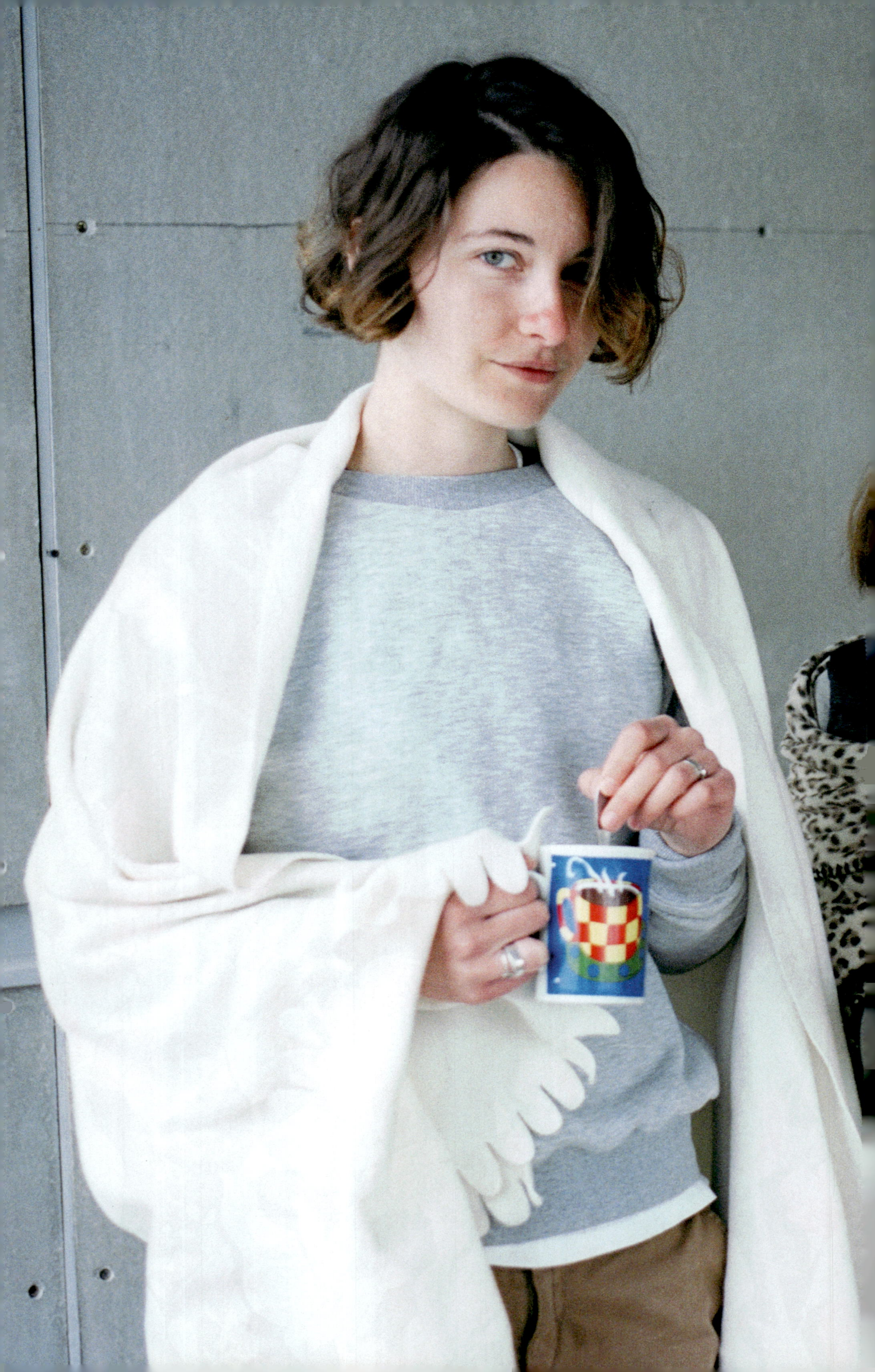

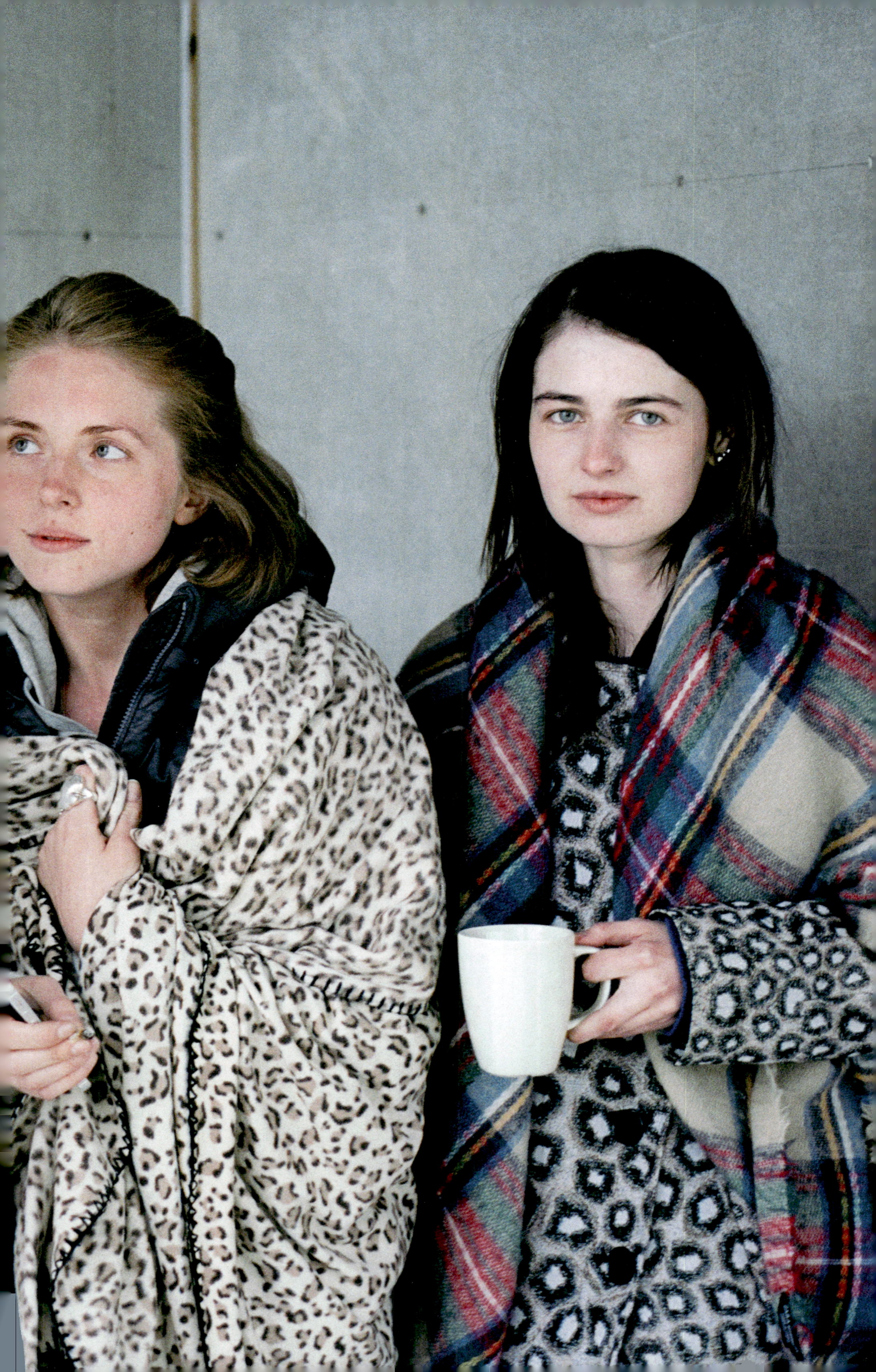

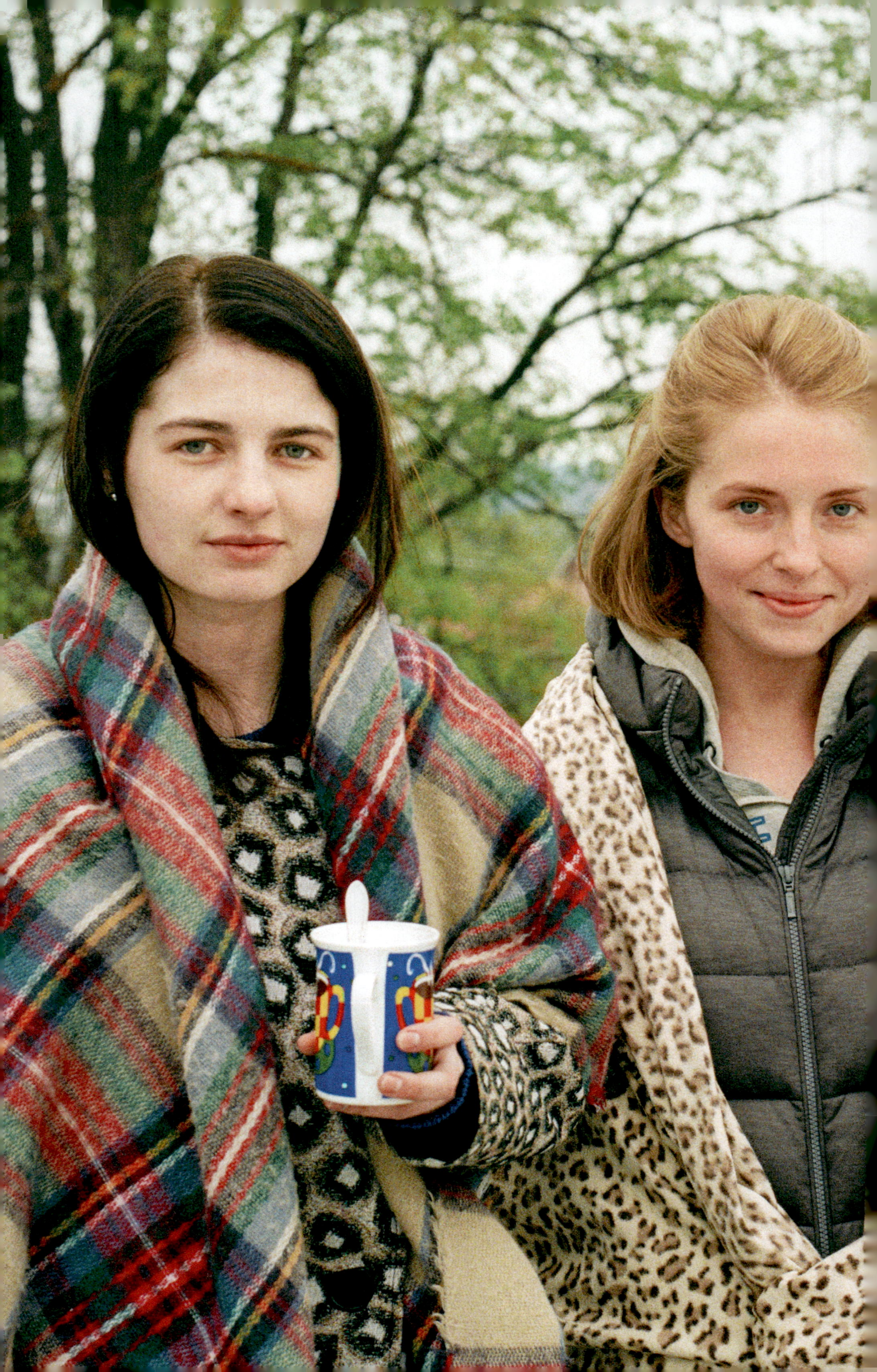

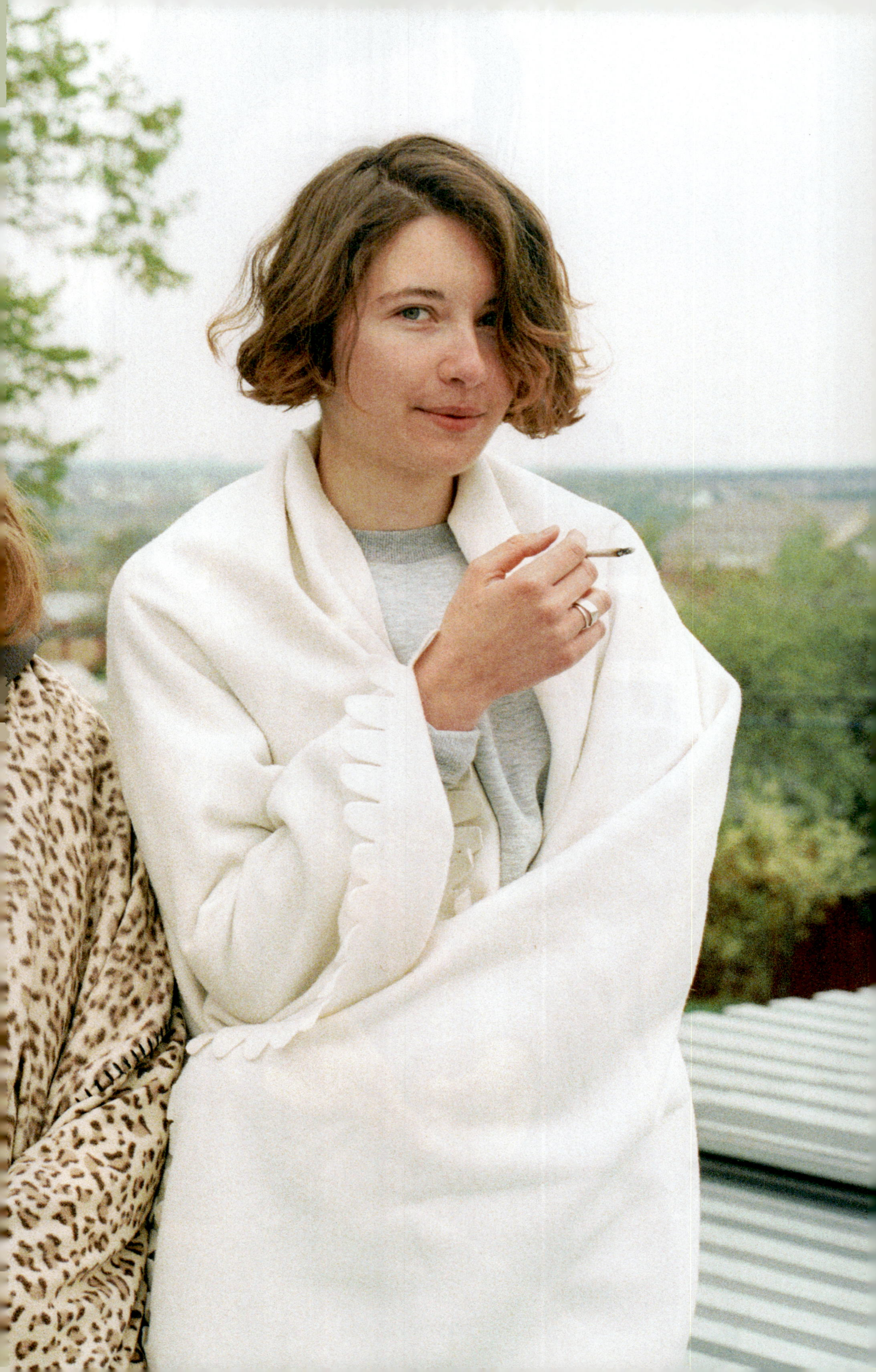

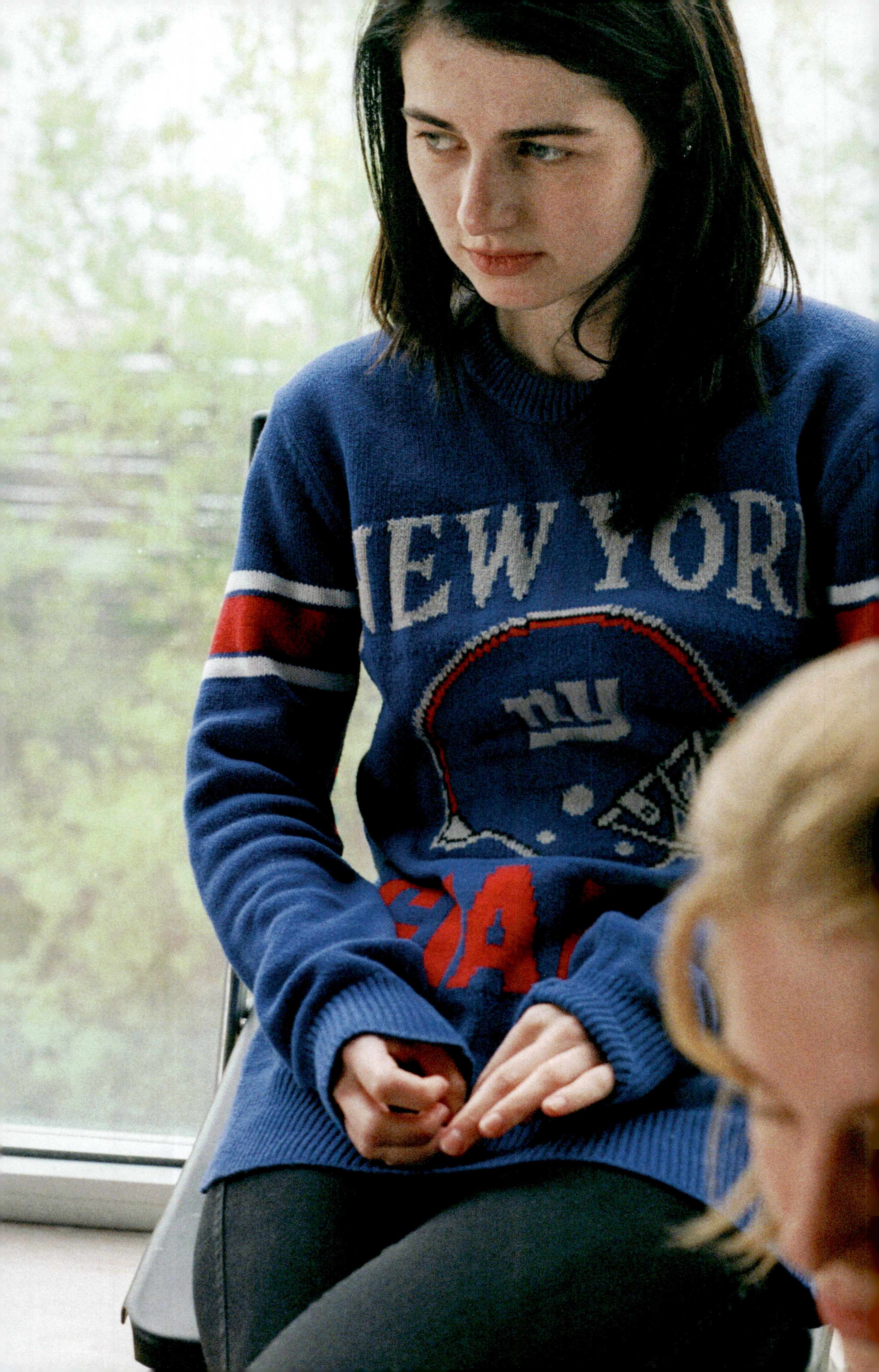
ny

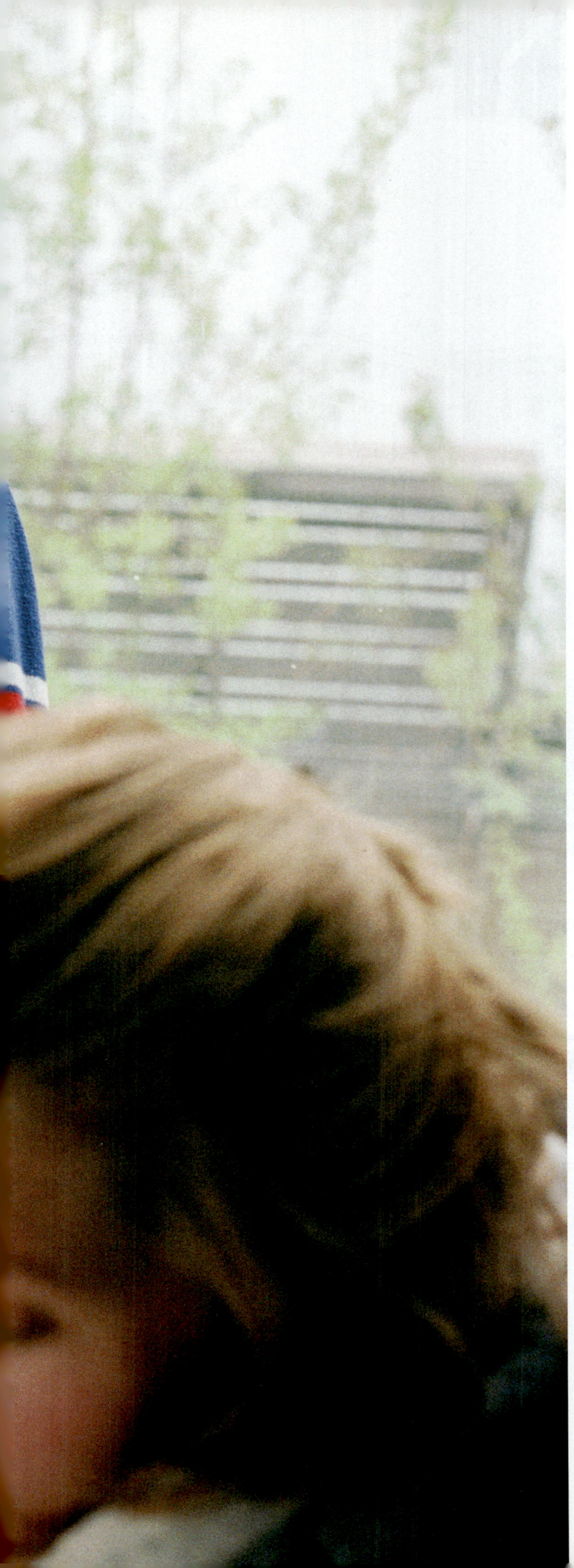

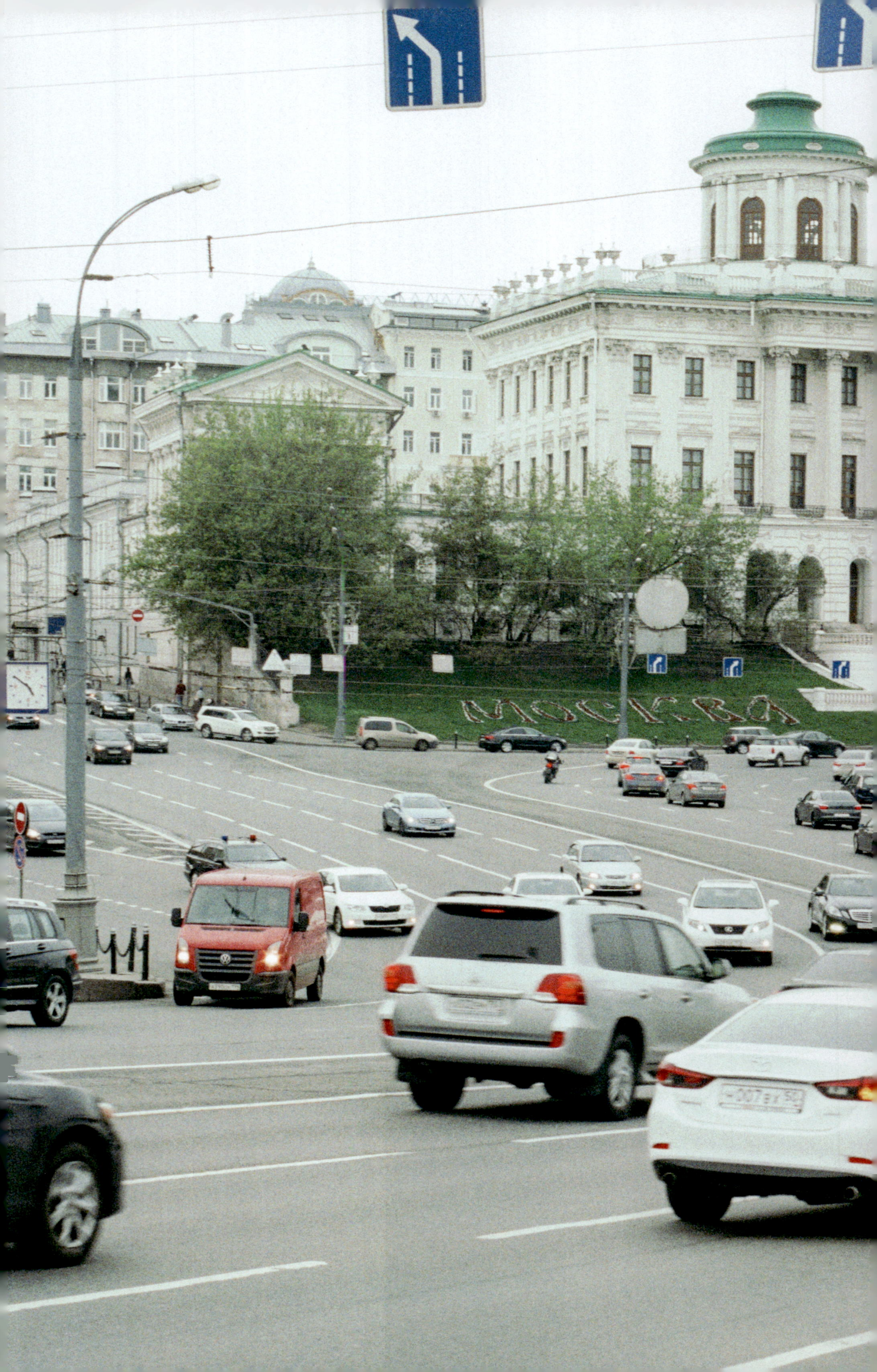
МОСКВА

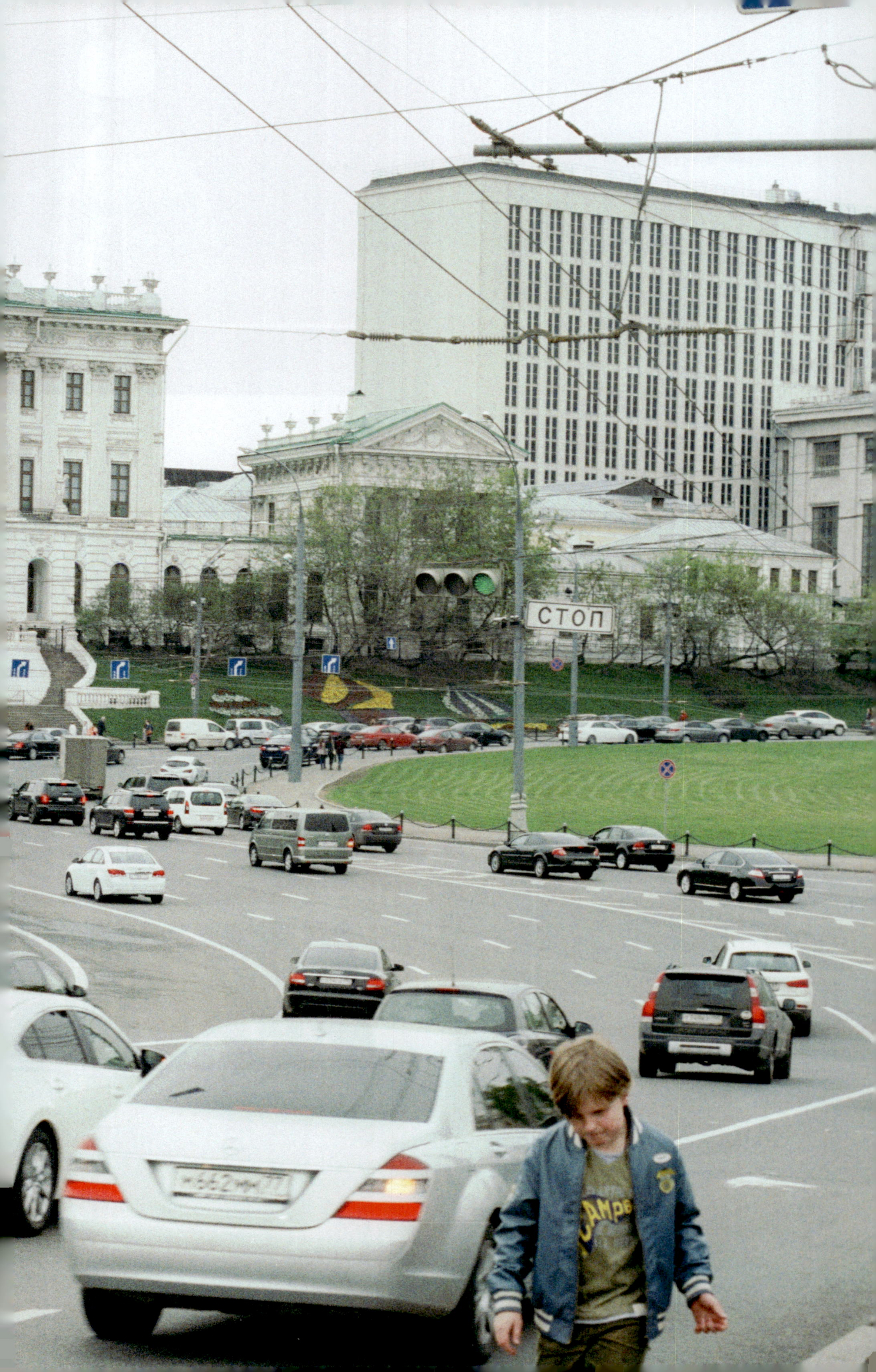
СТОП

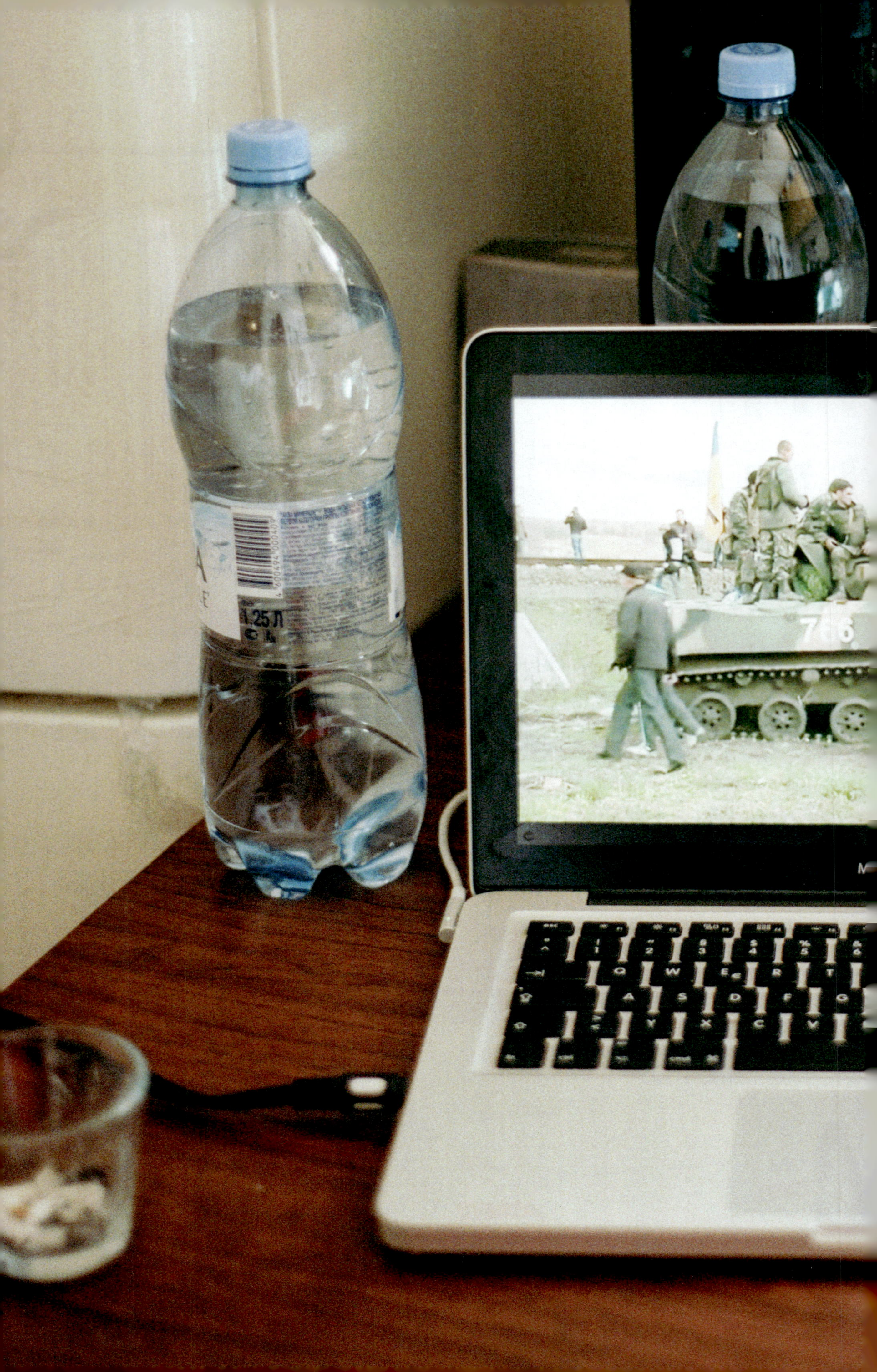

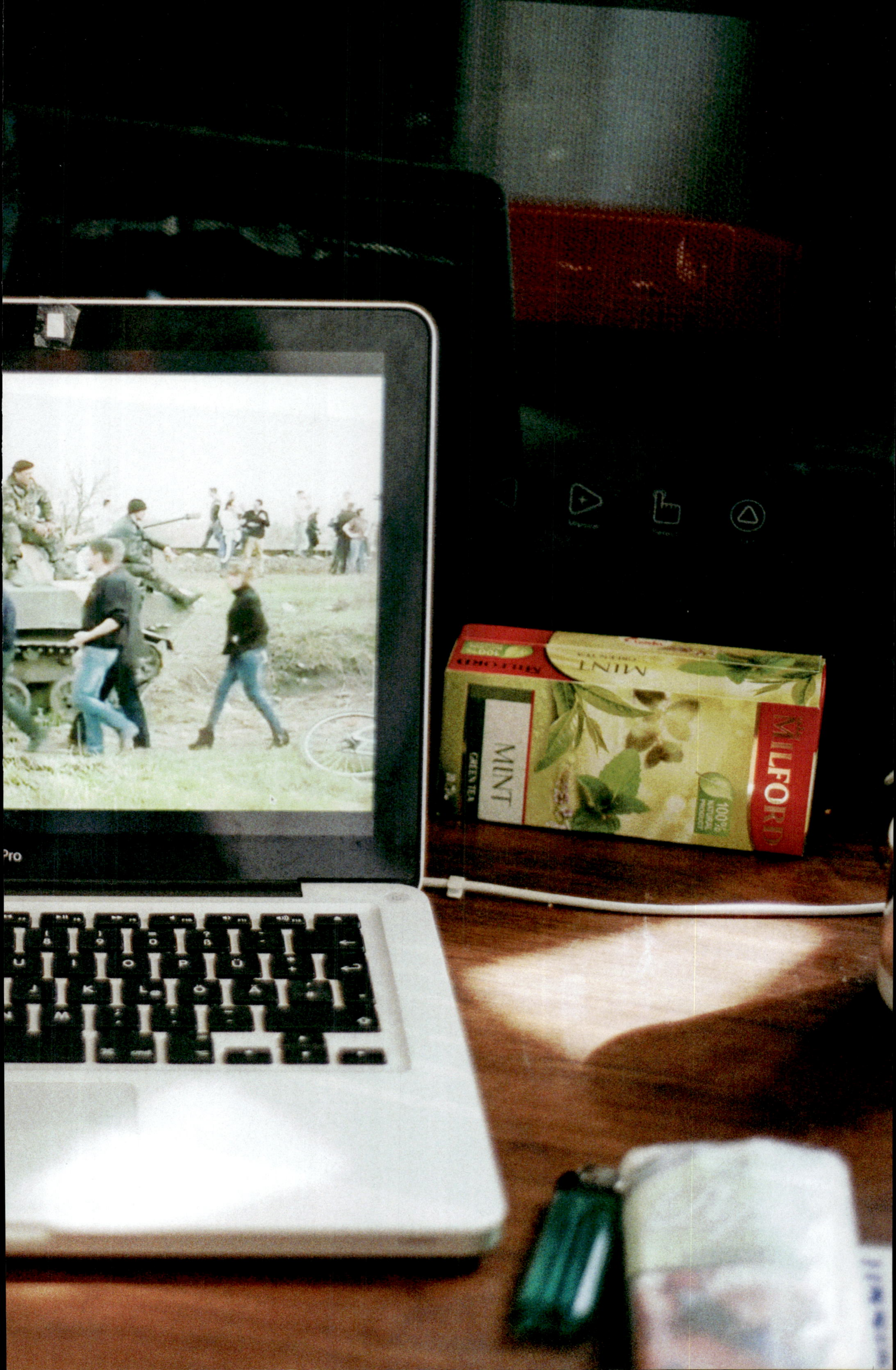
MILFORD
MINT
GREEN TEA
MILFORD

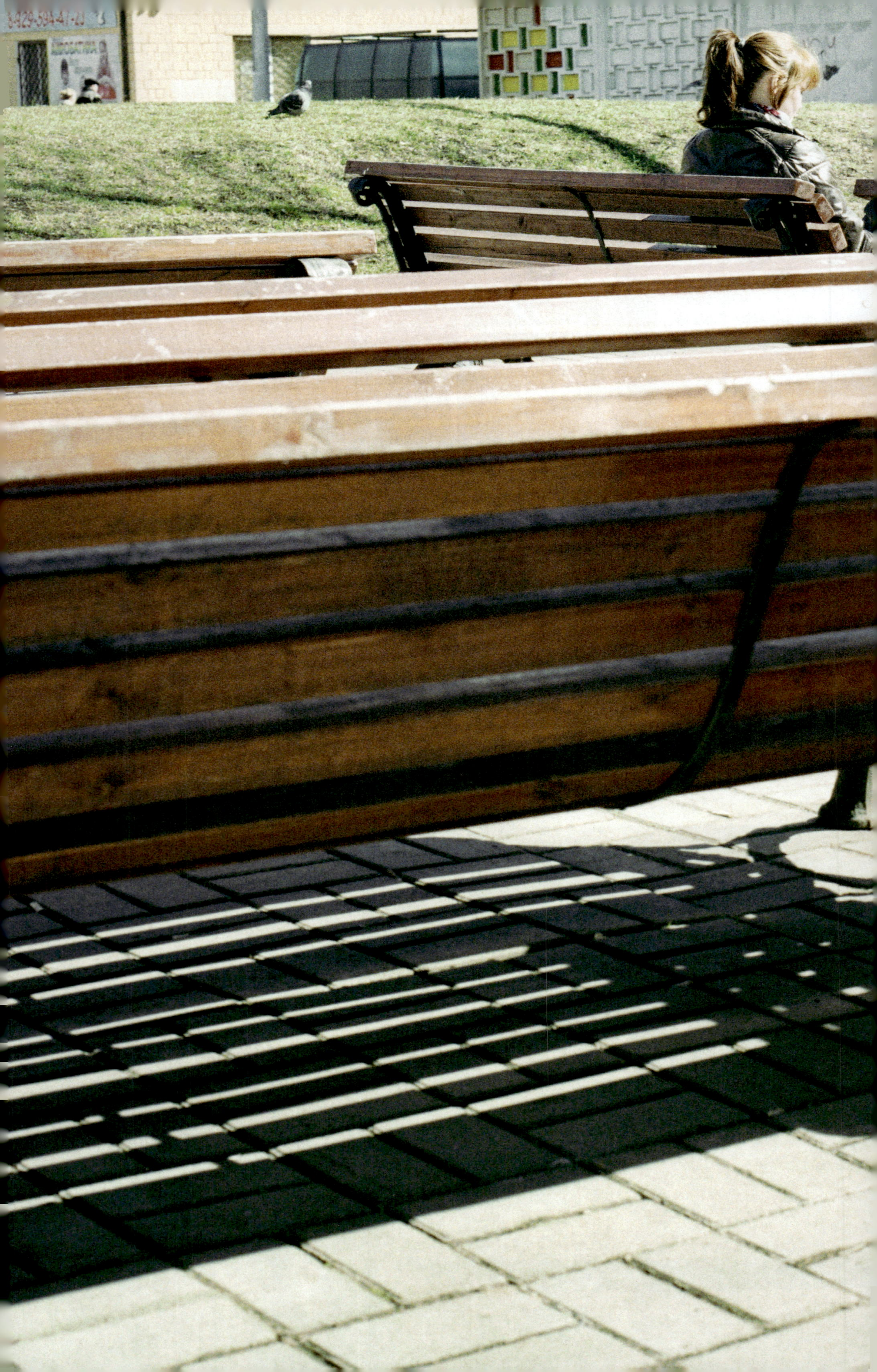

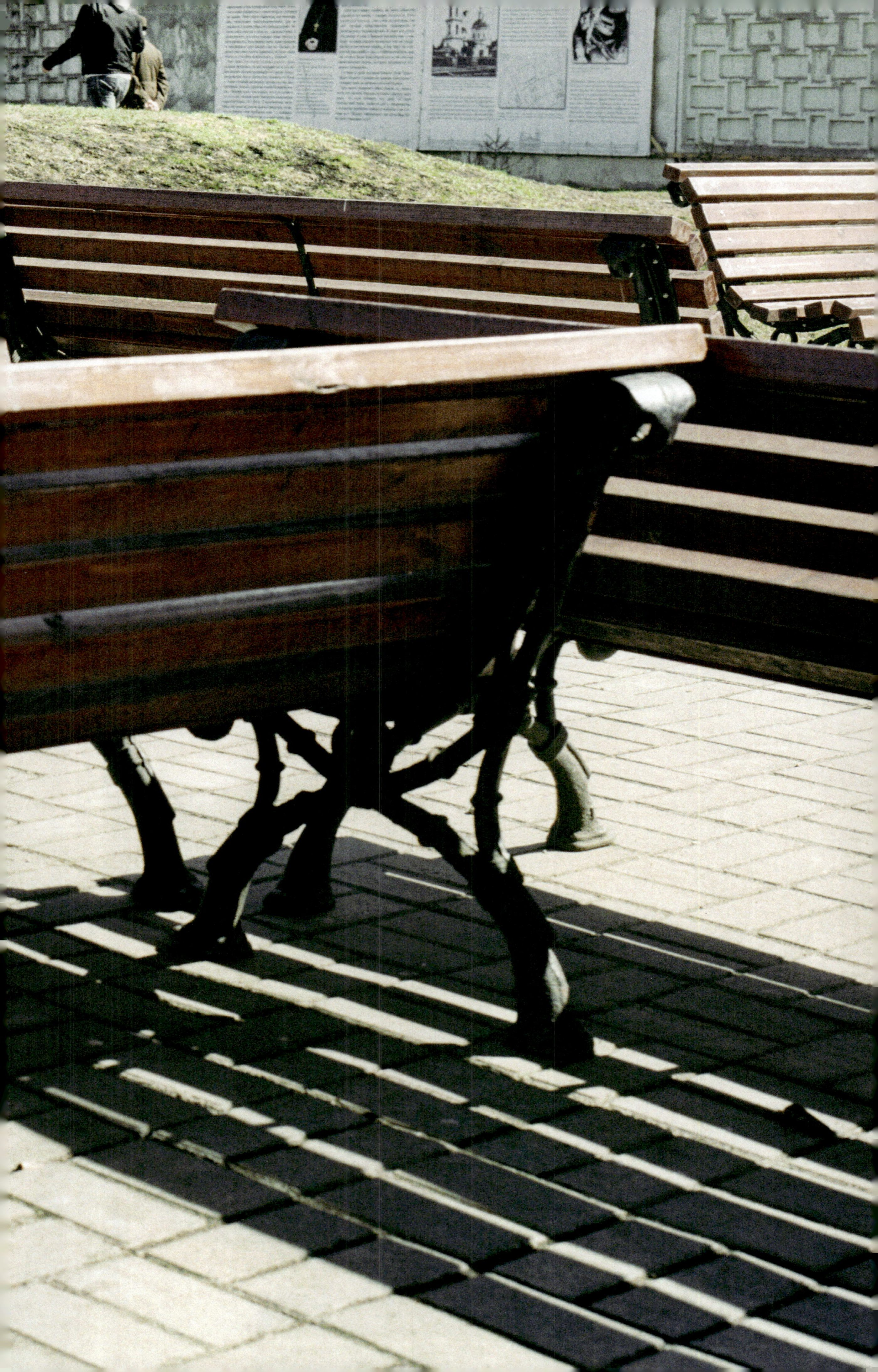

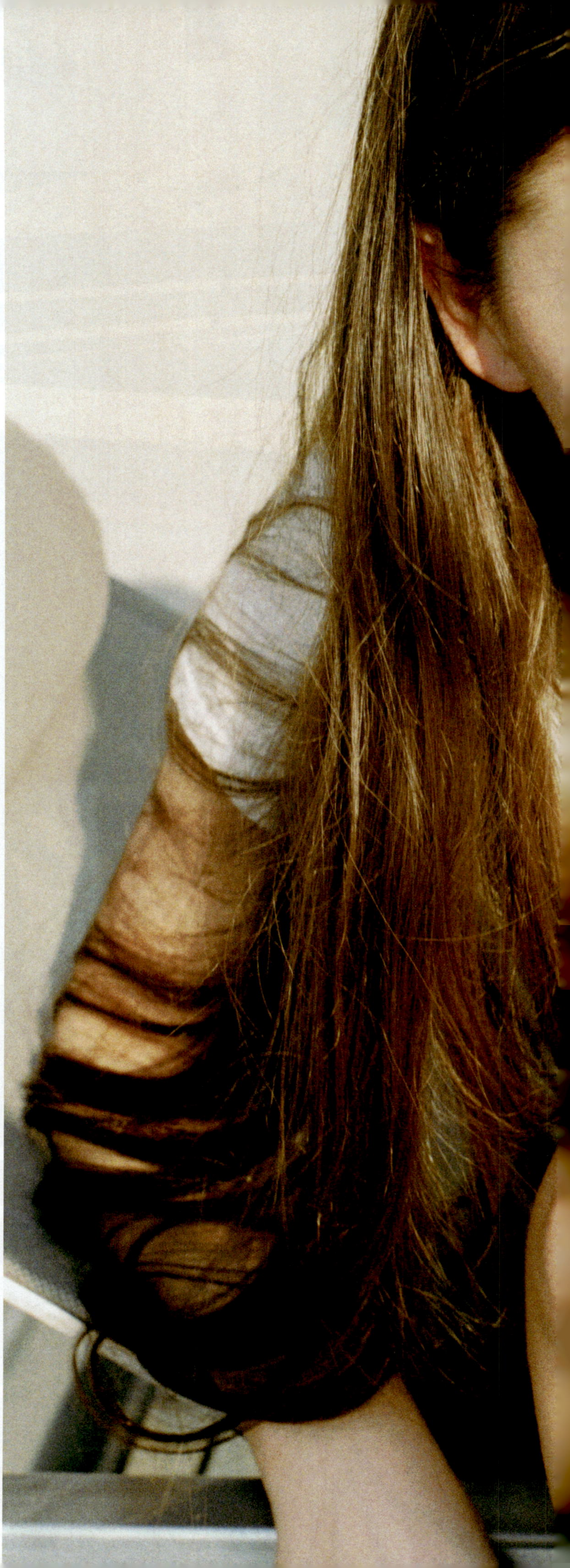

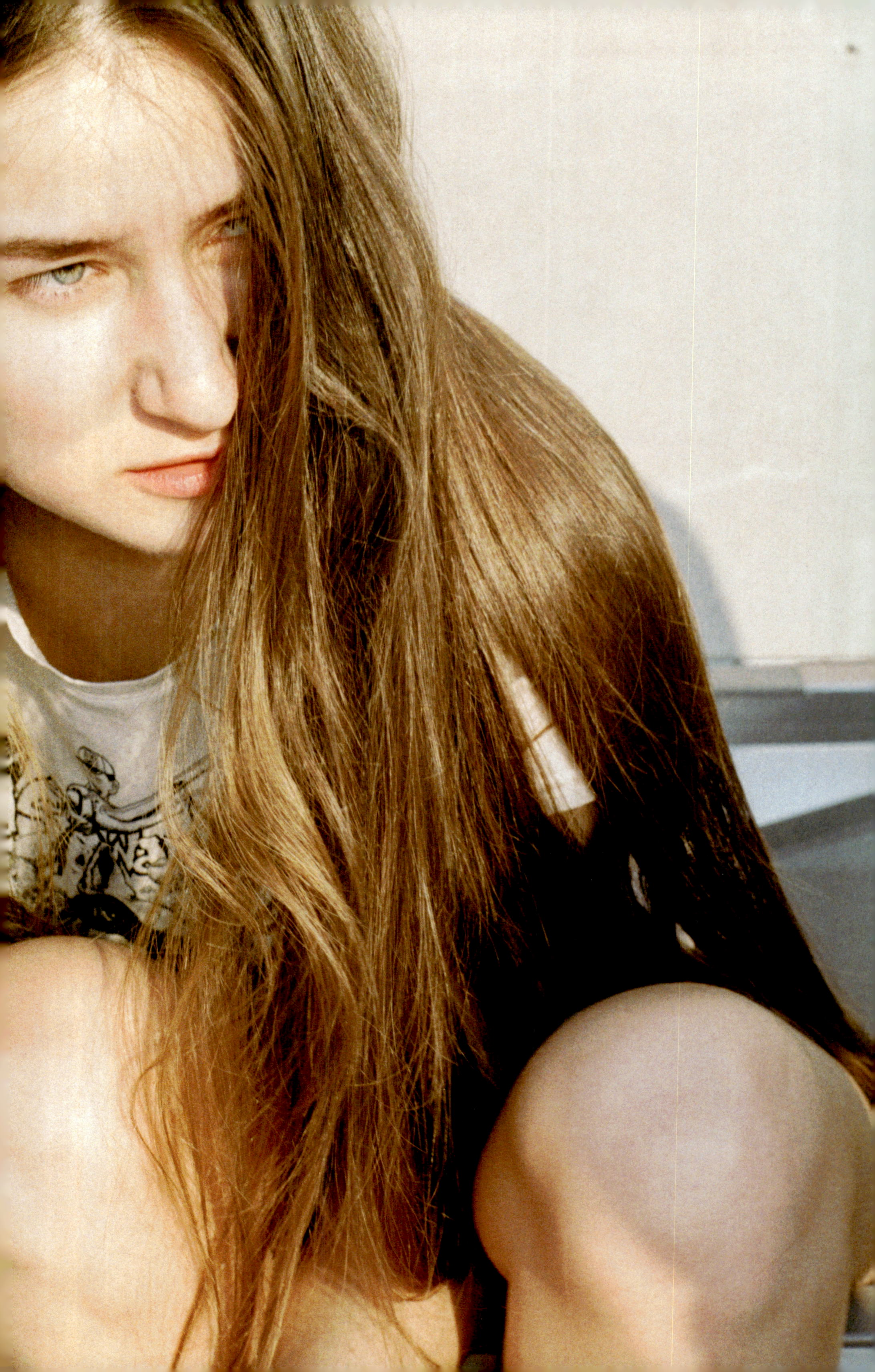

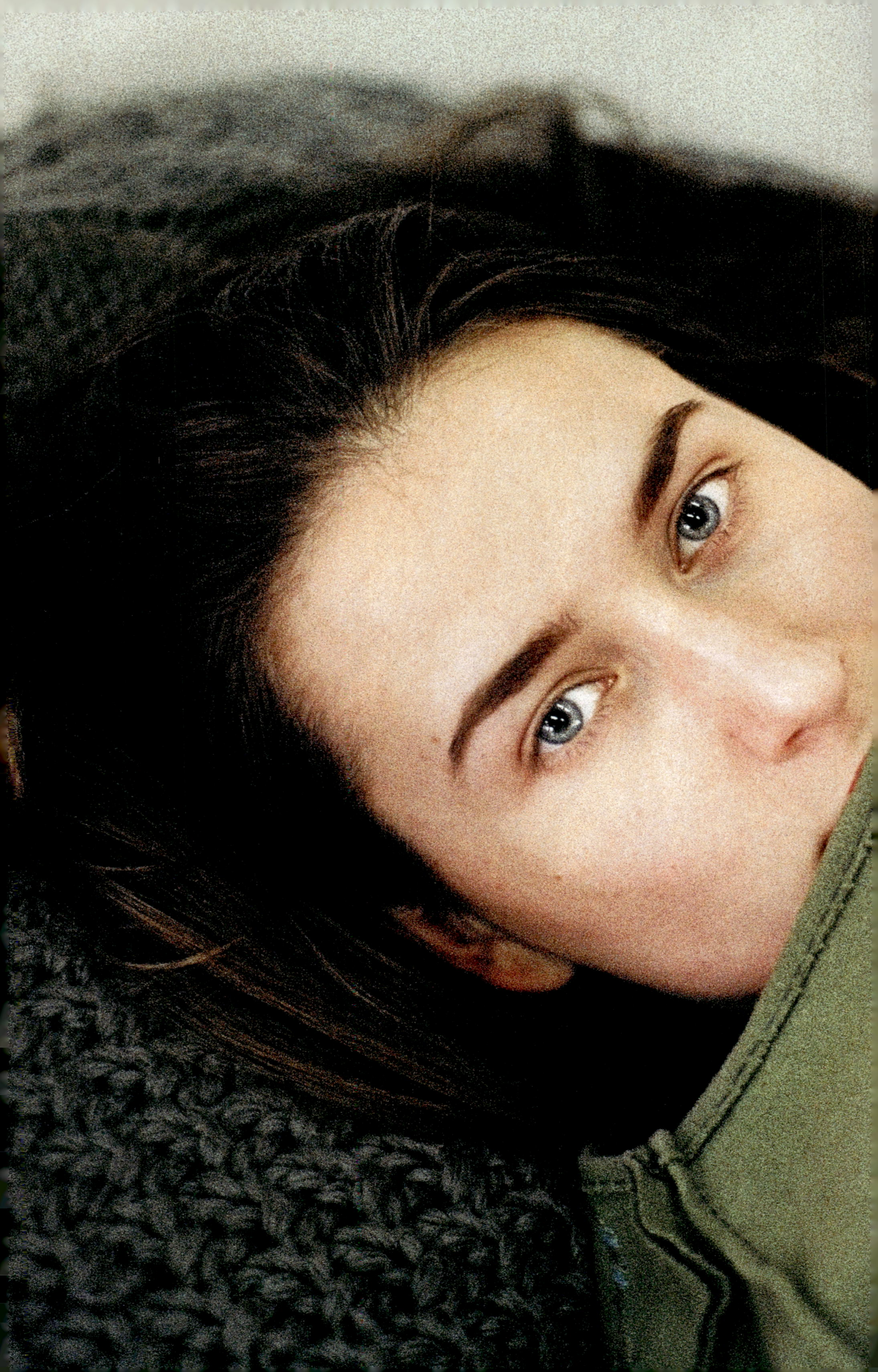

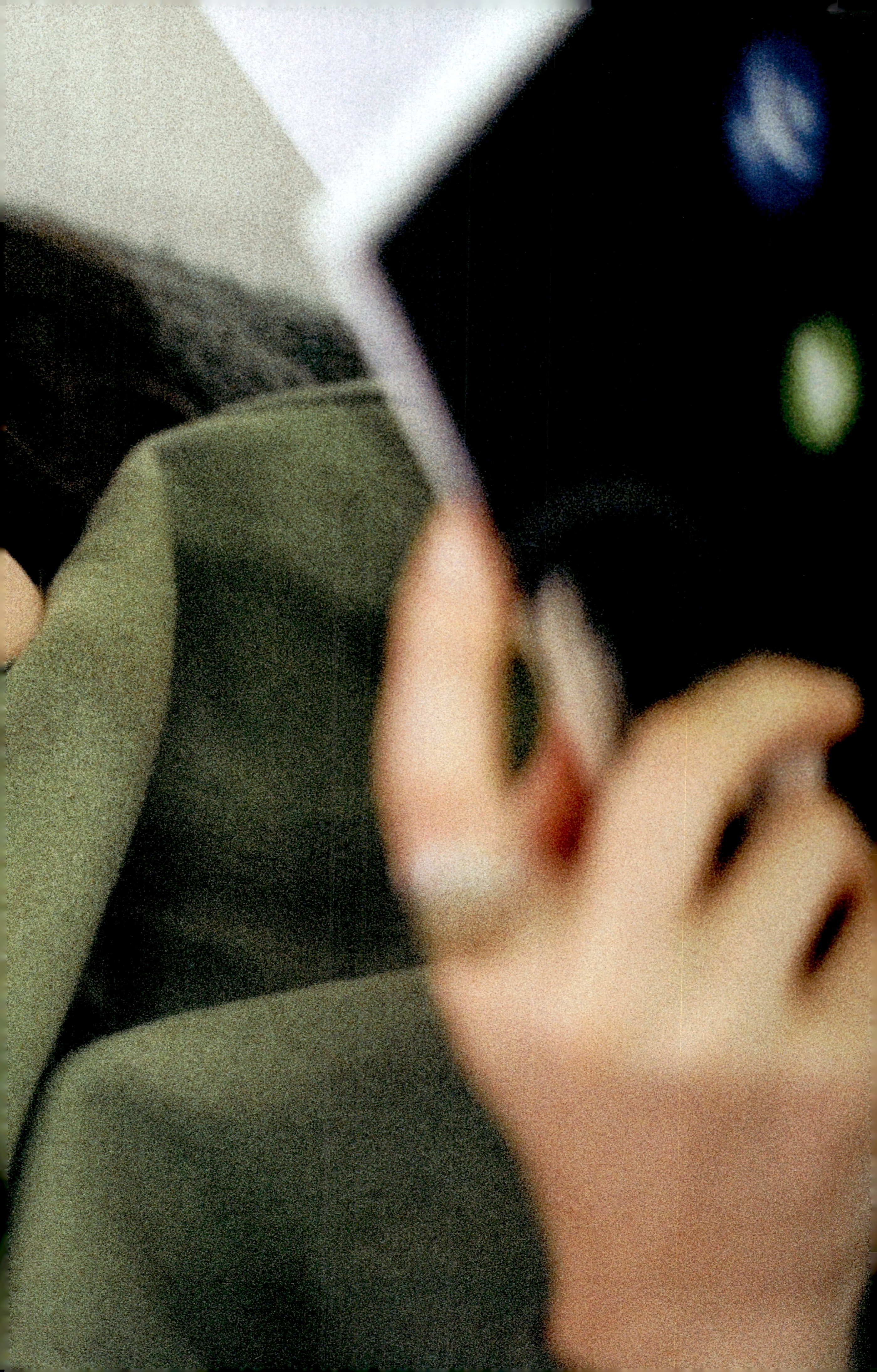

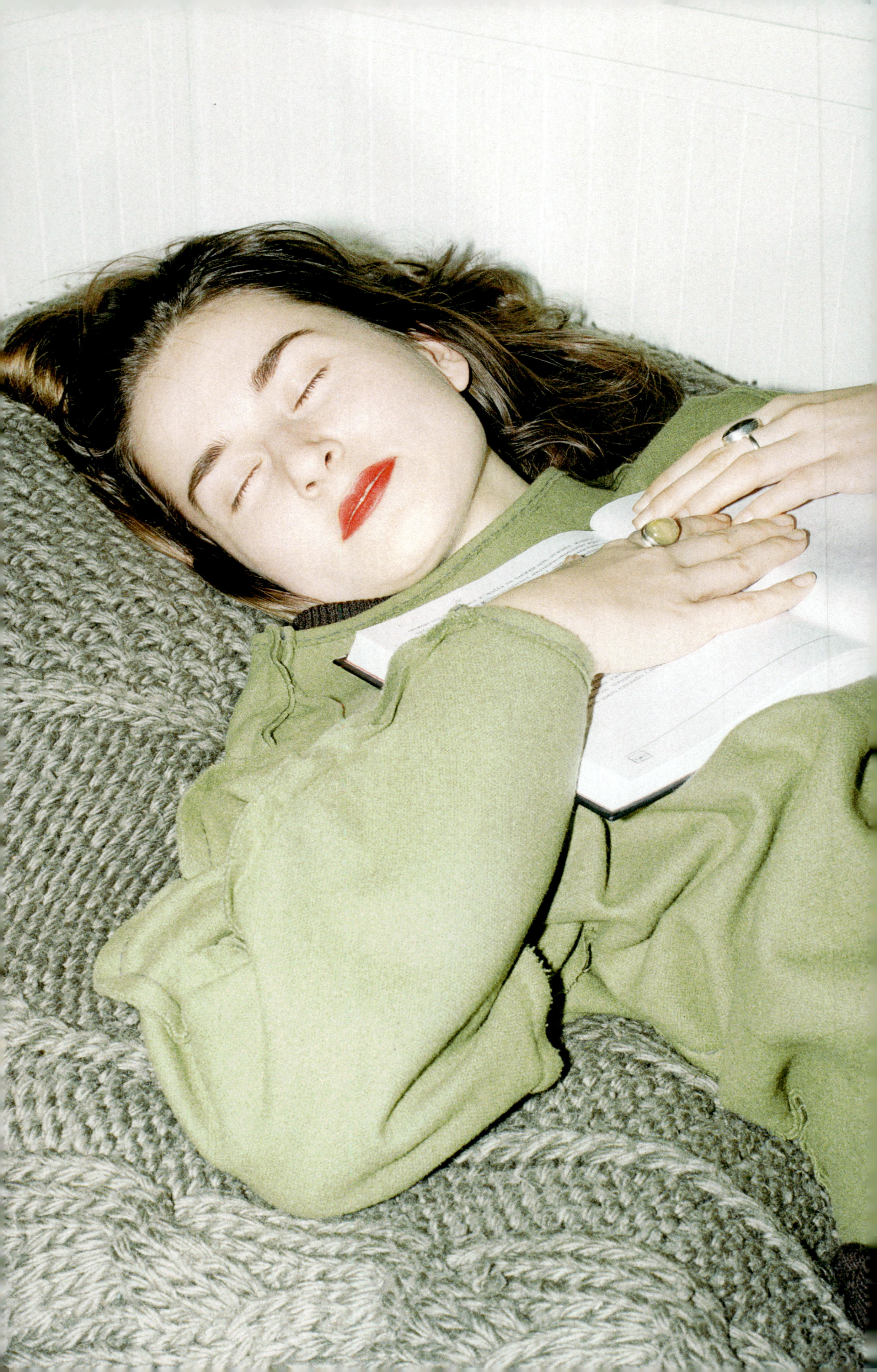

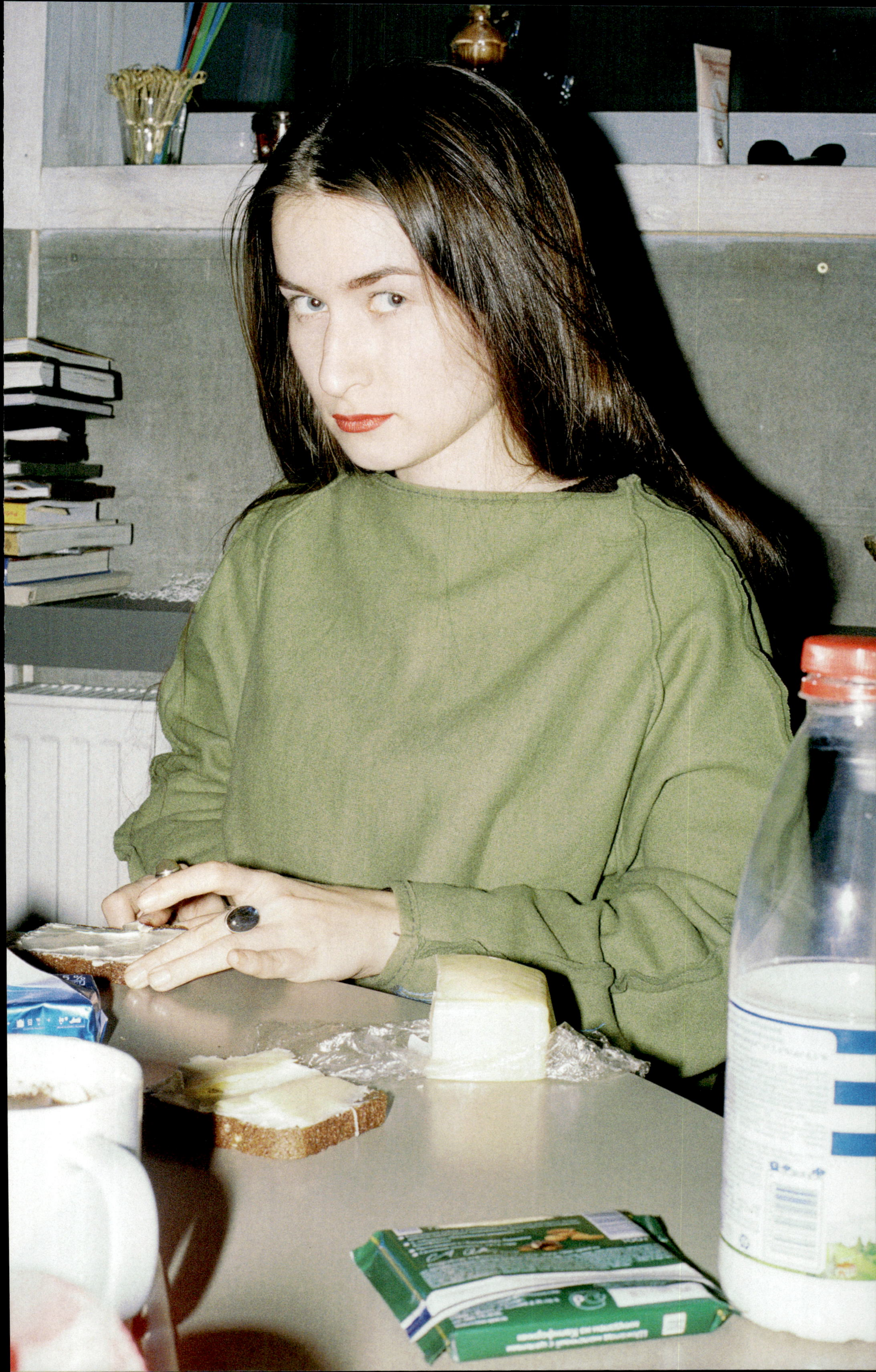

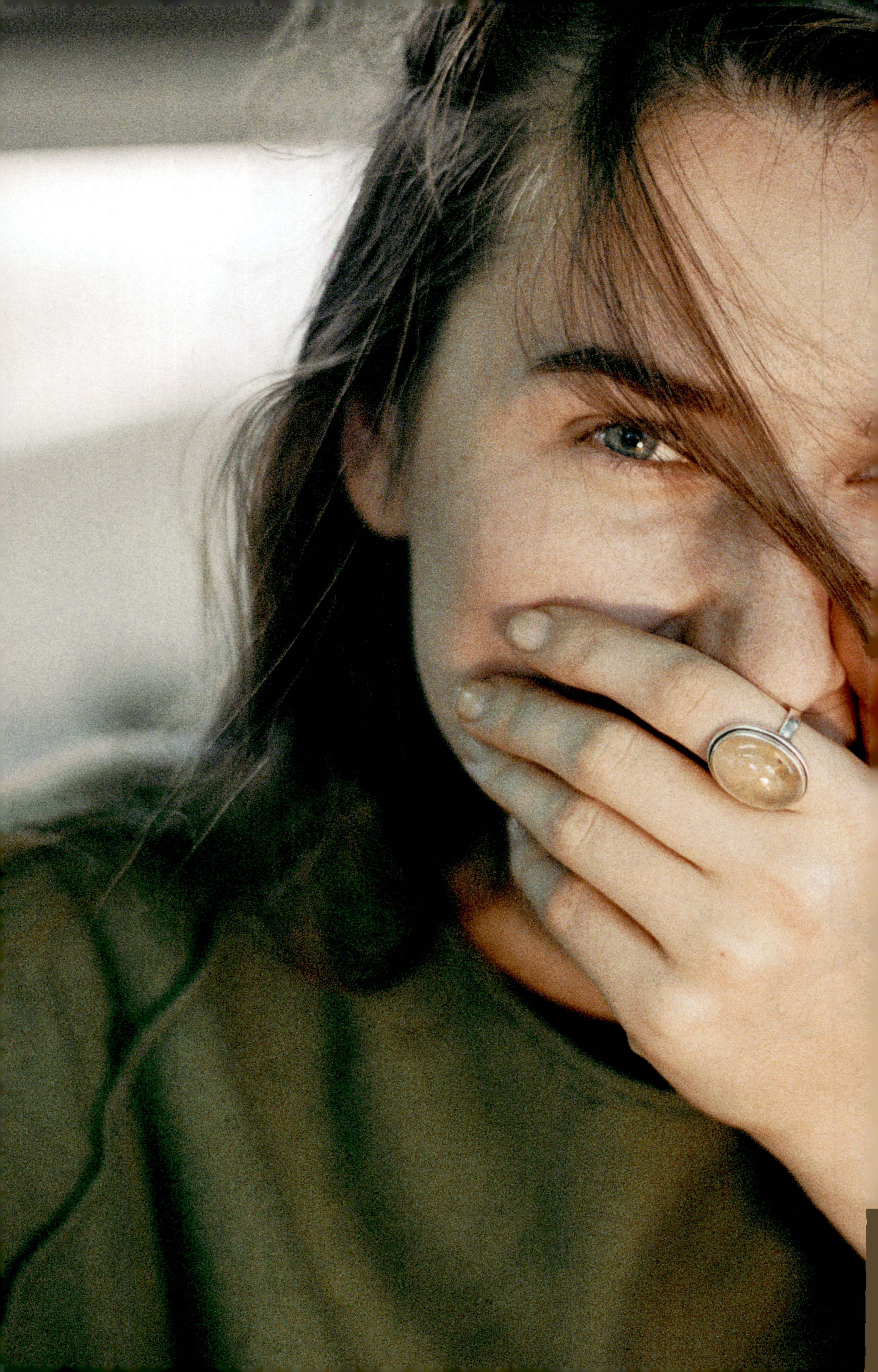

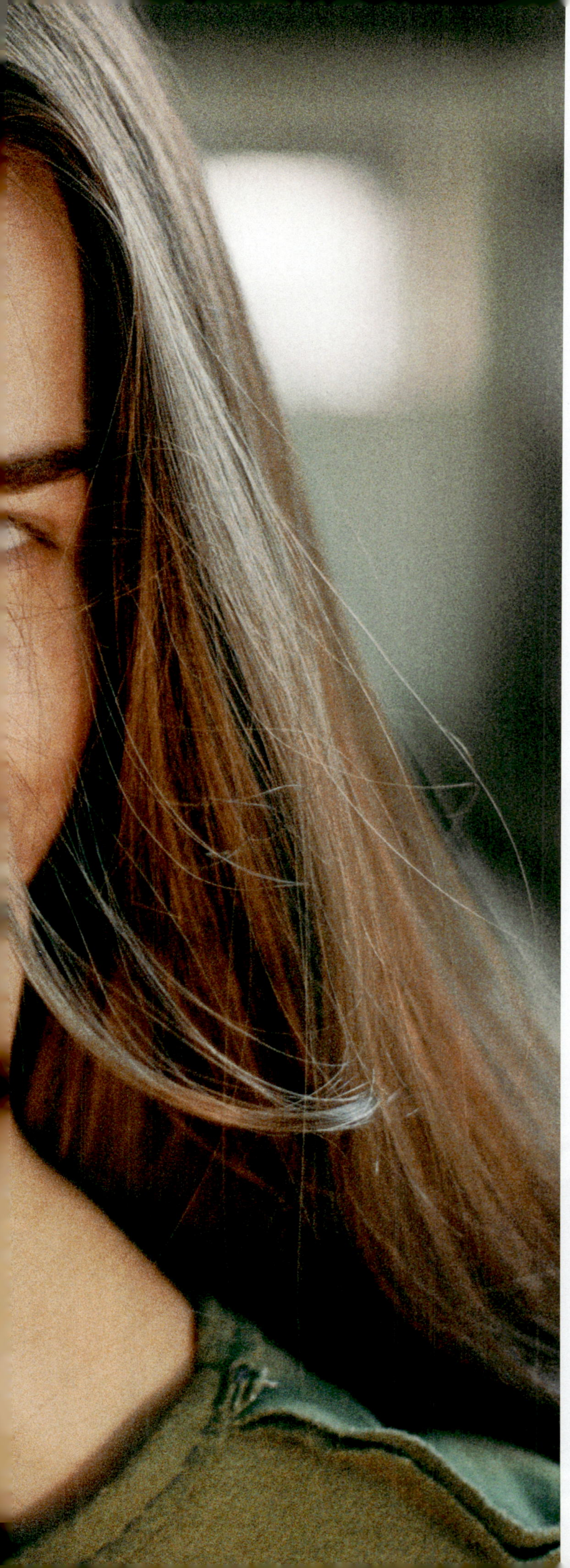

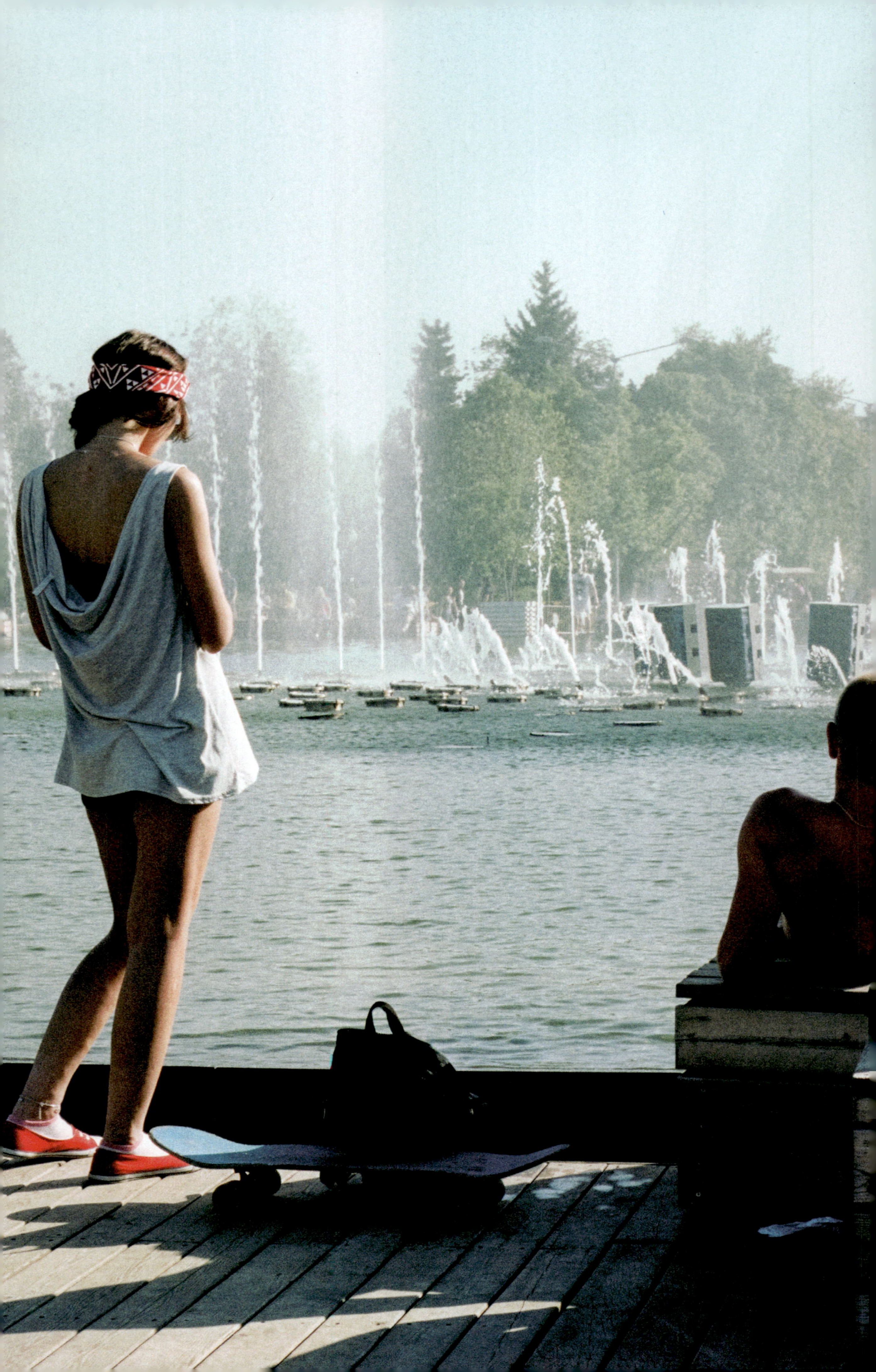

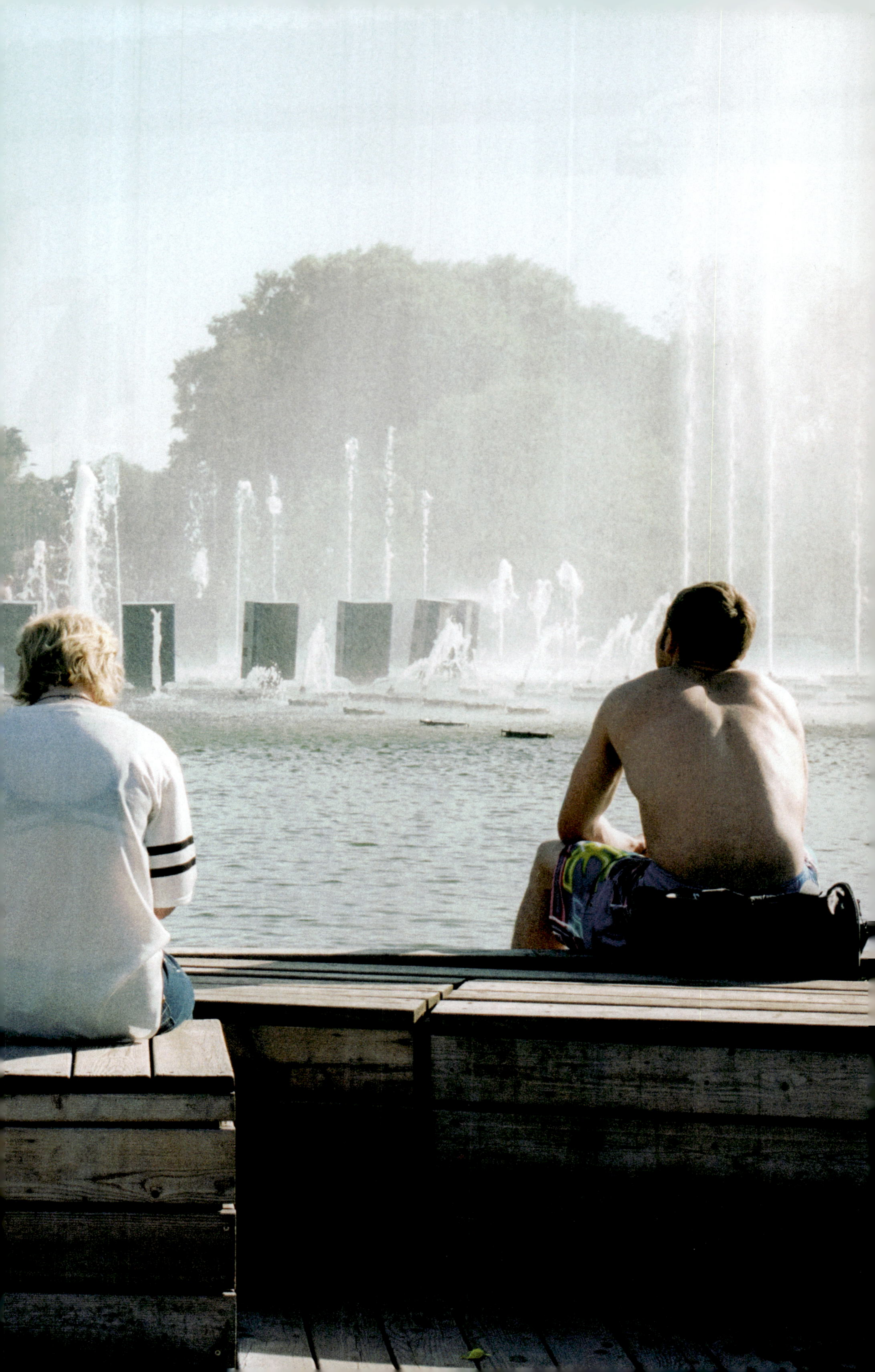

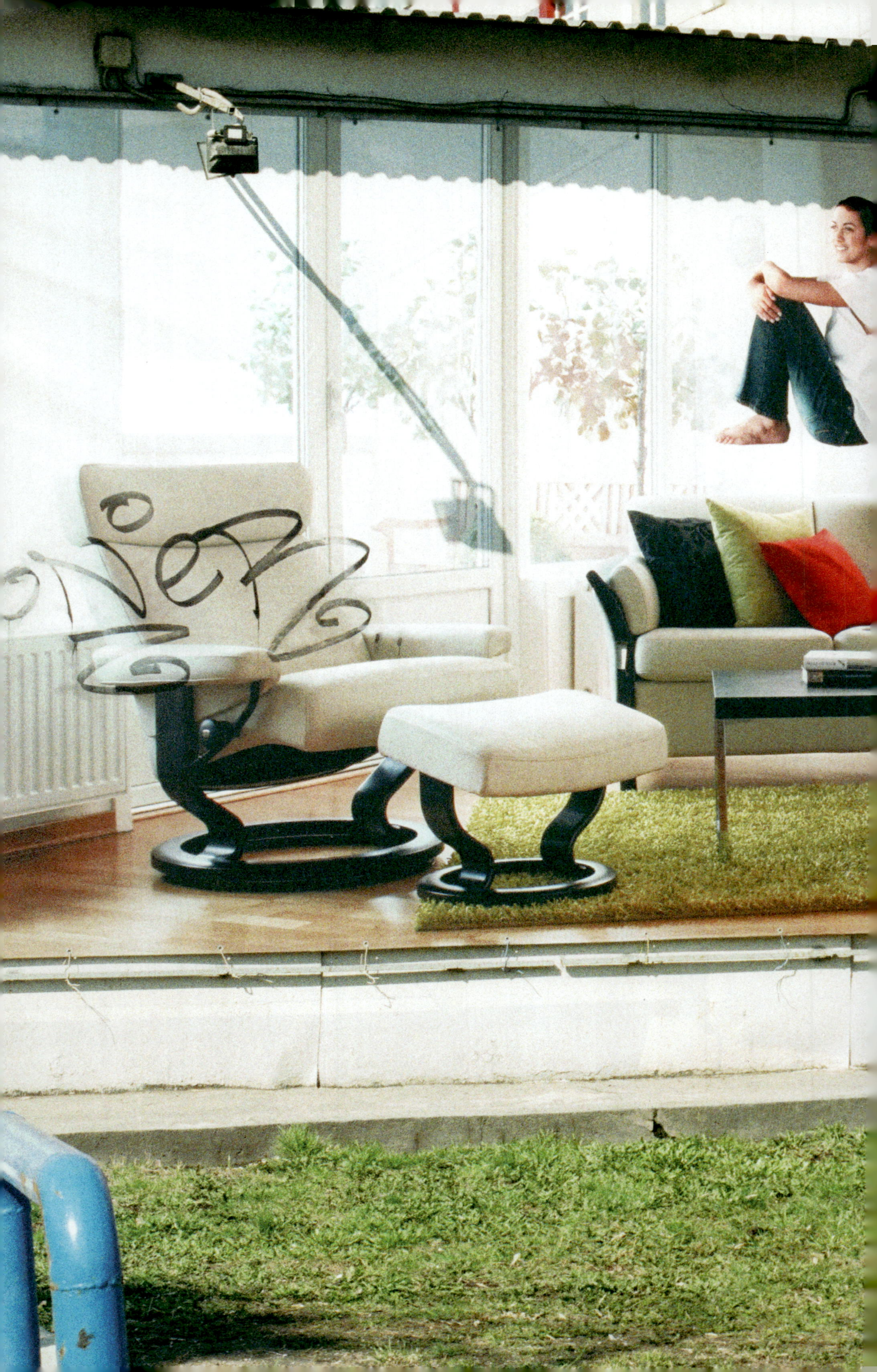

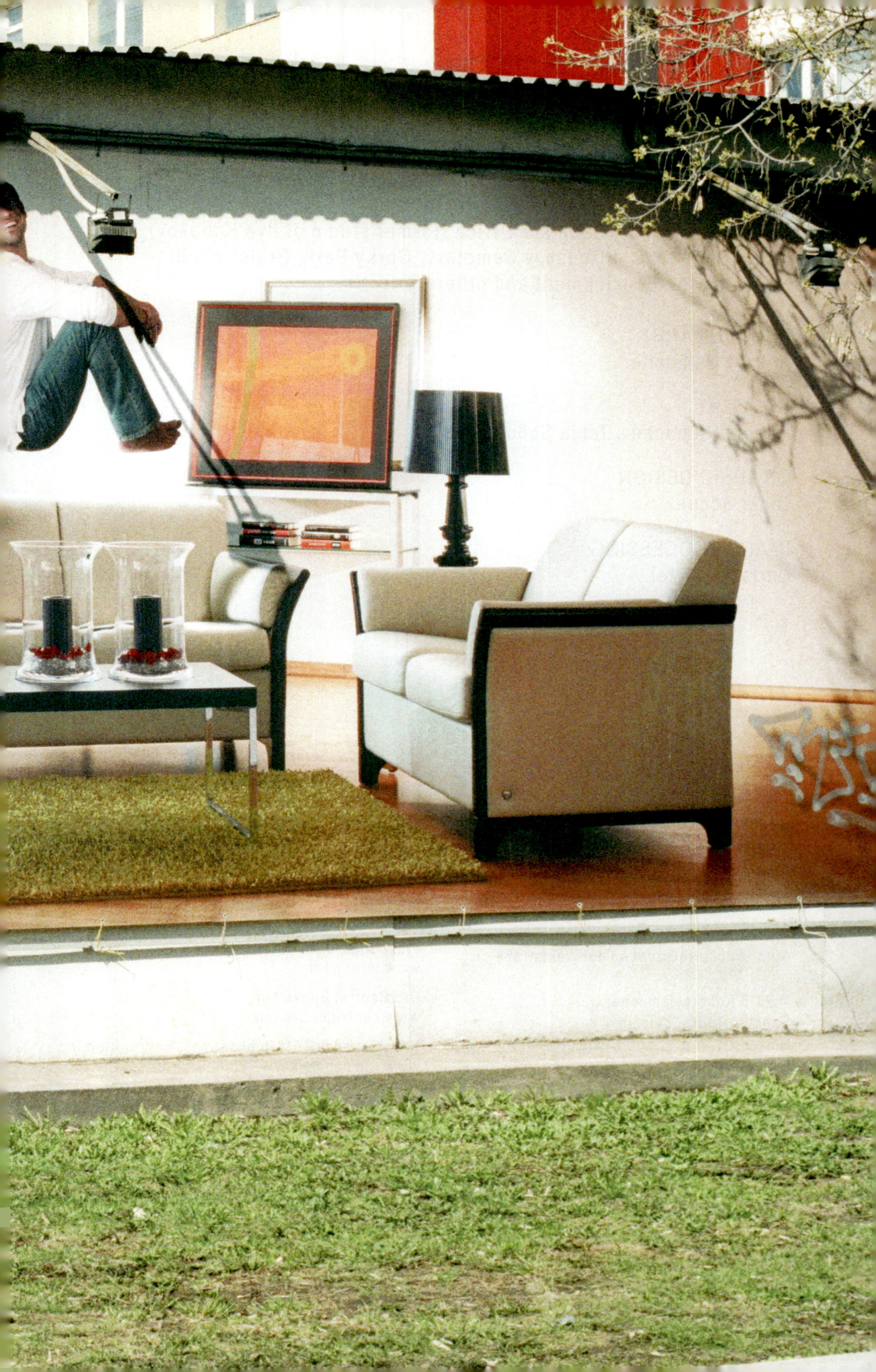

MOSCOW SPRING FEVER

QUOTES
Fedor, Ivan, Ksenia, Marina, Simon and Ustina

SCENES
Austrian Embassy, Biennale Office (former studio of Ilya Kabakov), Club ARMA 17, Old Donskoy Cemetery, Gorky Park, Gridchinhall, House on the Embankment and others

PHOTOGRAPHY
Robert Hamacher

CONCEPT
Robert Hamacher, Tanja Schuez

GRAPHIC DESIGN
Tanja Schuez

IMAGE PROCESSING
Christian Ertel

PUBLISHED BY
Spector Books
Harkortstraße 10
04107 Leipzig
www.spectorbooks.com

PRINTING AND BINDING
Nino Druck, Neustadt an der Weinstraße

First edition
Printed in Germany

ISBN 978-3-95905-062-3

DISTRIBUTION
Germany, Austria: GVA, Gemeinsame Verlagsauslieferung Göttingen GmbH&Co. KG
www.gva-verlage.de

Switzerland: AVA Verlagsauslieferung AG
www.ava.ch

France, Belgium: Interart Paris
www.interart.fr

UK: Central Books Ltd
www.centralbooks.com

USA, Canada: RAM Publications+Distribution Inc.
www.rampub.com

Australia, New Zealand: Perimeter Distribution
www.perimeterdistribution.com

Other countries: Motto Distribution
www.mottodistribution.com

RIEMSCHNEIDER Stiftung

GOETHE INSTITUT
Sprache. Kultur. Deutschland.

Stadt Karlsruhe
Kulturamt | Kulturbüro

LBBW
Stiftungen
Landesbank Baden-Württemberg